Tony

Thank you for all your help!

Greetings from the Norwegian group 2003
Høgskolen i Nord-Trøndelag

Kristin Buflaten

Signid Bakka

Ann Eve Harnes

Ellen Marie Rosvold

Ingeljorg Høydal

Lisa Mari Juliussen

Ingunn Laila Vodden

Håvard Okkulhaug

THE NORWEGIAN KITCHEN

THE NORWEGIAN KITCHEN, 2002

Norwegian Title: Vårt Norske Kjøkken
German Title: Die Norwegische Küche
French Title: La Cuisine Norvégienne

Publisher:
Svein Gran, KOM Forlag A/S
PB 865, 6501 Kristiansund
NORWAY
Phone: 71 57 33 10
Fax: 71 57 33 11
© KOM Forlag A/S

Graphic design:
Unni Dahl

Illustrations:
Christine Hoel

Translated by:
Melody Favish (English)
Lucie Fæste (German)
AAA Présentasjons (French)

Melody Favish has edited and adapted the recipes
Tone Solberg has contributed to Part I

Additional Photographers:
See page 224

Repro and Printing:
PDC Tangen, Norway

Norwegian edition: ISBN 8290 823 215
English edition: ISBN 8290 823 231
German edition: ISBN 8290 823 223
French edition: ISBN 8290 823 258

THE NORWEGIAN KITCHEN

Editor
Kjell E. Innli

Photographers
Per Eide and Bengt Wilson

Recipes
The Association of Norwegian Chefs

KOM
FORLAG

PREFACE

Many people have contributed to THE NORWE-GIAN KITCHEN and are eagerly awaiting its publication, especially now that interest in Norwegian food is increasing. THE NORWEGIAN KITCHEN adds to our understanding of Norway's rich cultural heritage, illustrating with both words and pictures the best that the Norwegian kitchen can offer.

The book is divided into two sections. The first covers the Norwegian kitchen in depth, examining the role climate and crops played in creating our culinary heritage. The historical perspective, contrasting a coastal culture with a quite different inland culture, is emphasized. Some of this development is traced to the present time, but to cover it all would take an entire book.

The Chefs' Guild in each county in Norway has collected recipes, and 350 of them have been selected for this book. They represent the Norwegian kitchen today, with a mixture of traditional dishes which still are popular, plus newer dishes based on Norwegian ingredients.

THE NORWEGIAN KITCHEN has been produced in cooperation with the Association of Norwegian Chefs, The Norwegian Kitchen, the Norwegian Department of Agriculture's "Good Norwegian" project and TINE Kitchens. Thanks for all help and enthusiasm! We would also like to thank the chefs at the Rauma school for chefs, the agricultural information offices, the fish information office and the Department of Fisheries for their contributions.

We hope that the flavors of THE NORWEGIAN KITCHEN will spread the enthusiasm and pleasure needed both to preserve and develop our unique culinary heritage in the years to come.

Good luck.

Kjell E. Innli

CONTENTS

Part I

Part II

NATURE'S OWN FLAVORS

In September, the sun is low on the horizon and trees, with their golden leaves, cast long shadows. Every day gets a few minutes shorter, and the nights are pitch dark. It is time to withdraw inside, to the cozy warmth of the hearth – this is the time for lamb and cabbage stew. Slices of lamb and wedges of cabbage are layered in a large pot, seasoned with salt and whole peppercorns and simmered. This is simple, traditional farm food, served throughout the country. On festive occasions, it is served with beer and Norwegian-produced aquavit.

The most appropriate dessert is veiled country lass: fall apples cooked into sauce and layered with breadcrumbs, which have been caramelized in butter and sugar, then topped with whipped cream – rich and good.

This autumn gathering around a steaming pot of lamb and cabbage stew tells a lot about Norwegian food culture. Not only is this dish a favorite, it also represents the importance of coming together for a good meal. Gathering around a table – at home or with friends – is an important part of Norwegian food culture. For centuries, it has been the custom to offer guests the best the house can offer. At holidays and celebrations, the home is the gathering place. Even though there has been an explosion in the number of cafés and restaurants, which we gladly visit, we still haven't forgotten that real Norwegian hospitality means inviting guests into our homes.

Most importantly, that pot of lamb and cabbage stew marks the transition to a new season. Summer is definitely over, and autumn has begun. That the Norwegian kitchen is seasonal is only natural, considering the country's geographic location and the dramatic changes which each season brings.

Norway is a long, thin country, with great variations both in the landscape and in the climate. Measured lengthwise, almost half of Norway lies above the Arctic Circle. The mountains, which separate the eastern and western parts of the country, also delineate the climatic differences between the two regions. Most of coastal Norway experiences mild winters and comparatively chilly summers, while the inland regions in the eastern part of the country and up north have cold winters and often warm summers. Some coastal areas get lots of rain, while others manage to blossom even with less precipitation per year than the Sahara desert.

The gulf stream and mild westerly winds give Norway a higher average temperature than any other area so far north. This has given us a climate which makes it possible to cultivate plants which normally could not grow at our latitude.

Norwegian master chefs are world class and have won many international competitions. They often use local ingredients, with particular emphasis on Norwegian fish, lamb and berries.

During the winter, much of Norway is covered with snow. Historically, this has meant that the entire summer is dedicated to gathering and storing food for the winter. This is not exclusive to Norway, but it is especially important here because of the climate. It used to be absolutely necessary to secure enough food to last through the winter, for the sake of survival. A poor crop could mean near starvation for both family and animals by springtime.

People ate what they had, not necessarily what they liked. Fish, dried meats, milk and grain were the mainstays of the winter diet. There was a lot of porridge and bread. It is an interesting curiosity that there is no single word translation for the Norwegian "pålegg," which means "something to put on bread." While bread elsewhere is an accompaniment to meat, fish and cheese, the Norwegian meal consists of bread with something on it.

Autumn's lamb and cabbage stew is also an example of the Norwegian way of emphasizing the natural qualities of the raw materials. The cool climate and strict import restrictions eliminate much of the potential for diseases and parasites. Norway is one of the leading countries in the world with regard to animal and plant health. We are in the lucky position that we can cultivate excellent products without using medicines and chemicals.

All this affects the taste. Vegetables and berries which grow slowly during summer, with light almost around the clock, are full of aroma and natural sweetness. We can safely say that Norwegian lamb is probably the best in the world: Norwegian lambs spend the entire summer up in the mountains eating wild herbs

Orchards full of apple, pear, plum and cherry trees line the fjords of western Norway. Apricots can be produced in some areas, while at the same latitude in other countries, it is difficult for even the hardiest plants to thrive.

and salty grass. Many chefs feel that the meat needs little more seasoning than a few grains of salt. Parsley, which grows wild in the Norwegian summer, can be used, but seldom such foreign flavors as garlic and rosemary.

The Norwegian kitchen, for obvious reasons, originally used very few herbs and spices. Some of the more exotic ingredients, which we take for granted today, were unknown to our forefathers. The most important seasoning was salt. Even though salt also intensified the flavor of food, it was used primarily as a preservative, and large quantities of it were consumed in earlier days.

Wild herbs, such as juniper, caraway seed and thyme, eventually found their way to the stew pot, but they were not used to any great degree. As trade with southern Europe increased, new seasonings were easier to obtain. They were introduced first in the cities, but these tastes of foreign cultures never spread widely.

Today, however, Norwegians have learned to appreciate both spices and wine. But still, the clean, true flavor of the basic ingredients is still most important in many dishes. The food is supposed to retain the taste of the raw materials. This is especially true for fish and shellfish. Fish is poached in saltwater or sautéed in butter. Shrimp and lobster are eaten on their own, while fresh water crayfish are cooked with dill.

We have always had to import sugar. It was expensive, and few could afford it. That is probably why less sugar is used in Norwegian recipes than in similar ones from other countries. Even though sugar consumption has increased in later years, and it is cheap to import, Norwegian cakes and desserts still are less sweet than those of other European kitchens.

Our attitude toward food has changed dramatically in the last 20-30 years. International trade, travel and technical development have given us year-round access to ingredients from around the world. And time has become an expensive, scarce resource. Everyday food preparation has become simpler, as the food industry has developed new products. In spite of this, the best Norwegian chefs prefer fresh ingredients, both traditional and new, and they treat them with respect. Many Norwegians, reacting against industrialization, search for their grandmothers' recipes for inspiration, for Norway does indeed have a rich tradition. It is through this consciousness that the new Norwegian kitchen takes form.

Sheep and other farm animals graze on the lush grasses of the Norwegian mountain regions. This makes for top quality meat.

THE SEA AS A FOOD SOURCE

Fish has always had a special place in the Norwegian kitchen. Historically speaking, dried fish was especially important – both for trade and table. When Christian IV was crowned in August, 1596, rumors spread regarding the coronation feast. The "shopping list" included the following quantities of dried fish: 30,000 flounder, 24,000 whiting, 400 skates, 200 ling, and 12 barrels of preserved fish (the kind which was exported from Bergen.)

Hans Strøm mentions in his "Descriptions of Sunnmøre" from 1762: "...and they also eat this fish, either fresh, salted or air-dried; and it is quite unusual that even though they eat this fish every day, at weddings and feasts it is considered the most important dish..."

The Norwegian coast is marked by mountains and fjords and a very narrow strip of arable land. The farms along the coast generally have been too small and unproductive to be able to feed a family. Most people, therefore, have relied upon fishing as their primary source of income.

Many who settled along the coast chose to live on islands near the good fishing spots. It goes without saying that it was difficult to cultivate anything on these windblown rocky plots. Islanders have always been dependent upon the gifts of the sea. In addition to fishing, they collected bird eggs and goose and duck down. What was not used for their own existence was sold.

Some people along the coast also used to rely on whaling and seal slaughtering for meat, fat and pelts. Hunting game, such as deer and birds, also contributed to the larders of coastal Norwegians. Around the turn of this century, fishing boats became motorized. Then the fishermen no longer had to live near the fishing grounds. They moved from the smaller islands and places with harsh climates to larger islands and the mainland, where new settlements were established. Fishing was combined with farming. The fisherman-farmer is a typical representative of the Norwegian coastal culture. The husband and

For thousands of years, the sea has provided a bounty of food. These resources will still be important in the future.

sons fished, while the wife, unmarried daughters and small boys ran the farm. Income from fishing varied greatly. In some families, the husband and sons could live at home and both fish and farm; in others, the men would travel with the fishing boats during the season to make ends meet. Others fished year-round and worked on the farms only during planting and harvesting.

Those who lived along the coast learned early on to live in harmony with nature, to listen to the wind and the weather and to adjust to the conditions. The struggle against the elements could be harsh and difficult, and many men were lost at sea.

The sea has always been a stable source of food for people along the coast. Even if other food was scarce, they could always catch enough fish to survive. Fish for dinner two or three times a week is still the norm for the better part of the population. Along our long coast are some of the world's richest fishing grounds. It is no wonder that fish is more important in the Norwegian kitchen than in that of most other countries.

Norwegians have high standards when it comes to fish. Along the coast, fish could be prepared almost straight from the sea. Two things were important for a successful fish dinner: The fish should be firm of flesh, and it should have no other taste than its own. Salt and vinegar were added, the salt to emphasize the flavor and the vinegar the keep the fish from falling apart during preparation. Even in today's kitchen, typical Norwegian fish dishes are known for their pure flavor, without the addition of other ingredients and seasonings, which diminish the flavor of the fish.

FACTORY FISHING ALONG THE COAST

Many writings from the early Middle Ages describe sea fishing as a solid pillar of the Norwegian economy during otherwise insecure times. Cod and herring always were of immense impor-

Including fjords and bays, Norway has a little over 21,000 km (13,000 miles) of coastline.
Many who live along the coast have their own boat and fish to provide for their own needs. For many, fishing provides a second income.

tance, both as part of the national diet and for export.

European markets bought all that could be provided. Fish also was of international political importance. Many – even foreigners, such as the Hansa league in Bergen – earned a fortune from the export of processed fish.

For the people along the coast, their life rhythm was connected to the sea-

sonal harvests of cod, herring and mackerel. For hundreds of years, fishing for the Lofoten islanders has meant catching mature cod which swim into the coastal region to spawn. These cod begin their journey toward Senja in December. From there, they follow the coast south, past Vesterålen to Lofoten. (In February, spawning cod swim to Sunnmøre, the popular Borgund cod, albeit in smaller numbers than in Lofo-

ten.) The great rush of spawning cod is the economic basis for the settlements along the outer side of Senja, Vesterålen and all of Lofoten. Processing plants were established on the shore, providing jobs for women.

Even though cod fishing along the coast of Finnmark is not so extensive as in Lofoten, it is still very important for that region. The rush of young cod comes in the spring, but along the Finnmark coast, there is often plenty of cod year-round. Some of this cod is filleted and sold fresh, lightly salted or smoked, but a great deal is sold frozen.

Dried Fish

Most cod was hung to dry – dried fish produced from Lofoten cod has always been considered the best in the world. It has been an important export since Viking times. Even today, Norwegian dried fish is exported to southern Europe, and large quantities also are sold to Africa and South America. Just how important cod was for the people of northern Norway can be understood from the following lines from "Nordland's Trumpet" of the poet-preacher, Petter Dass (1647-1707):

"If the cod should fail us
what would we have,
What would we bring to
Bergen from here?
No, the fish in the sea
is our daily bread,
and if we lose it,
then we are destitute."

The most common way to prepare dried fish is to soak it for several days and then poach it. Served with hot boiled potatoes, boiled kohlrabi and fried pork belly, it is delicious.

Dried fish is also snack food. In coastal districts, tenderized dried fish has always been considered a delicacy. Today, we can buy small bags of skinless and boneless dried fish, called Lofoten candy. Years ago, dried strips of halibut was a favorite snack food along the coast.

Lutefisk.

During the last weeks before Christmas, the aroma of lutefisk wafts out into the street from the most popular fish restaurants in Oslo. For one reason or another, lutefisk season is the coldest and darkest time of the year. Maybe it is because even though the fish itself is lean, all the side dishes make lutefisk a hearty meal, best served to happy groups and chased down with beer and whisky. Most Norwegians with respect for their food culture enjoy at least one lutefisk dinner before Christmas. When passionate lutefisk fans gather together around the table, it's one of the year's culinary highpoints.

Today, most dried fish is used to make lutefisk. This method of preserving fish goes back to the Middle Ages. Olaus Magnus gives a description of its preparation in his Nordic Cultural and Natural History from 1555. "Soak dried fish two days in a strong lye solution and

Fishing in Lofoten, 1936. Between the wars, most fishing was done with lines and nets from smaller boats.

Henningsvær. A weekend during the fishing season in one of the best known fishing villages in the Lofoten Islands.

one day in fresh water to make fine food."

Earlier, fish was soaked in lye made from birch ashes, while today, caustic soda is used. The cod soaks in lye-water for 2-3 days to soften. The fish is ready when a finger can be pressed through a medium-thick fillet without resistance. Then the cod should soak in running cold water for two days, until all the lye is rinsed out. After that, it is cut into rather large serving pieces, which are boiled or poached. Every lutefisk fan has his/her own favorite side dishes: Many like stewed green or yellow peas, some prefer white sauce with mustard, others butter or melted pork fat and/or fried bacon. Most serve it with lefse or flatbread.

Salt Fish

"Recipes for salt fish are as plentiful as the stars in the heavens or the grains of sand at the bottom of the sea," wrote Annemarta Borgen in her book, "Fish from the Kitchen at Knatten." In Portugal, the most important buyer of Norwegian salt fish, a bride is supposed to be able to prepare "bacalao" in at least 98 different ways. Our own bacalao was originally a Portuguese dish but has been adapted to suit our taste. The basics are the same: salt fish, sliced potatoes, onions, tomatoes and dried peppers prepared with good olive oil.

Even though Norway has been an important exporter of salt fish for hundreds of years, salt fish is not an essentially Norwegian invention. Salting of cod was not common in Norway before the 17th century. In 1691, a Dutch skipper, Jappe Ippe, was granted royal privilege to produce and export salt fish from Nordmøre, and since that time, salt fish production has been concentrated around the towns of Kristiansund and Ålesund. Salt fish from Lofoten and other areas is shipped to these towns, where they are washed carefully and laid to dry. The fish were placed on large flat boulders to dry during the day, then weighted down at night. In that way, the fish was pressed completely flat.

Today, about 80% of the salt fish consumed in the world is shipped from Ålesund. Most goes to Portugal but some is also sent to Spain and Italy.

Boknafisk

Another peculiar Norwegian tradition is boknafisk. Fresh or lightly salted cod, flounder or pollack is hung until half-dried. Boknafisk has to be soaked before cooking, and it tastes rather like soaked, poached dried fish. Years ago, boknafisk was popular in coastal districts. Poached boknafisk is served with boiled potatoes, fried bacon and mashed rutabagas and carrots.

Herring

Herring, often called the silver of the sea, has been an unreliable guest in Norwegian waters. Year after year, it might visit certain coastal areas, only to disappear completely and show up somewhere else.

When herring first came, it gave a livelihood to many – most importantly to the fishermen, but also to the farmer who owned the land where the nets were anchored, to the barrelmakers and the merchants who salted and sold the fish. People living along the coast, naturally, saw the herring as a blessing.

From the last century and up to the second world war, salt herring was the most common dinner dish for people of limited means. In many homes, salt herring was served once or twice a week. This is now history. Herring is becoming scarce and today costs as much as other fish.

A mountain of dried salt fish. Spreading salt fish to dry was heavy work. The fish was spread over the hills in the morning and stacked at night.

Washing salt fish. Many women were involved in the production of dried salt fish. These hard workers were the backbone of coastal society.

Mackerel

People north of Trøndelag don't appreciate mackerel, but in the southernmost part of the country, it is a delicacy, both fresh and processed.

If most of us associate lutefisk with the dark time of the year and parties inside, the first mackerel of the year is an equally important sign that summer is just around the corner. The chef who takes the time to remove every last little bone before dipping the fillets in egg and crumbs and frying them until golden in butter is popular, especially with children. With new potatoes, cucumber salad, sour cream and a sprinkling of dill and parsley, mackerel is a summer treat. Top the meal off with rhubarb soup or compote.

Mackerel can be both warm and cold smoked. In years past, it was also common to make boknefisk of mackerel.

A fish farm in Meløy in Nordland. Fish farms are located in fjords with good circulation of water.

Norwegian salmon is a wonderful starting point for a meal. Even prepared in the simplest way, it is a treat.

Fish farming has become an important livelihood in the coastal districts. Many farms are experimenting with farming other fish, such as cod, turbot and halibut, in addition to salmon. This is an exciting process for fish farmers, researchers and investors, as well as for the fish-loving consumer.

Norwegian fish is sold in many forms: Whole, round-cleaned or in fillets, frozen or fresh, lightly-salted, salted, smoked, half-dried, salted and dried, marinated and pickled. Improved freezing techniques and faster transport has revolutionized the fish industry. Now the consumer can buy top quality fresh fish even in places far from the sea. Between 80 and 90% of Norwegian fish is exported, a significant part of our total exports.

"Modern" Fish and Shellfish

The people along the coast have always concentrated on the most common varieties of fish. Lesser known varieties and unattractive fish were tossed back into the sea. Mollusks and shellfish were used for bait long before they were regarded as food fit for people. This attitude has changed in recent years. Ugly fish, such as monkfish and ocean catfish, are now regarded as gourmet food.

Norway's most popular shellfish is the shrimp. It is fished from the Oslo fjord in the south to the big fishing fields in the Barents sea in the north. Even though excellent quality frozen

Fish and Fish Farming

Until the 1980's, salmon and salmon-trout were the most popular fish served on special occasions, but they were seasonal, enjoyed from May to August. But then came fish farms, which changed all our preconceived ideas. During the 1980's, many fish farms were established along the coast. After years of trial and error, success finally came. Norwegian farmed salmon is one of our most successful exports – to the rest of Europe, USA and Japan.

It's no wonder that people didn't dare to eat ocean catfish until recently.

shrimp is available year-round, fresh are always best. When the shrimp boats dock, people gather round to buy newly cooked, succulent shrimp. Norwegians use shrimp in many ways – in shrimp cocktail, as a garnish in fish soup, but our favorite way is to eat them "as is," with fresh white bread, mayonnaise and lemon. It's the simplest and best party food.

Late summer and early fall is crab season. In the southern part of the country, boat-owners go out to catch crabs in the late evening hours. When both sky and water meld together in darkness, crabs creep high up on rocks, and all it takes to catch them with bare hands are simple tools and a flashlight. The most dedicated crab lovers build a fire on the beach and cook the crabs immediately, in seawater. Freshly cooked crabs are available in all fish shops from the beginning of September.

Lobster, on the other hand, is protected most of the year and has become an exclusive delicacy. With its fresh, slightly acidic meat, Norwegian lobster (regular European lobster, which should not be confused with the clawless langouste) needs nothing more than toast to make a fine meal.

Norwegians also have a taste for other shellfish. It is becoming more common to see people steaming mussels in the archipelago. Many return to the same spots to gather them year after year. Mussel and oyster farms dot the coastline in many places.

FRUITS OF THE EARTH

The climate along the fjords is mild. Precipitation can, however, cause problems, and it's important to get the hay inside as soon as it is dry. Most hay is stored in silos. From Utvik in Sogn and Fjordane.

Even on the most remote strips of coastline and the highest mountainsides, where only potatoes and the most hardy vegetables can grow, there are farms.

In the last century, the flatlands of Østlandet were dominated by large estates with tenant farmers. In the valleys, the large farms were in the lowlands, while smaller farms with a few tenants clung to the mountainside. (The tenant system was abolished in 1928, when all tenant farmers were allowed to claim their land. Most took advantage of this.) It is obvious that farming conditions vary from the valleys to the mountains.

In the valleys, it is possible to grow strawberries and vegetables, even such exotic delicacies as corn and asparagus, in addition to grain. The mountain farmer, however, is happy to harvest a decent crop of barley and potatoes. Otherwise, he, like most other small farmers, keeps sheep and dairy cattle.

Farmers in the inland districts always have had to depend upon their own production and have been, therefore, more vulnerable than fishermen-farmers during hard times. Those living inland have had to rely on more salt fish in their diets than those living along the coast. Dinner usually meant salted food, also salt meat. Fresh meat was served only on festive occasions, holidays and during the slaughtering season. Freshwater fish was served during the summer, in early fall and otherwise once in a while during the winter, if someone was lucky enough to catch any fish through a hole in the ice. Freshwater fish included whitefish, grayling, pike, pike-perch and trout. Catches were uneven and seasonal, so it was useful to have a supply of salt herring on hand.

Opposite page: Farms in Norway are small compared with those farther south in Europe. In spite of this, Norway has a thriving agriculture with strong traditions. Each field is the result of hard work removing trees and stones. From Skreia in Oppland.

Many coastal farms are of modest size, and agriculture provides only a part of the family income. From Vestvågøy in the Lofoten Islands.

LIFE ON THE FARM

Throughout history, farmers have wanted to be as self-sufficient as possible – and this meant meat, milk, butter, and cheese as well as grain, wool and skins. Farm animals were usually cows and maybe an bull, young animals, sheep, goats, pigs, a few chickens and a rooster, along with one horse or more, all dependent upon the size of the farm.

Usually, the women were responsible for the animals. They also were in charge of processing the milk. Not a drop was wasted. Milk was separated to remove the cream, which was churned into butter. The rest was used for drinking and cheese production. Years ago, most cheese was made on individual farms, most often during the summer,

at special dairy cabins high in the mountains. The most common kinds of cheese were a firm, mild white cheese, a pressed granular large-curd cheese called "old cheese," because of its rather burnished color and aged aroma, a kind of fermented cottage cheese, whey cheese and one made with beer.

The white cheese was made with either sweet or sour milk. Sweet milk was heated, then mixed with sour milk and rennet. The mixture was placed in a canvas bag or in a container with many small holes, for the whey to run out. The whey was then made into another kind of cheese.

The whey was cooked with milk and cream in an iron pot until it became thick and turned a rich brown color.

From Fekjastølen, Ål in Hallingdal. Production of sweet whey cheese.

Then it was poured into special molds. As soon as the cheese was cooked, it was ready to eat and could be sliced.

The fermented cottage cheese was both popular and easy to make from sour milk. The curds were rolled on a tray, pressed until broken down into very small curds. Then it was set in a warm place to ferment for three or four days. The mixture had to be stirred twice daily. Then it was kneaded together, seasoned with salt, caraway and chives and packed into wooden containers for storage.

Butter was churned from sour cream. In early days, churns were made of wood, but eventually metal churns became the norm. The butter was washed, then kneaded with salt for preservation. The liquid left after the butter was made, buttermilk, was used as a beverage and for making porridge. In coastal districts, it was also used as a marinade for lightly-salted fish.

The most Norwegian of all cheeses – red cheese, now called Gudbrandsdal cheese, exported as Ski Queen – was "invented" on one of the mountain dairies. Anne Solbrå (later married Hov)

from Fron in Gudbrandsdal was milkmaid for her parents in the 1850's. She felt that sour and skim milk cheeses were inadequate, especially for guests at her summer cabin in the mountains. She experimented by adding a little sour cream to the whey during cooking, which resulted in a tasty, caramel-brown cheese. When hard times set in several years later, and prices of butter and cheese were low, she began to "mass-produce" her distinctive brown cheese. Through a local merchant, it was sold to a dealer in Christiania, and eventually, it became so popular that other farm women in the valley began to produce it. In 1933, Anne Hov, age 87, was presented with the Royal service medal in silver, because her cheese had rescued the valley's economy from catastrophe.

Slaughtering

Slaughtering took place in October and November. The animals were heavy, and with the cold weather, it was easier to store the meat. Usually, a local butcher did the job, and the time was set according to tradition. Superstition said that it had to take place during a waxing moon and a rising tide.

Before the butcher arrived, all tools, containers and cups were scrubbed and rinsed with juniper-water. Children and sick people were not allowed to be present during the butchering.

The meat was hung to chill, either in the barn or another cool, airy place. When the meat was thoroughly chilled, it had to be divided. Some pieces were salted, then dried. Trimmings and other odd bits were ground or chopped and made into sausages. Organ meats also were made into sausages. Salted ribs of mutton, legs, split heads which were singed and salted, plus different kinds of sausages and salted hams were hung to dry. Eventually, they appeared on the table.

Everything was used, including innards, blood and fat, but also calf stomachs, intestines, horns, hooves, skin, tendons and bristles.

Kidneys and liver was washed and rinsed. The kidneys also were blanched in boiling, lightly salted water a few minutes, then prepared. The head and other organ meats were soaked in cold running water for 24 hours.

Blood was never wasted. It was strained, then stirred until it lightened in color. Then it could be used in pancakes, blood pudding, sausages and dumplings. The fat was trimmed, salted and fried together with meat or fish. It could also be rendered into cooking fat and used in potato dumplings, blood pudding and dumplings. Melted fat also could be mixed with lye to make soap.

Calf stomachs were used as rennet. They were washed and hung to dry on a clean birch branch. When it was time to make cheese, a chunk was cut off, soaked in water, and then added to the heated milk to separate the curds from the whey.

The intestines were cleaned carefully and used for sausages.

Dried Meats

The Baroque Era's preacher-poet, Petter Dass, was, literally, concerned with everything between heaven and earth, and ham was no exception:

Even small children had to help with the milking on the summer mountain dairy farms.

In the storehouse, dried meat hung from the rafters and lefse and flatbread were stacked.

*A ham that I own
if anyone wants it
has hung in the smoke
for its ninth autumn
it's pretty well smoked by now*

Here in Norway, we've eaten dried meat since Viking times. It was usually made in the late fall, as that was the best time for both salting and drying. By the time winter settled in, a good supply of dried mutton, ham and sausages of all kinds was in the larder.

For dry salting, large troughs were used. The meat was rubbed thoroughly with salt. It was important that the salt reach the bones. Then the meat in the trough was sprinkled generously with more salt. The brine which formed was used to baste the meat at regular intervals.

For salting in brine, wooden tubs and eventually barrels were used. It was important that the brine be strong enough, and to measure the salt content, a potato often was placed in the brine. If it floated to the surface, the brine was strong enough. For extra strong brine, it was normal to stick a large nail through the potato.

Our ancestors were miserly with many things, but not with salt. To be absolutely certain that the meat would keep, they were generous with salt, also between the chunks which were being salted.

Wooden planks or large rocks were placed on the meat to make sure that it was completely covered with brine.

When the meat was completely soaked, it was brushed to remove extra salt and then hung to dry.

Some dried meat also was smoked. Usually it was smoked before being hung to dry, but some preferred to dry first and smoke later. Low-temperature smoking was preferred, and the smoked meat kept very well. Such meat has been served as both everyday and festive food – summer and winter.

Our Daily Bread

Grain and grain products are an important part of the Norwegian kitchen. The most important grains are oats, wheat, rye and barley. Wheat is the most demanding and is cultivated only in the lowland regions. Rye and oats are not so sensitive, while barley is a more robust grain, which also can be grown on mountain farms.

According to tradition, the husband himself was supposed to sow the grain in the spring. It was considered a very formal act – a sower was required always to be bareheaded. Once the grain was in the earth, the rest was up to the Lord. Both old and young followed its development, from the first green shoots which sprang up from the earth in the spring, until the sheaves of grain stood tall and golden and ready to harvest in the autumn breezes. In Sep-

tember, the grain was cut, tied and dried. When it was completely dried – in the field, on hayracks or poles – it had to be threshed and cleaned. Women were in charge of grinding, so long as the work was done by hand. When mills began to spring up along the streams and the work became mechanized, men took over.

The Norwegian diet has changed in many ways during the past few years, but it is still not unusual to have up to three meals which include bread – breakfast, a packed lunch at school or

work, and a slice or two in the evening. In spite of the vast selection at most bakeries, it is still popular to bake bread at home – most often coarse, whole-grain varieties. Norwegian flour is coarser and contains more of the whole grain than flour in most other countries, a result of the tradition of coarse flour from hand-milling or from small mills. Coarse, hearty flour is still the bread flour of choice in Norway. In addition, politics also play a role, and Norwegian authorities insist that flour contain as much as possible of the whole grain. While desirable for bread, it is less so for cakes, but cakes play a small role in the Norwegian kitchen.

In addition to bread, porridge also has had an important role in the Norwegian diet, for it is cheap, easy to prepare and nourishing.

Years ago, people ate porridge at least once a day, often barley gruel served with sour milk. Today, porridge is less popular, although many do eat oatmeal for breakfast, rice porridge for Saturday dinner, and sour cream porridge on special occasions.

Bread frequently is served as an accompaniment to meat and fish dishes, especially in the country, usually flatbread. Fish and meat soups often were stretched with barley or oats. In that way, sometimes every meal of the day included grain.

Bread Baking

Long ago, people were completely dependent on their yearly crops of grain, and even if farmers tried to set aside a little in case of hard times, this was not always possible. A bad harvest generally meant hunger and misery. During a bad year, perhaps because of frost, it was common to eek out the grain with bark, which was shredded, dried and ground. The innermost, light part of the bark was used, generally from elm, rowan, mountain ash, willow and pine trees. Otherwise it was common to use elm bark which had been soaked for a while in flatbread dough. That made it more pliable and easier to knead.

The farmer himself sowed the grain. This was considered a religious task, always done bareheaded.

In early days, bread was baked on a griddle or in an iron. Flatbread and lefse were the most important breads. At many meals, flatbread and lefse were served instead of porridge. Flatbread varied according to type of flour and thickness, and to eek out the grain, potatoes often were used in the dough, along with water, milk or whey. For Christmas, the flatbread was rolled out thinner than usual.

Flatbread was baked twice a year, in the spring and just before or after slaughtering time in the fall. Normally, many farm wives got together to roll out sheets of flatbread on one large table. These baking women often traveled from farm to farm, carrying their own irons with them.

Flatbread dough, which was best made with freshly ground oats and water, was kneaded in a large trough. When the dough was stiff and thoroughly kneaded, it was divided into small balls of equal size, which then were pressed into 12 cm (5") discs. These were rolled out with grooved or latticed rolling pins into thin round sheets, about 50 cm (20") in diameter. Then they were ready to bake. Each sheet was rolled onto a thin wooden pin and then rolled out again onto a hot baking stone or griddle. The bread was baked lightly on both sides and then set aside to cool quickly, before it was returned to the griddle to bake completely. Then the sheets were stacked under light weights. When the stacks were completely cool, they were stored in the larder.

Everyone needed a good supply of flatbread. Flatbread was on the table for all meals – especially before the potato came to Scandinavia – and it was considered shameful to run out of it.

It is unknown whether lefse or flatbread is the oldest kind of bread. Lefse is baked either hard or soft. Oat lefse was made of coarse flour, rolled thick and baked at such low heat that it became crisp or hard. It usually was baked in great quantities and stored with the flatbread.

Soft lefse has a much shorter shelf life.

Baking flatbread in Rogaland, about 1912, with one woman in charge of rolling, the other of baking.

A barley field from Helgøya. Many farms in eastern Norway concentrate on grain and are run by a single person, while a few generations ago, farms were small societies with many workers.

These were made of fine flour, cream and other good things. Lefse can be festive food if made and topped with the right ingredients. The most popular topping is lightly-salted butter and cinnamon sugar.

The Ubiquitous Potato

Today, the potato is such a common ingredient in the Norwegian kitchen that it is strange to think that it hasn't always been available. It was introduced to Europe in the 16th Century, and first arrived in Norway in the 18th. When we know how difficult it was for people in Norway years ago to have enough grain for food, it is easy to understand that the potato quickly became an important part of the diet.

Government employees and the upper classes, almost out of curiosity, were the first to plant potatoes in their gardens. The clergy soon realized that this was an important resource, and they used their position to spread word of the benefits of the vegetable. The "potato preachers" eventually convinced the farmers that these strange root vegetables were really worth cultivating. This was realized to the utmost during the famine years from 1807 to 1814, when hunger forced people to grow potatoes for their own use. During World War II, the potato helped people to ward off hunger – it was used with great ingenuity and served in many interesting ways.

For the most part, the potato can be grown all over the country. It has been cultivated in addition to grain or instead of it. Even in more prosperous times, the potato is still found on most Norwegian dinner tables. Although now prepared in other ways than the traditional boiled, and sometimes replaced with rice or pasta, the potato and the average Norwegian's love of it will never die.

Fruit and Vegetables

Monks were the first to practice organized planting of fruit and berries in Norway. The knowledge of new varieties and improved methods of cultivation spread from cloistered gardens to the rest of the population. In low-lying inland settlements and along the coast as far north as Romsdal, apples, pears, plums and sweet and sour cherries have been cultivated for hundreds of years. Red and black currants, gooseberries, blackberries, raspberries and strawberries also have been grown, where climate and terrain allow.

Thanks to an effective production system and well-developed chilling and freezing techniques, it takes only a few hours to get peas from the field to the freezer. Frozen vegetables are a good alternative to fresh during the winter.

Along with the potato, root vegetables, such as the carrot, rutabaga, turnip, onion and cabbage, have the oldest tradition in the Norwegian kitchen. Until the 1960's, these were the only fresh vegetables found in the winter. Lately, more fresh vegetables are available, especially salad vegetables. But it is still a pleasure to welcome the first green signs of spring, and to sprinkle food with chives from the garden. Many people also search for the first wild spring greens. Young caraway shoots, nettles, dandelion leaves and sorrel are all delicious in soups and salads. The best is probably caraway, which tastes wonderful in oxtail soup.

Otherwise, the selection of fruit and vegetables has expanded greatly in the past 20 years. Increased travel has given us a taste of exotic fruits and vegetables. Air freight and improved transportation and communication allows us to bring home most of what is available on the world market. Cooking is more exciting, thanks to colorful and interesting fruits and vegetables, such as pineapple, artichokes, avocados, eggplants, grapes, chilis, endives, kiwi fruit, bell peppers, squash and others. Fresh herbs can be bought in pots, ready to add flavor to all kinds of dishes.

Jæren, on the southwest coast, is one of the best farming regions in the country. The flat fields are separated with stone fences.

Meat and Poultry

Today, Norwegian agriculture has become more specialized. Farmers produce what is most natural, considering climate and geography. Most grain is cultivated in Jæren, the lowlands of Østlandet and in Trøndelag. Others are primarily dairy farmers, often in combination with meat, while others concentrate on meat alone, with sheep, pigs or poultry. Few old-fashioned self-sufficient farms have survived to this day.

Norway has strict rules regarding production of meat and poultry. Breeding is done according to defined ethic norms which are based upon biology's natural laws, with no gene manipulation or other controversial research methods. Neither hormones nor growth-stimulating drugs are allowed – not directly or through the feed. In addition, antibiotics in cattle production are prohibited.

Norwegian red cattle are a result of thorough and lengthy planned breeding. This race suits Norwegian conditions and produces a great quantity of milk as well as meat.

Extensive and goal-oriented research also have yielded good results with breeding of pigs. The good old pig, short, fat and stubby, has become long and slim, with a thin layer of fat, and with streaky bacon. The long back provides lovely, juicy chops.

Most consumers already have noticed that the selection of fresh, tender meat has improved. This is particularly true for beef and pork.

Norwegian sheep have good grazing pastures, both on the mountainside and in fields – by the sea or on islands. That the animals can stay outside and graze on fresh grass from June to late September has a positive effect on the quality of the meat. Norwegian lamb is top quality, a gourmet product. Autumn is butchering time for sheep and lambs. In recent years, it has become normal to deliver fresh lamb at other times of the year, especially at Easter.

Norway has a long tradition of respect for animals. Small herds allow farmers to get to know their animals, and most Norwegian cows have names. Each cow has her own diary, where the farmer records information about her health and the amount of milk produced. Summer grazing makes for happy, healthy cows.

Norwegian lamb is a favorite among gourmets.

Norwegian poultry, particularly chicken, has improved. Castration of chickens has never been allowed. Now, it is possible to obtain free-range chickens raised exclusively on vegetarian feed (as opposed to the fishmeal-based feed of many battery hens). These chickens are allowed to peck around the farmyard, just like in the olden days. This combination of diet and nature gives the best meat.

In some parts of Norway, it is possible to buy fresh chicken, but unfortunately, most poultry is sold frozen. Sales of fresh chickens are growing, and chicken is experiencing a renaissance, now that people have learned to appreciate this lean and juicy meat.

Milk and Cheese

Milk is a special drink in Norway, appreciated by both young and old. Norwegians love milk. When we are abroad, we can accept that milk is good food for calves and that it is used in food preparation and as an addition to coffee, but it is always good to come home to cold fresh milk.

All milk produced in Norway goes to central dairies owned by the milk producers (co-ops). These dairies are associated with the Norwegian Milk Producers' Organization, which has established Norwegian Dairies as a sales and marketing apparatus. Lately, Norwegian dairies have been revamped. They have been made more specialized, and the most modern equipment available has been installed.

Most milk produced in Norway goes directly from the milking machine through a closed pipeline to the farm's own cooling tank. This maintains a temperature just under 4°C (39°F). The milk is picked up by dairy trucks with big cooling tanks, to insure that the milk stays cold on the way to the dairy. To test the quality, samples are taken at every link of the production chain.

Norwegian Dairies market about 20 different varieties of milk, in addition to three types each of cream and sour cream, ice cream, dessert puddings and sauces. In addition to three kinds of butter, they also produce a margarine-butter blend.

Norwegian Dairies produce more than 70 different cheeses, with new varieties being developed all the time. Many are local versions of foreign specialties, which include Cheddar, Edam, Mozzarella, Emmenthaler (Sveitser), Gouda (Norvegia), caraway-clove, Tilsit, Port Salut, Saint Paulin, Gorgonzola (Norzola), Roquefort (Normanna), Camembert, Brie and cottage cheese. In addition, the Norwegian Dairies also have developed 100% Norwegian cheeses, such as Gudbrandsdal (Ski Queen), Gamalost, Pultost, Jarlsberg, Ridder and other goat milk and dessert cheese variations.

Norwegian processed cheese spread is made from hard white cheese, which is ground and melted with special salts, which bind protein, fat and water to a homogeneous mass. These are flavored with bacon, shrimp, ham and spices. They are among the most popular spreads for bread. In addition, Norway also produces processed cheese in blocks and two dessert cheeses, one flavored with cherry, the other with blue cheese.

"Ekte Geitost" (real goat cheese) is produced from goat milk. "Gudbrandsdalsost" (Ski Queen) is a blend of cow and goat milk. Fløtemysost (cream whey cheese) is made from cow milk alone.

Norway is a land of milk drinkers. The average Norwegian drinks over 150 liters (quarts) of milk per year.

Norwegian Dairies have developed many different cheeses, some of which are based on our rich cheese traditions. Pictured from the left:

ROYAL BLUE, a semi-hard, smooth blue cheese with an aromatic flavor.
AGED NORVEGIA is easy to recognize, with its black wax covering. It is aged eight to 10 months before it is sent to market. It has a rich, aromatic, slightly sour flavor.
JARLSBERG is the flagship of Norwegian Dairies. This successful combination of flavor and consistency has made this cheese popular, at home and abroad.
ROSENDAL is a pure white goat cheese with a clean, rich goatmilk taste.
RIDDER has an aromatic and piquant taste, which can be quite sharp if it is well-aged. This cheese has become popular in many other European countries.
BALSFJORD is a semi-soft aged goat cheese with a milk flavor.
NAMDALSGOMME is one of many local varieties of gomme which has found its niche. Gomme has a sweet whey flavor, with the spiciness of cardamom and cinnamon.
GAMALOST has roots back to viking times. It is rather granular in consistency, with a sharp flavor.
PULTOST from Hedemark has a sharp, slightly fermented flavor. It, too, has a long tradition.
G 35 GUDBRANDSDALSOST (Ski Queen) was first made in Gudbrandsdalen over 130 years ago and is the most popular cheese on the Norwegian breakfast table. It has a clean, sweet, caramelized flavor.
REAL GOAT CHEESE is similar to G 35 but it is made with 100% goat milk. Goat cheese has long traditions in Norway.

FORESTS, MOUNTAINS AND PLATEAUS

Norway is dominated by nature, and Norwegians have always been good at taking advantage of what nature has to offer in the way of food. Compared with other countries, Norwegians have the perfect chance the use nature. All of our vast, untouched natural areas are public domain. In the autumn, everyone can go out and gather berries to freeze or to make into juice and jam. The forests are full of blueberries, wild raspberries and lingonberries.

A particularly Scandinavian delicacy is the golden cloudberry, which grows in swamps and high up the mountainsides in southern Norway. The supply is not always reliable, for the young plants and flowers are very susceptible to frost. In rich cloudberry years, a good income is waiting out there for the picking. For many Norwegians, cloudberries are synonymous with feasts and cloudberries and cream are often served on Christmas Eve.

The forests are also full of mushrooms, a resource we don't always appreciate as much as southern Europeans. Many feel that mushrooms are a less than worthy food, until they find out the price of fresh porcini mushrooms in Rome, or even at the outdoor market in Oslo, for that matter. More and more people are learning to recognize the best mushrooms. A few baskets of mushrooms can yield many happy meals during the winter.

Hunting and Fishing

Hunting has always played a major role in self-sufficient households. It is most important in the inland regions of the country and in mountain settlements. Hunting always has been regarded pri-

In July, the forest is full of juicy blueberries just waiting to be picked.

marily as a source of food, but it also has a culling effect.

Deer, such as moose and wild reindeer (in southern Norway, only), along with hart and roedeer are the most common kinds of game. Moose, reindeer and hart are heavy animals, and the meat which the hunter does not need usually is sold. From 1986 to 1991, the yearly yield of big game increased steadily – from 4,760 to 5,836 tons. Every year, a large number of small game, such as ptarmigan, grouse, hare, geese, ducks, and pigeons are landed.

Although coastal fishing is the most important, freshwater fishing has always been popular – in lakes, moun-

tain streams and rivers. The salmon is the king among river fish, and for hundreds of years, it was regarded as the most noble of fish. It was caught on its way up the rivers to spawn. Only decades ago, salmon were so abundant in certain areas that farmworkers had it written in their contracts that they not be served salmon more than four or five times a week. Salmon was salted and packed in barrels, and salt salmon was everyday food. Now, many rivers are almost emptied of salmon, making wild salmon luxury food. Today, extensive fish farming has put salmon within the reach of just about everyone. Smoked or marinated salmon is a delicacy, perfect for the festive table.

Fermented Fish

Old written sources indicate that fermentation of trout and whitefish has been common in Norway as far back as 1428. It is made primarily in Østlandet and is one of many delicacies often reserved for Christmas. In days of old, the fish was buried near where it was caught. It was packed in birch bark, buried alongside the water and covered with stones. It was important to maintain an even temperature. When the first snow had fallen, the fish was retrieved and brought back to the farm with a horse-drawn sleigh. Then it was layered in open wooden containers and weighted down. In this way, the fish could keep until late winter.

In earlier times, relatively little salt was used in the brine, partly because it was still rather difficult to obtain, and partly because it was so heavy to transport. Today, more salt is used, but the amount varies according to the consistency the fish is supposed to have.

Many people hunt small game to fill the freezer and to earn extra money. Hunting hare, about 1930.

The usual method is as follows: The fish is cleaned and washed, then placed in newly-scrubbed wooden containers. It is important that the stomach cavities of the fish be as clean as possible, and that all the fish in any single container be about the same size. Sprinkle a layer of coarse salt in the bottom of the container, then sprinkle salt into the stomach cavity and on the skin of each fish. Place the fish, stomach cavity up, in the container, sprinkling each layer of fish with salt and with a tablespoon of sugar. When the container is full, weight the fish down with boards and a stone, both of which have been cleaned with boiling water. Eventually, brine accumulates in the bottom of the container, and it is important that the fish be covered with brine. If there isn't enough, additional brine should be cooked from 70 grams (2 1/2 ounces) salt per liter water then chilled before adding. Fermented fish should be stored at 2-8° C (34-44° F) for about three months. The fish needs to be "aired" several times

Fishing for trout in Langtjønna in the Sunndal alps. A good catch means fermented trout for Christmas. Many people make their own fermented fish.

Reindeer-herding Sami have lived for hundreds of years as nomads, following their flocks to different grazing fields.

during storage, which just means lifting the boards and stirring a little.

As soon as the fish is ready, it is time for a party. This dish is an acquired taste even for many Norwegians, but it has its fan clubs. In Valdres and Østerdalen, it provides an added income for many farmers, who fight to

be able to offer the best fish during the short season, which lasts from mid-November until the middle of January.

Sami Reindeer Culture

In old times, the Sami were a hunting people, who lived from fishing, trapping and hunting. When the wild reindeer flocks were just about wiped out, early

in the 17th century, the Sami domesticated the reindeer and followed the flocks to different pastures. In this way, the Sami developed a nomad culture. Until the 1950's, the life of the reindeer-herding Sami could be considered a natural existence. Similar to other nomad peoples, their production was relatively one-sided. They had to barter

with other groups of people. The nomad Sami both traded and sold reindeer and its products.

Traditionally, the Sami have used the entire animal. Horn and bone were the raw materials for making tools and handicrafts. Pelts and tanned skins were made into clothing and shoes. The sinews were used for thread and the furs as blankets and mattresses. Their food consisted primarily of reindeer. They either roasted the meat over an open fire, or they cooked it in large pots which were heated over the fire. Boiling was the most common method of preparing meat.

When an animal was slaughtered, nothing was wasted. Blood, liver, and other organ meats were valuable resources. To satisfy the need for a warm beverage, the Sami often brewed a cup of blood-bouillon. They kneaded blood and fat into small balls, which they dissolved in boiling water to make a strong and nourishing drink. They

The family assembled around the hearth. It was tradition among the Sami that the men should make all dinners which included meat, while the women and girls should prepare the dairy dishes. It was considered bad manners to crack a meat bone. All bones were collected after a meal and deposited in a special place.

of the western Finnish peoples. The largest colony in northern Norway was founded at the end of the 17th century-beginning of the 18th, but even later, particularly in hard times, Finns have come over the border.

The other main area for Finnish immigration is Finnskogen (Finnish forest) in Solør (Hedmark). The largest colony was settled from 1620-1660. These were descendants of Finnish immigrants who had settled in Sweden in the 1570's. They settled in the areas around the Great Røden and Øyeren lakes. In contrast to smaller groups of Finnish immigrants who settled in other communities in eastern Norway, the Finns in Solør took much longer to assimilate. They continued to speak their own language, build according to Finnish custom and eat their traditional foods. Even after 250 years, there was very little intermarriage between Finns and Norwegians in the district.

probably preferred hot meat bouillon, though.

The meat was partitioned and prepared in a special way. If the meat was to be smoked or dried, the thickest muscles in the leg and arm were spread out. Roast, flank and shoulder in a long strip was hung over the smoke source in the tent or, if the meat were to be dried, over a pole outdoors.

The most important meal of the day was in the evening. During the winter, it consisted mostly of boiled reindeer meat and fish, while in the summer, it could be freshwater fish and reindeer milk. The Sami used little bread. They always had enough fish, birds, game, berries and other wild plants. Cloudberries have always been an important source of income for reindeer-herding Sami, and they picked sorrel as well. Angelica was another popular and tasty plant, where both the stalk and the blossoms were used. It was considered a snack, a vegetable and a seasoning.

One Sami specialty is boiled reindeer with marrow bones, tongue and bouillon. Marrow bones cooked with meat make a rich broth. It is important to

skim well, but otherwise, it is simple to make a hearty drink or soup. Only a little salt is needed to bring out the flavor. The bones are split and the marrow is eaten with the meat. In earlier days, the Sami often used to make "reindeer fondue." It is easy to make our own variation by adding grated cheese and toasted croutons to bouillon.

Finnish Beef

Finnish Beef is probably the best known Sami specialty for the average Norwegian. It is both easy to make and tasty. Thinly shaved reindeer meat (either bought already shaved or shaved with a sharp knife from a half-frozen reindeer shoulder) is browned in butter and seasoned with salt and pepper. When the meat begins to color, chopped onion is added and cooked until golden. Then the dish is rounded off with sour cream, a few slices of brown goat cheese (Ski Queen), and crushed juniper berries. After a few minutes' simmering, it is ready to serve with boiled or mashed potatoes and lingonberry compote.

Finnish Immigrant Culture

For centuries, Finnmark and Nord-Troms have absorbed a steady stream

Motti and silpo are two dishes from Finnskogen. Motti is made of 2 dl (3/4 cup) water, 1 teaspoon salt and 4 dl (1 2/3 cups) oat or barley flour. Water and salt are brought to a boil. Flour is sprinkled over the water until the entire surface is covered. When the water begins to boil, small "volcanos" are formed. Stir carefully with a slotted spoon until the flour forms small (1 – 1 1/2 cm (1/2") lumps. If the mixture is stirred too early, the motti are raw and big, and if it is stirred to late, they can be small, dry and floury. Fried fresh bacon slices are good with this dish. Leftover motti can be served for dessert with buttermilk and sugar.

Silpo is made of cubed pork and potatoes with milk. Equal amounts of fresh and lightly salted pork belly are cubed and browned in a frying pan, then removed with a slotted spoon and set aside. Afterwards, potato cubes are browned in the pork fat. Then milk is poured over them and cooked until thickened. The pork is added and heated just before serving.

THE HISTORIC MENU

The Norwegian historical menu is held together by a long thread tied to the natural resources: Fish from the sea and lakes, game from forests and mountains, and grain, milk and meat from one of Europe's most marginal agricultural societies. Through the centuries, the menu has, of course, changed, influenced by the economy, climactic changes and impulses from without. But even if pizza can be considered a "national dish," the basic theme of the Norwegian kitchen is still traditional ingredients and customs.

The development of the Norwegian menu can be divided roughly into thirds: subsistence farming, traditional country food, and the bourgeois kitchen. Today's kitchen is based on the latter two, with further development through new preservation methods and knowledge about diet. Refinement has come via other lands' kitchens, especially the French. Many of our chefs have worked in France and have brought back impulses.

EARLY NORWEGIANS MENU

Even if the journey to today's Norwegian kitchen has been long, finds from prehistoric settlements indicate that even early Norwegians had quite a varied menu. A dig in Vistehulen in Jæren from about 4000-5000 BC shows great variation in the diet. Bones from more than 50 kinds of animals have been found, about half from birds, a third mammals, and the rest fish. The amount of bones points to a deliberate concentration of the hunt to animals which yielded the most meat. Wild pigs, seals and moose were the most important animals. Of birds, the guillemot, and the now extinct great auk, were the most popular, while cod was the favorite fish. People collected hazelnuts, and we can deduct that they also gathered roots and berries. In the earliest settlements, mollusks were hardly consumed, but later they became an important part of the menu. Shells from oysters, sand snails, and mussels were found during the dig.

The first traces of farming date to about 4000 BC, but not until about 2000 BC did it became dominant. Cultivation of grain and raising animals did not provide enough to feed a family, so hunting and fishing continued to be important. From Nordfjord and Sunnfjord, 2100 carvings indicate just how important hunting and fishing were for the people. These carvings probably had religious significance, but in modern times, we look at them as the first Norwegian menu. Big game animals, such as moose, deer and reindeer, are the most common motifs. Otherwise, carvings depict bears, whales, salmon, halibut, birds and seals. With the exception of bear, all of these are part of the Norwegian kitchen today, although whale and seal have an insignificant role.

NORWEGIAN FARM FOOD

The establishment of farm settlements gave the second theme to the Norwegian kitchen. Grain (usually barley and oats) meant porridge, bread and beer. Farm animals gave milk, cheese and, of course, meat. From viking times, we know that the diet was simple, and that most farms were self-sustaining. Only one commodity was needed from without: Salt. It was extracted from seawater along the coast, but it also was imported. It is no coincidence that a salt center such as Moirmoutier in France became a Viking base.

The Norwegian menu changed little during the Middle Ages, and it was not until the potato gained in popularity at the beginning of the 19th Century that any important changes occurred. By taking a close look at the Norwegian farm household during the last century, we can get a good idea of the historic Norwegian menu.

In the old days, there was a more pronounced difference between workdays and feast days than there is today. Everyday food was often herring and gruel or porridge, while on feast days both fresh meat and sour cream porridge were served. Flour was a gift of God, and the cow was needed for survival. This reveals the important role of grain and milk in the Norwegian diet.

In coastal settlements, herring and other fish were an important part of the daily diet. Inland, people ate some salt fish, but salt herring was more common. Salt herring was eaten with flatbread, gruel and butter, if one could afford it. Freshwater fish was a welcome addition to the diet.

Herring was not often served for dinner in the settlements at Hedmark, but herring, potatoes, flatbread and gruel or milk often was served in the evening.

In Ringsaker, Thursday was designated meat day, with salt meat, bacon and

A fisherman's meal. From Portør, near Kragerø, 1909. Everyday food was simple, and many meals consisted of bread and gruel.

soup. Tuesday and Sunday also could be meat days. Otherwise, dinner food was porridge, dried meats, stew, flatbread with buttermilk, sausages, blood pudding and dumplings and other things.

In Telemark, meat was eaten once a day, but this was not the norm in the rest of the country. Generally, porridge was eaten two or three times a day.

Around 1870, farm workers in Gudbrandsdal were given a rye cake and some whisky or beer before they started work at 4 a.m. They had to eat this meal standing, but they were allowed to sit down for the next meal.

In some settlements in Østerdal, butter was served only on designated days. On other days, butter was mixed with fat, concentrated whey, milk or buttermilk or a mixture of potatoes and butter.

Sometimes there were considerable differences in the diet from one region to another during the 19th century. The number of meals per day and their names varied according to the district. Breakfast and dinner were new words which eventually took over. The most common meals during the 1860's are listed below.

Coastal Cultures
(Møre and Romsdal)

Early breakfast was served from 5-6 a.m. and consisted of ersatz coffee or warm milk, a barley cake with butter and cheese or whey spread.

Breakfast was served from 8-9 a.m. and consisted of cold porridge with warm milk and dried halibut, or shark cooked over the coals; flatbread and warm sour milk (usually this meant buttermilk or cultured milk); dried meat, dried bacon or sausage. Flatbread with sour milk was often served in the summer.

Dinner was served at noon. It could be halibut soup, herring soup, herring and barley, barley soup, stew, meat and potato dumplings, poached fresh or salt fish, soaked dried peas and pork, flatbread mixed with soup, fish dumplings stuffed with fish liver or plain.

The afternoon meal was served from 4-5 p.m. and consisted of ersatz coffee or warm sour milk, a flat bread, barley or rye bread, potato pancakes, raised pancakes or lefse with butter and whey spread. There might also be fried shark, fried dried herring, dried halibut cooked over the coals or fried pork belly with porridge and flatbread.

The evening meal, from 7-8 p.m. consisted of milk and porridge, herring and potatoes, or cooked yellow peas with sour milk and soup.

Inland Cultures
(Inner Trøndelag)

Early breakfast was served around 6 a.m. Among the many dishes which could be served, the most common were milk, barley cake, butter and several cheeses; fried pork belly and potatoes or blood sausage in the fall; porridge with warm milk; fried pork belly and potatoes, dumplings with fat, dried meats with milk, fried blood pudding and flatbread or milk, bread, fried pork belly and potatoes.

At around 11 a.m., any of the following could be served: Herring, potatoes and flatbread; milk soup with barley; milk soup with dumplings, dried meat, potatoes and flatbread, porridge and milk; boiled meat, pork and mashed potatoes or vegetables; bread porridge or soup with potatoes.

At about 5 p.m., barley cake and potato pancakes or waffles, butter and cheeses were served.

The evening meal was served at about 8 p.m. and consisted of milk and porridge; milk, herring, potatoes and flatbread; yogurt and potatoes; yogurt and porridge; milk and flatbread; milk soup and dried sausages or other dried meats.

Seljord in Telemark

For the first meal of the day, cheese and flatbread were served in the settlements, and cold porridge and sour milk (usually buttermilk or cultured milk) in the high mountain cabins in the summer.

The next meal, at about 9:30 a.m., consisted of warm porridge and sour milk (usually buttermilk or cultured milk) in the settlements, and flatbread with butter and whey spread in the mountains.

Dinner was at 3 p.m. In the mountains, it consisted of either milk soup with milk; meat and soup; flatbread with buttermilk, flatbread with broth, veal in broth or fermented fish, meat, sausages, gruel and boiled fish. If this meal was served earlier in the day, there

A meal of coffee and flatbread in Setesdal in 1910. Bunads (national costumes) were not everyday clothing, so this must be a special occasion.

Many Norwegian families still gather around the breakfast table.

The packed lunch is typically Norwegian. Norwegians pack lunches for work and for a walk in the mountains or forest. This always consists of slices of bread with cheese or meat.

The Daily Meals

In most families, meals are still times for everyone to come together, even though the changes in society have given us another family pattern. Family members are also more on the go, with many more activities than in earlier days. For that reason, it is even more important to get together at mealtime. Food preparation is much easier than it used to be, because industry has taken over much of the work. Now, we can devote more time to enjoying those meals.

The breakfast table is an important occasion. A table set with bread, butter, cheese, jam and other sandwich fillings, milk and juice, is a good start to a busy day. Even though Norwegians travel a lot and enjoy a warm lunch when abroad, he always returns to his cold packed lunch at home.

When the workday is over, the family once again meets around the table, at dinnertime, with a meal of meat or fish, potatoes and a vegetable or two, and maybe some fruit for dessert. Norwegians eat dinner much earlier than southern Europeans, so they end the day with either coffee and maybe even an informal evening meal of open-face sandwiches.

Holiday Food Traditions

Many of today's Norwegian food traditions go back to heathen times. Others are connected to Christian feasts or secular holidays, such as May 17, Norway's Constitution Day.

Lent, the seven weeks before Easter, is a period of fasting for most Christians,

could also be a meal at 5 p.m., which consisted of porridge or flatbread with buttermilk.

The nightly meal was served around 9 p.m. and consisted of porridge and milk.

Setting the Table and Serving

During the last century, it was still uncommon to use plates for everyday meals, although food was served on wooden plates for festive occasions. On workdays, the food was set in the mid-

dle of the table, and flatbread served as a plate. Cutlery was scarce, but everyone had a spoon. In days of old, spoons were made of horn or wood. The table knife was uncommon. Men had a knife in a sheath hanging from their belt, and eventually, the folding pocketknife was introduced. Those who didn't have knives ate with their fingers. The fork, which came into use in the 16th century elsewhere in Europe, was not common in the Norwegian countryside until around 1850.

but the Norwegian Lutheran church has no official rules regarding the fast. Nonetheless, we do have certain food traditions connected with Lent.

Rich food always was served on the days leading up to Lent. Palm Sunday was once called Pork Sunday, followed by Pork Monday and Fat Tuesday. On Pork Sunday, buns filled with cream or jelly doughnuts deep fried in lard were served. The following day's menu featured split buns spread with butter and sprinkled with sugar and cinnamon. These were served in soup bowls and doused with boiling milk.

Fat Tuesday was also called White Tuesday, an indication of the different traditions connected with that day. In places where it was called White Tuesday, sour cream porridge was on the menu, and sometimes the day was referred to as Porridge Tuesday. Where it was called Fat Tuesday, the menu consisted of fatty food, such as peas, meat and pork.

Norwegian Easter food traditions are of relatively recent date. Most people serve boiled eggs for breakfast on Easter Sunday, and lamb for dinner either the night before Easter or for Easter Sunday dinner.

Whereas national days in many countries are celebrated with military parades, Norway's Constitution Day is first and foremost a day for children. On May 17, children march in parades wearing national costumes, and they have parties, with ice cream, hot dogs and soda pop, in between all the other activities. For grown-ups, May 17 means cream cakes, egg cream, sour cream porridge and coffee.

In the Christian tradition, we celebrate the feast of St. John, in honor of St. John the Baptist, while in the heathen tradition, that day is midsummer-night, the shortest night of the year. This feast is celebrated with bonfires, sour cream porridge and dried meats, hotdogs and dancing.

Olsok, in memory of St. Olav, who Christianized Norway, is celebrated on

On May 17, Norway's Constitution Day, children parade up Karl Johans gate to the Royal Palace to pay their respects to the king. It is a festive day for every Norwegian.

Midsummer Night at Rotevatnet in Volda.

July 19. This is marked by more bonfires, dancing, and grilling. Sour cream porridge is served on this day, too, but by the end of July, the nights are already getting longer.

A_{dvent} is the time between the fourth Sunday before Christmas and Christmas Eve. In a religious context, it represents the preparations before the holiday, which, for the Catholic church, is a period of fasting. In Norway, it has been the tradition that all food which was to be consumed during the Christmas holiday had to be made during Advent. It was therefore a busy time, dedicated to preparing meat and hams and baking breads and cakes. It was also time for cleaning, as everything had to be scrubbed before the holiday.

T_{oday}, we have retained many of those same traditions. Much of the food which was produced on the farm is now industrially made, but still, Advent means cleaning, baking and making dishes which have special significance

in the family, such as mutton roll, head cheese, lefse, flatbread, Christmas cakes and cookies.

A_{dvent} is also a time for social get-togethers. Often, people go to special Christmas buffets together with friends and colleagues. The menu usually features lutefisk, pork ribs, steamed dried ribs of mutton or fermented fish.

$C_{hristmas}$ is the most important of our Christian holidays, and it is celebrated at home with the family. Many old customs connected with the celebration are still honored. The home is made festive with a Christmas tree and decorations. It's a time for the family to get together around the dinner table with the best food the kitchen can offer. It's a time of roaring fires, candles, games and fun. The dinner table is always laid carefully and decorated.

M_{ost} families have their own special food traditions which have been handed down through the generations.

Some eat Christmas porridge, usually a rich sour cream or rice porridge. Porridge is served both inland and along the coast. Some place an almond in the porridge, and the person who finds it gets a prize. Fish dishes, such as lutefisk, poached cod or halibut, are served most often in coastal districts, especially in northern Norway. Pork ribs, pork patties and sausages are most popular in eastern regions, while steamed dried ribs of mutton with mutton sausage are most popular in the western part of the country. For dessert, rice cream, prune compote and cloudberry cream are popular all over the land. Head cheese, ham, coarse liver paté, mutton roll, anchovies, fermented trout and other good food also have their places on the Christmas table. Christmas beer (stronger than that available the rest of the year) and aquavit are the beverages of choice.

Opposite page: In many homes, the Christmas tree is decorated on Christmas Eve. Years ago, candles were used, and when the tree was lit, Christmas had begun.

In days of old, special customs were connected with Christmas. In grain-producing areas, a special cake was baked. It was decorated with signs pertaining to the district. It was supposed to be made from the last sheaf of wheat harvested from the fields, and it was to remain on the Christmas table throughout the holiday. When Christmas was over, it was stored in the silo until spring. Then it was either cooked in a soup pot, given to the farmhands, or just crumbled and sprinkled over the fields with hopes of a good crop.

In many places in the country, people set a bowl of porridge in the barn on Christmas Eve for the Christmas elf. This was to thank the elf for looking after the farm animals throughout the year.

In northern Norway, it was said that if the husband couldn't get fresh halibut for Christmas dinner, he would have to spend the night on the barn roof.

Christmas celebration started after the church bells rang in the holiday at 5 p.m. Then the family could gather to hear the Christmas story before dinner or coffee and cookies were served. After the meal, they joined hands and sang songs around the Christmas tree and passed out presents. These often were homemade and less expensive than the gifts of today. But even if both gifts and food today are more impressive, most families still follow the traditional pattern on Christmas Eve. Families of all ages get together to celebrate.

Earlier, most people attended church on Christmas day, the most important religious day of the year. Now, it is a family day for most, and people often journey a long distance to get together over a brunch buffet or dinner. The buffet can include pork ribs, pork patties, cheeses, headcheese, ham, coarse liver paté, mutton roll, beef roll, anchovies, different herring dishes, fermented trout, lefse, bread and flatbread, all according to tradition.

New Year's Eve is a family holiday for many. For others, it is time for parties with friends or dances. Turkey, ptarmigan, fish, reindeer or roast moose are featured on the menu. Here, too, families make their own traditions, which still are important, even in our own times.

Family Celebrations

It has always been the tradition in Norway to celebrate all important days in the family with a festive meal, with the best food and drink the family can offer, along with lots of good conversation around the table.

Weddings are such occasions. Before, it ws usual for the bride and groom to travel from farm to farm and invite guests to the wedding. Both wore their best clothes for this, and all the people in the area wondered who would be on the guest list. A master of ceremonies and cooks had to be found. Usually a neighbor lady was placed in charge of the food, a job which commanded respect.

In days of old, a wedding always lasted three days: The eve of the wedding, the wedding day and the second day. Everyone who had participated in the preparations before the wedding were guests on the second day. The cooks came to the farm the day before the wedding to make porridge and bake different kinds of lefse and sour cream wafers. Cheese was often served with the lefse, otherwise salt meat, pork and sausages were on the menu.

The guests came together the eve of the wedding. In addition to the food which the hosts had prepared, the guests brought with them special foods, which might be molded butter, lefse, waffles, cakes, milk and sour cream. Everyone competed to bring the best food.

It was scandalous to run out of food, so dishes were made in great quantity. The person in charge of food had a lot to do. She had to keep track of all the food in boxes and baskets. Everything had its appointed place on the table. When the wedding was over, cakes, lefse and cheese were set aside for those who had been unable to attend.

THE BOURGEOIS KITCHEN

It is normal to emphasize the importance of the country kitchen whenever discussing Norwegian food. For the most part, this is correct. But from the beginning of the 19th Century, we note considerable influence from what we call the bourgeois or urban kitchen. The Norwegian upper class (really bourgeoisie and mercantile class), consisting of merchants and civil servants, was tiny, and compared with that of other countries, not particularly wealthy. But the outward-oriented Norwegian economy, with considerable shipping and export of timber and fish, encouraged many to bring back

A farm wedding around 1885 in Tydal in Sør-Trøndelag.

impulses from other countries. It is said that the timber-baron, Bernt Anker, sent his collars to London to be starched, and that at Bogstad Manor, outside Christiania (Oslo), guests could help themselves from a Madeira fountain.

Little has been written about the development of the bourgeois kitchen. We have reason to believe that the most important impulses came from England and France via Denmark. Foreign customs were blended with Norwegian traditions and ingredients. Such Norwegian specialties as ptarmigan in cream and the many different kinds of cream cake are examples of this. And these are worthy of even the most sophisticated culinary nation.

The pioneer of the modern Norwegian kitchen is undoubtedly Hanna Winsnes (1789-1872), a minister's wife. Her "Manual in the Many Aspects of the Household" was not only the first systematic Norwegian cookbook, it set the standard for the bourgeois/urban kitchen right up to our own time. Hanna Winsnes writes of the well-to-do kitchen, with no shortage of ingredients: "Use what you have on hand – 12 eggs." Although there are some recipes for simple dishes (for the servants), the book is aimed at the bourgeoisie. Winsnes also had a political message in her book, which was generally the case with the cookbook writers who followed her. In the preface, she mentions that she had "missed having a simple and thorough instruction book in running a household and wondered why there were no books in the only trade open for women, while all kinds of books existed for men."

Everybody wasn't equally enthusiastic, either for the food or for the careful statement regarding women's rights. The radical poet, Arne Garborg, attacked her on both points, exclaiming: "This is just women's rights, she's just like Camilla Collett (a writer and outspoken suffragette)." In his tirade against the Winsnes kitchen, he writes: "The upper classes certainly live well.

They wallow in eggs, sugar and butter, their larders and cellars are full; they take... take...take..., never questioning from whom they are taking. For the world is in order. Go into the servants' quarters and look at them eating porridge and herring, without envying the people upstairs either the salmon or the steak. There's an aroma over her book which is enough to make you believe in the good things in life."

But the protests were nothing more than a footnote. While Garborg oozed with irony over the capable preacher's wife, her cookbook sold 50,000 copies, an unbelievable number for the last century.

Many other women followed in Hanna Winsnes' footsteps. Of these, Henriette Schønberg-Erken probably was the most influential, with her "Big Cookbook," published in 1914. This was the heyday of the bourgeoisie, and even the most humble members of the

Hanna Winsnes, pioneer of the modern Norwegian kitchen, in 1866.

Henriette Schønberg-Erken enjoyed working in her kitchen.

middle class had servants. They were certainly needed to prepare some of Schønberg-Erken's many-course dinners. These contrast with the simple customs of farm kitchens. Here are Henriette Schønberg-Erken's own suggestions for four dinner party menus:

DINNER I
Molded Cream
Soup a la Bismarck with Cheese Straws
Fillet of Fish a la Marquise with White Wine Sauce and Geneva Sauce
Salt Tongue with Macaroni Timbale and Russian Peas or Turkey a la Daube
Sorbet
Roast Fowl
Pears a la Helene or Chestnut Cream

DINNER II
Spinach Soup with Egg Dumplings
Lobster with Mayonnaise
Mushroom Tartlets
Roast Duck
Lemon Ice Cream
Crackers with Parmesan Cheese
Fruit, Chocolates

DINNER III
Turtle Soup with Milk Punch
Poached Flounder with Hollandaise Sauce
Egg Croquettes or Asparagus
Hazel Grouse
Pistachio Ice Cream
Fruit, Chocolates
Cheese, Crackers

DINNER IV
Brown Soup with Madeira
Salmon in Mousseline Sauce
Tournedos
Artichokes with Melted Butter
Roast Chicken
Strawberries with Frozen Cream
Cookies, Chocolates

The classic bourgeois kitchen disappeared, along with the servants, around 1940, but some of the typical dishes live on and are served on special occasions. Restaurant chefs are renewing their acquaintance with the bourgeois kitchen, and a few years ago, Henriette Schønberg-Erken's cookbook was published in a facsimile edition.

THE NORWEGIAN TABLE

The Norwegian buffet has long roots. Foreigners often find the cold table the most fascinating part of their stay in Norway. Many hotels serve buffets daily, and on special occasions, buffet tables are set up both at home and at restaurants.

Food is always fresh, and it is seldom covered with sauce. A Norwegian buffet can seem rather simple in form, but simple food is the essence of the Norwegian kitchen. The raw materials play the most important role.

Breakfast

Every hotel guest, especially at mountain resorts, meets the Norwegian buffet tradition at the breakfast table. A roll and jam just won't do for a hungry Norwegian. On a hotel breakfast table, you will find different kinds of bread and cereal, milk and juice, along with all kinds of sliced meat, eggs, cheese, jam and marmalade.

Lunch

Most foreigners find the lunch table a great culinary experience. It is a real feast for the eye as well as the palate, with all kinds of beautifully prepared and arranged food. On a lunch table, you will find:
• different kinds of bread
• milk and juice
• salads with dressings
• many herring dishes
• fish and shellfish
• sliced meat

A Norwegian lunch buffet is a sight to behold. The food is the focal point.

Herring, beer and aquavit is festive food today, whereas many years ago, herring was poor man's food.

Herring Buffet

- dried meats with side dishes
- hot dishes made with fish, meat and occasionally, pasta
- cheese and fruit
- rice cream, caramel and chocolate pudding, gelatin, Bavarian creams, cakes, berries and fruit

Only a few decades ago, salt herring was regarded as poor man's food. Times have changed, and now that we no longer have to eat salt herring every day, most people think it tastes very good indeed – so good that this one time poor man's food has now entered the gourmet temple. We still have not adopted Sweden's rich traditions re-

garding herring tables, but even here, it is becoming more popular to invite guests to enjoy several herring dishes, accompanied by beer and aquavit.
Many kinds of dishes can be made from salted or spiced herring. When the fish is cleaned and filleted, it is cut into pieces and combined with different sauces or dressings. A well-appointed

herring table might include the following: Marinated herring, herring in tomato, mustard or curry sauce, glazier's herring, herring salads, a warm dish or two, dark bread, onions, pickled beets, butter and sour cream.

Dried Meats

Dried ham has always been festive food. It is both easy to serve and popular with guests of all ages. A festive table of dried meats includes: Ham, dried leg of mutton, salami, mutton sausage, horsemeat sausage, mixed meat sausage, flatbread, lefse, sour heavy cream, scrambled eggs, creamed potatoes and bread. Sometimes, salad is served alongside. This food tastes good with beer and aquavit.

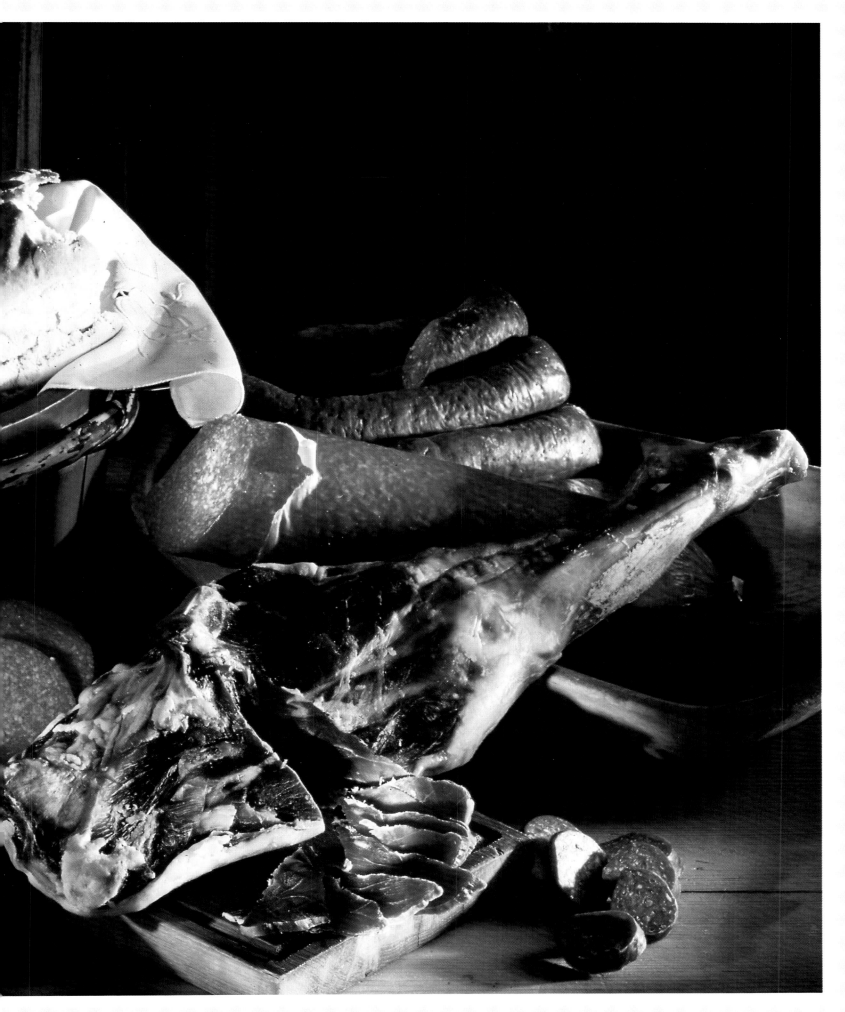

Dried meats have always been considered festive food.

According to tradition, the Christmas buffet is supposed to be one great horn of plenty. Everything good in the house is placed on the table. At hotels, the Christmas buffet is the most extensive one served.

Christmas Table

Many connect the term "Christmas table" with the meals served at home during the holiday. For most people, though, it is synonymous with the big cold and hot tables featured at hotels and restaurants from the end of November through the holiday period, primarily at the week-end. It has become a tradition for pairs, friends, business associates and colleagues to meet for an evening of eating during the Christmas season.

The Christmas table builds on the luncheon cold table. In addition come many special Christmas dishes, such as pork ribs, pork patties and sauerkraut, turkey, steamed dried ribs of mutton, smoked leg of lamb, ham, headcheese, mutton roll, liver paté and pigs' trotters. There is also a selection of cheeses, along with desserts such as cream cake, almond ring cake and an assortment of Christmas cookies.

Cakes and desserts have a central place in home entertaining.

Cake Table

Desserts and cakes always have had a central place on all festive occasions. They are a natural part of birthday and Christmas celebrations, as well as less for formal get-togethers. Decorated cakes are served at Christenings, confirmations and weddings. The Norwegian kitchen has a rich cake tradition, with many local variations.

TO DRINK WITH FOOD

Norwegian drinking customs have developed through the interaction of the country's natural raw materials, its trading partners, and the governmental alcohol policy. There is a good balance between the traditional dishes and the appropriate drinks. Salted or smoked foods go well with beer and aquavit, and both of these are produced from raw materials and flavoring agents which can be cultivated in Norway.

Parallel with the development of the typical national drinks, Norwegians have imported drinks and drinking customs from the Continent and from America (coffee, chocolate). We have imported wine since viking times, for the sagas tell us that French wine was the province of the king and his court. Trade with abroad insured a steady supply of wine, and later, whisky. This import of drink followed the export of fish and timber to France, Germany, Spain and England. By the end of the 18th century, foreign wine and spirits were well-established in Norway.

But these wares were exclusive to the small number of upper class Norwegians, mostly merchants and civil servants. Most Norwegians drank water or milk with everyday meals. This tradition has been maintained up to the present day.

Otherwise, beer was and is the most typical drink for both work days and feasts in Norway and in the rest of northern Europe.

The peculiarly Norwegian alcohol policy has had an enormous effect on the development of Norwegian drinking habits. After the unrestricted production of whisky resulted in severe social problems in the middle of the 19th century, a strong temperance movement emerged. As a political entity, its biggest achievement was the implementation of prohibition against fortified wine and whisky in 1916. When these restrictions were rescinded in 1927, all sales of wine and spirits had to go through a monopoly, with a restrictive policy regarding number of sales outlets and liquor licences. By the middle of the 1980's, the policy was liberalized, a development which probably will be reinforced through Norway's connections with the EEC.

DAILY DRINKS

It wasn't long ago that our water was so clean that it could be drunk straight from the river or stream even in populous areas. Away from the cities and towns and plowed fields, rivers and streams are still clean, and the water is

Norwegian mountain water, drunk directly from the river, is for many, the ultimate natural experience – clean, cold, fresh and delicious.

safe to drink. For many Norwegians, a drink straight from a mountain stream is almost a ritual of pleasure and unity with nature. Tap water in Norway is delicious, and cold water is often the drink of choice at dinner.

In days of old, milk was the most common daily drink. It was mostly drunk sour (cultured). Fresh milk was cooked before serving. It was often mixed with water to eek out the quantity. Milk was a logical accompaniment to many dinner dishes, among them, potato dumplings and salty fish dishes. Milk still has its place on the table for all the other meals. Even though most adults drink coffee or tea for breakfast, lunch and the evening snack, they often drink a glass of milk as well.

Coffee first came to Norway about 250 years ago, but it wasn't generally accepted until the 1870's. Nor was it a drink for just anyone, to begin with, for it was both foreign and expensive. People soon found out that they could stretch it with different things, and before long, the butcher, shoemaker, tailor and baker enjoyed coffee after each meal.

Even today, coffee is a popular drink. In fact, Norwegians are among the world's biggest consumers of coffee per inhabitant. Coffee is comparatively reasonable in price, and the cold winter climate creates a need for a hot drink. Coffee is the perfect accompaniment to meals where bread is consumed, and

Norwegian are world-class coffee drinkers.

there's a hot pot in every office. After work and after dinner, a cup of coffee tastes good. Festive dinners are often concluded with a cup of strong coffee and a glass of cognac or liqueur.

Coffee also can have political significance. Alongside the political or religious message, coffee has been a drawing card for mission organizations, women's groups and political meetings. Former prime minister, Einar Gerhardsen, relates in his autobiography, that what he enjoyed most was being together with his fellow Social Democrats over a pot of coffee brewed over an open fire in the forest or in the mountains.

Tea came to Norway at about the same time as coffee, but it never has achieved the same status or popularity. Earlier, it was used on formal occasions and served to the infirm, but as an ordinary drink, it wasn't used much. In the 1970's, in the wake of the hippie movement and the new political left, young people started to drink tea. Both regular and herbal varieties increased in popularity. Today, tea consumption is at an all time high and the selection has improved.

Cocoa and chocolate have long been popular drinks, especially among children, but a thermos of hot cocoa in the middle of a long walk or ski expedition hits the spot for all generations. And it tastes especially good with buns and cookies.

NO HOLIDAY WITHOUT BEER

Beer is a typical Nordic drink, even though it stems from ancient Babylon and Egypt. But beer couldn't compete with wine. It was not until it came to northern Europe and Scandinavia that it found its true home.

Norwegian cultural history is full of beer. Even in preChristian times, beer played an important role in society, especially in connection with sacrifices.

The sagas of the Norwegian kings and old Norwegian laws have numerous descriptions and rules regarding beer. Olav Kyrre's saga notes the following: "King Harald and other kings before him used to drink from animal horns and carried the beer from the throne around the fire and shared the drink with those who desired."

It was no joke to neglect to brew beer, or to brew bad beer. The Gulating law states that a man who does not brew for three winters has sinned against Christianity and should lose all his property – half to be given to the king, the other half to the bishop.

Both in viking times and during the Middle Ages, the beer bowl was the center of attraction. To celebrate a birth, a wedding or a funeral, beer was drunk. Beer had to be served to make an agreement legally binding. The Gulating law also states that nobody should be declared incompetent, so long as he has his senses, can ride a horse and drink beer.

Brewing took place on the farms and was especially connected with holidays. Strong Hardanger and Sogn beer are still brewed in those places and are descendants of what we call original Norwegian beer. Although brewing beer was up to the individual households, as early as the 1200's, beer was sold in the cities. But such retail beer was not common before the modern industrial brewery took over production at the beginning of the 19th Century. In 1857, there were 343 breweries in Norway, while today, only 16 are left.

Brewing beer was an elaborate process. When we see how much work it was, it is easy to understand why it was appreciated so much.

Preparations began as soon as the grain was threshed. Barley with the best sprouting ability was sorted, cleaned and stored until it was time to brew the bear. When that time came, half-full sacks of barley were placed in running water for three days, to allow the grain to swell. When the shoots were 3 cm (1") long, the tangled grain was separated and then spread out over the loft floor to dry. The grain had to be turned with a rake daily. The last part of the drying process took place in the kitchen. It was very important that the grain be completely dry. When that happened, the grain was transformed into malt, which could be stored for many years.

Extensive equipment is needed to brew beer, and everything has to be thoroughly clean. The night before the brewing was to start, malt was added to a wooden tub and covered with luke-warm water. Then a large vat was filled with water and juniper – everything had to be prepared in advance to be ready and waiting the next morning. Then a fire was lit to cook the juniper. When the juniper-water was almost at the boiling point, it was poured over the malt. Then more juniper-water was cooked and poured into kegs.

The next step was to make brewer's yeast in a large tub with a hole connected to a valve or a tap near the bottom. The malt-juniper-water mixture was then transferred to the large vat and heated to 80°C (175°F). Then it was poured into the tub with the tap and topped off with additional hot juniper-water. After standing long enough, the mixture became known as brewer's

Brewing beer at Mølstertun at Voss. There was prestige in brewing good beer.

wort. The wort was brought to a boil and canvas bags of hops were added. In the Middle Ages, hop gardens were fairly widespread in Norway. When the wort had cooled to about 30°C (80°F), yeast was added, along with a little sugar.

The first beer which was ready after fermentation was called "good beer." The alcohol content was medium to high, dependent upon how much sugar had been added. The beer which resulted from the second addition of juniper-water was called "light beer." It

Beer is a traditional drink which suits many of the dishes in the Norwegian kitchen, especially those made with salted or smoked foods. Beer has been considered the appropriate festive drink since viking times.

A half-liter of beer at an outdoor restaurant is a sure sign of summer.

had, much like the light beer of today, a very low alcohol percentage. Even back then, people understood the importance of "light" products.

Commercial Production

Norwegian breweries make all beer according to the so-called purity law, which means that only malt, water, yeast and hops are allowed to be used in production. In connection with the European Trade Agreement, this law probably will be rescinded, but there is still reason to believe that Norwegian breweries in the future will continue to brew beer in the traditional way.

Industrial beer production is similar to the traditional but adapted to suit modern techniques and in much larger volume. Norwegian breweries produce many varieties of beer, the most important being pilsner and light beer. Beer with a higher alcohol content has become less popular in recent years, and its future is uncertain, now that the sale of the beverage has been transferred from grocery stores to the wine monopoly. Another developmental trend is rapid growth in the sale of alcohol-free beer.

Beer is always best when it is newly tapped, and it should not be stored longer than three months. It is served in a glass or tankard, dependent upon the atmosphere and the food on the menu. Weak beer should be served colder than beer with a higher alcohol content.

NORWEGIAN SPIRITS

What would lutefisk, lamb and cabbage stew, dried meats or a herring table be without beer and aquavit? Not a lot, many Norwegians would say. For even if Norwegians are deluged with dishes and drinks from other countries, they prefer their traditional dishes, accompanied by aquavit. The special thing about the Nordic aquavit tradition is that it is seldom consumed alone. It just about always accompanies food.

Imported spirits have always been luxury articles in Norway, but most people, at least until World War II, could afford aquavit. Now the price difference is minimal, but aquavit's popularity is still growing, also on the export market. Aquavit is the Nordic countries' most important contribution to the liquor cabinet (although some berry liqueurs also are unique). But it took several hundred years before aquavit, as we know it, got its own identity. Perhaps aquavit's history began in 1531, when the Danish leader at Bergenhus castle, Eske Bille, sent archbishop Olav Engelbrektsson some liquor, which he called Aqua Vitae. According to Bille, this drink could help cure all kinds of ills. Since then, the archbishop himself has been credited with introducing liquor to Norway.

The first liquor was sold as medicine by local apothecaries. The medical expertise at the time claimed that there was an herb for every illness. Therefore, it was important for it to include as many herbal extracts as possible. It tasted accordingly, but that did not affect the belief in its healing powers, rather the opposite was true. Eventually, people discovered its other powers, and the size of the doses administered by the apothecaries was adjusted. With that, liquor as a stimulant was born.

The first Norwegian spirits were made with grain, and people built all kinds of contraptions to distill it at home. With the exception of the period 1756-1816, when home-distilling was forbidden to secure the availability of grain for planting (but also to favor Danish breweries), moonshine was produced in every town and settlement, until it was forbidden completely in 1845. By then, the production and consumption of spirits was completely out of control. In 1827, it was estimated that 11,000 distillation apparatuses were in use in Norway, and drunkenness had become a big social problem. 30 years later, only 450 home stills were left.

This is not wholly due to the law of prohibition. Another reason was that

grain was replaced by the potato as the basic ingredient. Making spirits from potatoes required more advanced equipment and a greater volume of production. That's how modern aquavit evolved.

Aquavit is a flavored liquor, with caraway the most important seasoning. Other herbs and spices used in the production of aquavit include anise, fennel, coriander, star anise and bitter orange peel. In addition to small amounts of Oloroso sherry, sugar and salt also is added. All these ingredients contribute to the well-rounded, developed taste of the pure caraway distillate. The exact recipe for the different blends of herbs and spices in the aquavit produced by the Norwegian wine monopoly is, of course, a well-guarded secret.

Today, aquavit is made from neutral potato spirits. The filtered alcohol is blended with distillates to a strength of

Aquavit is aged in used sherry barrels. Its development is controlled at set intervals.

60%. The mixture is aged for three to five years in 500 liter (quart) oak barrels which previously were used in sherry production. During that period, the product takes shape. The many

Potato alcohol is used in the production of Norwegian spirits. Aquavits available in Norway include, from the left, Simers Taffel, Oplandske Gammel, Gilde Non Plus Ultra, Løiten Linie and Lysholm Linie.

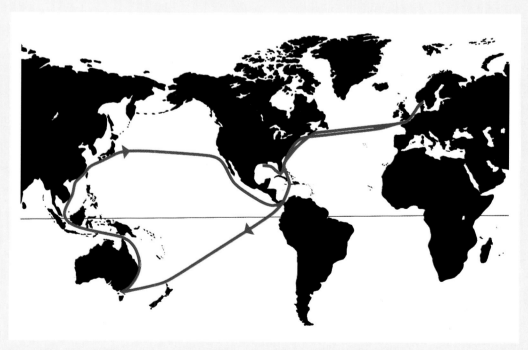

For more than 100 years, aquavit which has sailed over the equator has been a Norwegian specialty. Even today, both Lysholm Linie and Løyten Linie are transported over "the line" and travel around the world via Australia.

different ingredients meld together, but it takes time before they find one another and unify. The flavorings also probably develop due to the absorption of oxygen through the pores of the barrel and through the bunghole. At the end of the aging process, the aquavit from different barrels is blended (equalized) to give the finished product a uniform character.

Linje aquavit is the flagship of Norwegian spirits, and not without reason. It is called "Linie Aquevit" because the aquavit has passed over the equator or "the line." The explanation of this is as follows: Years ago, sailing ships from Trøndelag used to transport Norwegian liquor to foreign countries. On some voyages, not all was sold or consumed, and what was left had to be brought back to Norway. Once in port, these bottles were sampled, and the tasters noticed that the long journey over the equator had given the liquor a completely new and wonderful aroma. From the 1850's, aquavit was aged on board – the oak vats were sent between Norway and Australia. That tradition has continued until the present time. The back label on each bottle notes the name of the ship used to transport the aquavit, where it has been and how long it has been en route.

Both white and brown aquavit are produced in Norway. The white variety is younger and suits rich and fatty food. Brown aquavit is uniquely Norwegian, and the prestige label Gilde Non Plus Ultra, has been aged at least 10 years. It should be served at room temperature (the same is true for most aquavits) and is a good alternative to cognac.

Mead – the Drink that Disappeared

When the vikings feasted, they toasted with mead. They regarded mead as a "substantially strong drink" that was better than beer. Old recipes indicate that mead was usually made from water, sugar, lemons, syrup, ginger, raisins and yeast. Today, mead is brewed privately by a very few fans.

The Berry – Northern Europe's Substitute for the Grape

Making wine of fruit and berries has long been a popular hobby here in Norway. It is time-consuming, for the wine has to be aged at least a year. For that reason, many have turned to "quick wines," where chemicals shorten the aging time. But true fruit wines are both interesting and delicious. Fruit and berries often used in winemaking are red currants, apples, rhubarb and blueberries. And whoever has the patience to pick kilos of dandelions in the spring can make an excellent aperitif wine.

Norway is too far north for the successful cultivation of grapes on a large scale. Apart from a certain amount of industrial production of fruit wines and vermouth, wine is imported. All wine and liquor is sold by law through the government monopoly. All Norwegians have a relationship with this institution, whether they drink or not. From a consumer's point of view, the wine monopoly provides a wide assortment of high-quality wine and spirits. The disadvantages are that the outlets are few and far-between, concentrated in the cities and towns, and that the wares are very expensive.

Consumption of alcohol has shifted from liquor to wine during the last few years. All the major newspapers now have wine columns, and the most interested have organized clubs. The selection of wine at restaurants has improved, and many have cellars which can compare with those of the best restaurants on the Continent. Young people seem to prefer wine, so it is possible that a wine culture finally has sprung up in Norway.

NORWEGIAN DRINKS

BISHOP

7 1/2 dl (3 cups) water
1 vanilla bean
2 sticks cinnamon
12 whole black peppercorns
1 1/2 dl (2/3 cup) sugar
1 bottle (3/4 liter, 3 cups) red wine
1/2 dl (3 1/2 tablespoons) 60% alcohol

Bring water, spices and sugar to a boil. Simmer over low heat about 90 minutes. Strain. Add red wine and alcohol. Bishop also can be made with blueberry or cherry wine. An alcohol-free version can be made with black currant or blueberry juice. Serve warm in high glasses.

MULLED WINE

14 cl (2/3 cup) Port wine
14 cl (2/3 cup) Sherry
14 cl (2/3 cup) Madeira
7 cl (1/3 cup) red wine
4 whole cloves
2 cardamom pods

Combine in a saucepan and slowly bring to a boil. Serve warm in cups with raisins and blanched almonds. Place a teaspoon in each glass.

MOUNTAIN STREAM

2 cl (1 1/2 tablespoons) Norwegian vodka
2 cl (1 1/2 tablespoons) aquavit
1 cl (2 1/4 teaspoons) lime juice
Seven-Up or other soda

Combine spirits and juice with ice in a shaker. Pour into a tall glass and add soda.

NORWEGIAN OLYMPIC COFFEE

4 cl (3 tablespoons) aquavit
1 1/2 dl (2/3 cup) strong brewed coffee
2 teaspoons brown sugar
whipped cream

Combine aquavit, coffee and sugar and pour into a tall glass. Top with whipped cream.

SOUTHERN KISS

4-6 cl (3 – 4 1/2 tablespoons) rhubarb wine
whipped cream
grated chocolate

Pour cold rhubarb wine into a glass. Top with whipped cream and grated chocolate.

Mulled wine

APPETIZERS

STUFFED EGGS

Serves 4

4 hard-cooked eggs
about 1 1/2 tablespoons chopped ham,
tongue, anchovy fillets or smoked salmon
1 teaspoon butter
3 tablespoons grated cheese

Peel the eggs and halve lengthwise. Carefully remove the yolks and combine with the remaining ingredients. Stuff the egg whites with the mixture.

SEAGULL EGG OMELET

Serves 6

6 seagull eggs
1 dl (1/3 cup) whipping cream
salt
pepper
4 tablespoons (1/4 cup) chopped chives
200 g (7 ounces) dried reindeer meat
butter

Crack each egg into a cup to check for freshness. Combine in a bowl with the cream, salt, pepper and chives and whisk lightly. Cut the meat into thin strips and sauté lightly in butter. Melt a small amount of butter in an omelet pan and pour in the egg mixture. Stir with the back of a fork until creamy and soft set. Sprinkle the meat over the omelet, then fold. Serve with toast and butter.

TOMATO EGGS

Serves 4

4 hard-cooked eggs
2 tablespoons tomato paste
1 tablespoon grated cheese

Stuffed eggs on a bed of lettuce.

chopped parsley
salt
pepper
4 tomatoes, halved
75 g (3 ounces, 1/3 cup) butter
1 dl (scant 1/2 cup) flour
5 dl (2 cups) full fat milk
100 g (4 ounces) mushrooms
butter
1 1/2 dl (2/3 cup) grated cheese

Preheat the oven to 250°C (500°F).
Peel the eggs and halve lengthwise.
Carefully remove the yolks and sieve.
Combine with tomato paste, grated cheese and parsley and season with salt and pepper to taste. Stuff the egg whites with the mixture.
Place the tomato halves, rounded side down, in a greased ovenproof dish. Top with the egg halves.
Melt the butter and stir in the flour. Gradually add the milk and simmer until thickened. Season to taste. Sauté the mushrooms in butter and stir into the sauce with the grated cheese. Pour over the eggs and bake until golden, about 2 minutes.

Juniper-marinated Arctic char is a typical dish from the mountain villages.

JUNIPER-MARINATED INDIVIDUAL ARCTIC CHAR

individual char or trout, about 100-200 g (4-8 ounces) each
fresh juniper
2 tablespoons salt per kg (1 tablespoon per pound) fish
1-2 tablespoons sugar per kg (1/2-1 tablespoon per pound) fish
1 teaspoon ground white pepper per kg (1/2 teaspoon per pound) fish
1 tablespoon cognac per kg (1 1/2 teaspoons per pound) fish
1 apple per kg (1/2 per pound) fish
blueberries
sour cream

Clean, fillet and freeze the fish. Defrost the fish. Place on a bed of juniper and layer the fish with salt, sugar, pepper, cognac and apple peelings. Refrigerate 48 hours, turning several times. Cut the fillets into 2 cm (3/4") lengths and serve with a dressing made from sour cream, finely chopped juniper needles and

chopped apple. Garnish with apple wedges which have been poached in blueberry juice and serve with flatbread.

MARINATED FISH FROM LIERNE

This dish was often served at harvest time with sour cream porridge.

Serves 4

500 g (18 ounces) trout or char
1 tablespoon salt
1 teaspoon sugar

Brine:
1 liter (quart) whey
2 tablespoons salt
about 1 tablespoon sugar

Clean and rinse the fish well.
Combine salt and sugar and sprinkle into the cavity of the fish. Layer with salt/sugar in a plastic pail, cavity up.
Cover with a clean cloth and marinate one week at 10-12°C (50-54°F).
Reduce the whey with salt and sugar

until about half remains. Cool. Rinse the fish and place in a clean plastic pail. Pour over the cold brine. The fish should be completely covered with brine. Place a weight over the fish to hold it down. Store in a cold celler or refrigerate 7-8 weeks. Wash, skin and fillet the fish before serving.
Serve with boiled almond potatoes, flatbread and butter.

CAVIAR AND SEAGULL EGG COMPOSITION

Serves 1

1 tablespoon red trout or salmon caviar
1 tablespoon golden capelin caviar
1 tablespoon black caviar
1 seagull egg (cooked 12-15 minutes), quartered lengthwise
1 1/2 tablespoons sour cream
2 tablespoons red onion rings

Arrange the caviar, egg wedges, sour cream and onion rings on a plate.
Serve with toast, butter and beer.

SHERRY-MARINATED SHRIMP

Serves 2-3

200 g (8 ounces, 2 cups) shelled, cooked shrimp
1 tablespoon chopped fresh dill
1 1/4 dl (1/2 cup) dry sherry
4 teaspoons lemon juice
chopped fresh dill
6-8 lettuce leaves, shredded
Mustard sauce:
1 dl (1/3 cup) mayonnaise
1 dl (1/3 cup) sour cream
2 teaspoons coarse grain mustard
2 teaspoons sugar
2 tablespoons sherry
2 tablespoons chopped fresh dill

Combine shrimp, dill and sherry and marinate 10 minutes. Dip the edges of 4 high, footed glasses in lemon juice, then in chopped dill. Make a bed of shredded lettuce in the bottom of each glass, then top with the marinated shrimp. Combine the ingredients for the dressing and serve alongside. Serve with toast and butter.

Sherry-marinated shrimp flavored with dill on a bed of lettuce served with a piquant mustard sauce.

Trout, capelin and lumpfish caviar with hard-cooked seagull eggs is a popular summer dish along the coast.

SMOKED SALMON QUICHE

Serves 8

Pastry:
250 g (4 1/4 dl, 1 3/4 cups) flour
250 g (8 ounces, 1 cup) butter or margarine
1 dl (up to 1/3 cup) water
1 1/4 dl (1/2 cup) finely chopped onion
2 1/2 tablespoons butter
400 g (14 ounces) chopped smoked salmon
2 teaspoons chopped fresh chives
1/2 clove garlic, chopped
2 teaspoons chopped fresh basil
5 eggs
2 1/2 dl (1 cup) milk
2 1/2 dl (1 cup) whipping cream
pepper

Quickly combine all pastry ingredients in a food processor. Gather into a ball, cover with plastic wrap and chill 1 hour. Preheat the oven to 200°C (400°F). Roll out the dough to fit a 24 cm (10") tart pan. Prick with a fork. Cover edges with foil and bake 10 minutes. Reduce temperature to 160°C (325°F). Sauté onion until shiny in the butter. Stir in salmon, chives, garlic and basil. Cool. Arrange the salmon mixture in the pre-baked tart shell. Whisk eggs with milk and cream, season with pepper and pour in the tart shell. Bake about 30 minutes, until puffed and golden.

WARM LOBSTER SALAD

Serves 4

60 g (4 tablespoons, 1/4 cup) butter
4 tablespoons (1/4 cup) flour
2 dl (3/4 cup) boiling milk or fish stock
5 dl (2 cups) cooked lobster meat, chopped
1 egg, lightly beaten
1 teaspoon lemon juice
salt
1 lettuce, separated into leaves, dipped in boiling water until wilted
Poaching liquid:
1 liter (quart) fish stock
Sauce:
2 dl (3/4 cup) fish stock
1 dl (1/3 cup) whipping cream
1 dl (1/3 cup) dry white wine
2 tablespoons unsalted butter

Preheat the oven to 200°C (400°F). Melt the butter and stir in the flour. Gradually whisk in the milk or stock. Bring to a boil. Stir the lobster into the sauce. Whisk together the egg and lemon juice and add. Season with salt, if necessary. Place spoonfuls of lobster mixture on the lettuce leaves and wrap up, covering the filling entirely. Place, seam side down, in a greased ovenproof dish. Pour over stock, cover with foil and heat about 20 minutes. Combine fish stock, cream and wine and reduce by half. Cool slightly, then stir in the butter. Serve the lobster rolls hot with the sauce.

Smoked salmon quiche is a new way to serve smoked salmon in the Norwegian kitchen.

Warm lobster-lettuce rolls on a mirror of creamy butter sauce garnished with lobster caviar.

DELICATE HERRING

Serves 8

5 salt herring
5 dl (2 cups) full fat milk
1 1/2 tablespoons sugar
1/4 teaspoon saltpeter
sliced onion
sliced leek

Rinse the herring, but do not clean. Layer in a jar.
Bring the milk, sugar and saltpeter to a boil. Cool, then pour over the herring. Refrigerate 10-14 days.
Remove the herring from the brine. Clean, skin and bone the herring.
Arrange on a serving platter with onion and leek rings.
Serve with pickled beets, Bergen kringle, beer and aquavit.

OVEN-POACHED FRESH HERRING

Serves 8

1 kg (2 1/4 pounds) fresh herring
1 teaspoon salt
1/4 teaspoon pepper
1 onion
4-5 black peppercorns
1-2 bay leaves, crushed

Preheat the oven to 150°C (300°F).
Scale, clean and rinse the fish. Bone and cut into fillets.
Sprinkle fillets with salt and pepper. Roll them up, beginning at the tail end. Place tightly together in a jar.
Peel and slice the onion. Place between and over the herring rolls. Sprinkle with peppercorns and bay leaves.
Cover with a lid or foil.
Place the jar on a towel (to keep it from moving) in an oven pan. Add hot water to reach halfway up the sides. Bake 10-12 minutes, until the fish is done.
Serve directly from the jar with rye bread, boiled potatoes and horseradish cream, or with sour cream and chives.

FURULY SALAD

Serves 4

small wedge raw cabbage
2 medium raw carrots
2 apples
15 pitted prunes
1 tablespoon sugar
juice of 1/2 lemon
1 dl (1/3 cup) nuts
fresh herbs

Clean the vegetables and fruit. Do not peel the apple.
Shred cabbage, carrots, apples and prunes. Combine.
Dissolve the sugar in the lemon juice and stir in.
Arrange the salad on a platter or in a bowl. Sprinkle with nuts and fresh herbs.

MARINATED HERRING

Serves 6

4 spiced herring (packed in a rosy brine in large tins)
4 tablespoons (1/4 cup) 7% vinegar
1 dl (1/3 cup) water
2-3 tablespoons sugar
1-2 onions
1-2 bay leaves

Soak the herring in cold water overnight.
Bring vinegar, water, sugar and bay leaves to a boil. Cool.
Clean the herring and rinse well. Skin and fillet the fish.
Dry the fillets well. Cut into 2 cm (3/4") lengths. Peel and slice the onion.
Layer herring and onion in a jar. Pour over the cold brine. Chill 24 hours before serving.
Serve with bread or Bergen kringle.

Herring in a barrel.

KJELLAND'S PICKLED HERRING

Serves 4

*6 spiced herring fillets (packed in rosy
brine in large tins)*
milk or water
3 large onions
3 dl (1 1/4 cups) water
3/4 dl (1/3 cup) 7% vinegar
1 1/2 dl (2/3 cup) sugar
1 teaspoon ground allspice
1 teaspoon black peppercorns
3 bay leaves
1/2 dl (3 1/2 tablespoons) aquavit

Soak herring fillets in milk overnight.
Peel and thinly slice the onions.
Bring water, vinegar, sugar and season-
ings to a boil. Cool.
Cut the herring fillets into 12 mm
(1/2") slices and layer with the onion in
a jar. Pour over brine to cover.
Refrigerate at least 24 hours before
serving.
Just before serving, pour over the
aquavit.
Serve with rye bread.

MATJES HERRING SALAD

Serves 4

1 medium onion
1 medium pickled beet
1/2 large apple
10 cm (4") cucumber
150 g (5 ounces) matjes herring fillets
3 hard-cooked eggs
2 tablespoons capers
fresh dill
grated horseradish

An assortment of herring dishes for lunch, pictured in a maritime setting.

Marinade:
1 dl (1/3 cup) vegetable oil
2 tablespoons white wine vinegar
1 tablespoon matjes herring brine
pepper

Cube onion, beet, apple, cucumber and herring.

Cut the egg lengthwise into wedges. Arrange each ingredient in small piles on a serving platter. Combine ingredients for marinade and drizzle over. Serve with cold, whipped sour cream, coarse bread, beer and aquavit.

NARVIK HERRING

Serves 12

12 pre-soaked salt herring fillets
6 large dill pickles
6 onions
Sauce:
1/2 dl (3 1/2 tablespoons) tomato paste
1/2 dl (3 1/2 tablespoons) ketchup
2 dl (3/4 cup) sugar
1 dl (1/3 cup) olive oil
1 dl (1/3 cup) 5% vinegar

Cut the herring, pickles and onions into 3 mm (1/8") cubes and combine.

Combine ingredients for the sauce and add enough to coat all ingredients. Refrigerate 48 hours.

Drain off as much liquid from the salad as possible and add new dressing to coat.

Refrigerate an additional 24 hours before serving.

SALTED BRISLING

Serves 8

1 1/2 kg (3 pounds) brisling
200 g (7 ounces, 1 3/4 dl, 2/3 cup) salt
2 tablespoons sugar

Layer the brisling with the salt and sugar in a jar or bowl. Place a weight on top and marinate 10 days. Stir carefully once a day. The brine should cover the fish completely.

Clean and rinse the fish. Skin, bone and cut into fillets.

Dry well before arranging on a serving plate.

Serve with boiled potatoes, flatbread, butter, beer and aquavit.

STAVANGER HERRING

Serves 10

5 salt herring
2 hard-cooked egg yolks
1/2 teaspoon mustard
1/2 teaspoon pepper
2 tablespoons soy oil
1 tablespoon 7% vinegar
1-2 teaspoons sugar
3 tablespoons chopped parsley

Soak the herring in cold water overnight.

Clean and rinse the herring. Skin, bone and cut into fillets.

Cut each fillet diagonally into 3-4 pieces. Arrange on a flat dish.

Mash the egg yolks. Add mustard and pepper. Stir in oil and vinegar, a little at a time. Season with sugar. The sauce should be smooth and shiny.

Pour the sauce over the herring and garnish with parsley.

Serve with bread or boiled potatoes and beer.

CURED SALMON

Serves 10

1 kg (2 1/4 pounds) frozen salmon fillet
with the skin
4 tablespoons salt
2 tablespoons sugar
1 teaspoon coarsely ground pepper

Defrost the salmon in the refrigerator. Remove all bones with a tweezers and remove the fins.

Turn the fish skin side up and make small slits in the skin, in the middle and down the length, so that the salt and seasonings can penetrate from both sides.

Combine salt, sugar and pepper and rub the mixture into both sides of the fish. If there are two fillets, place them on top of one another, meaty sides touching. Cover with plastic and refrigerate. Turn the fish twice daily. The salmon is cured after 2-3 days.

A composition of cured, smoked and marinated salmon.

TRIPLE SALMON STARTER

Serves 4

8 large lettuce leaves
4 slices cured salmon
4 slices smoked salmon
4 slices marinated salmon
4 tablespoons (1/4 cup) sour cream
1 tablespoon chopped chives
1 teaspoon minced onion
1 teaspoon mustard
4 leek slices
4 dill sprigs
4 lemon slices

Shred the lettuce leaves.
Make a bed of lettuce on four individual plates.
Arrange the salmon slices on the lettuce.
Combine sour cream, chives, onion and mustard and spoon carefully over the salmon.
Garnish with leek, dill and lemon.

HARE PATÉ

Serves 8

1 hare
1 onion
2 teaspoon cognac
200 g (7 ounces) fresh pork fat, half in thin slices
salt
pepper
3 eggs
3 dl (1 1/4 cups) whipping cream
parsley
rosemary
300 g (10 ounces) spinach leaves, blanched
Currant jelly sauce:
1 dl (1/3 cup) currant jelly
1 teaspoon minced onion
juice and shredded peel (no pith) of 1/2 orange
1 dl (1/3 cup) port wine
cayenne pepper
salt

Remove the thighs. Carefully remove the outer filets from the backbone. Each filet should weigh about 70 g (2 1/2 ounces). Mince half the onion and sprinkle over the filets. Sprinkle with cognac and marinate about 40 minutes. Remove thigh meat and remaining meat from the carcass. Place in a food processor with half the fat, half an onion and salt. With the motor running, add pepper, eggs, cream and herbs. Spoon a 2 cm (3/4") layer onto a sheet of plastic wrap. Top with thin slices of fat. Cover the filets with blanched spinach leaves and place on the fat. Enclose the filet with the ground meat. Wrap completely in plastic wrap. Preheat the oven to 120°C (250°F). Place in a greased pan and bake until an instant thermometer reads 60°C (140°F), about 40 minutes. Cool. Melt the jelly and combine with the remaining ingredients for the sauce. Serve on a lettuce leaf with green asparagus, tomato boats, lingonberries and currant sauce.

Hare paté with the filet wrapped in spinach on a bed of lettuce.

FERMENTED FISH

Serve 150 g (5 ounces) per person

10 kg (22 pounds) trout or whitefish
700 g (1 2/3 pounds, 5 1/2 dl, 2 1/3
cups) salt
1 tablespoon sugar
1/4 teaspoon saltpeter

Prepare according to the main recipe on page 32.
Rinse the fish well, Skin, bone and cut into fillets.
Cut the fillets on the diagonal into 3 cm (1") pieces. Arrange as a whole fillet with red onion rings.
Serve with boiled potatoes, butter, lefse and sour cream.

"Rakfisk" is trout or whitefish which has undergone a special fermentation process. This dish has many "fan clubs" and "rakfisk" evenings are often held just before or after Christmas.

STUFFED LOBSTER

Serves 8

300 g (10 ounces) fish forcemeat
6 dl (2 1/2 cups) whipping cream
6-7 dl (3 - 3 1/2 cups) lobster meat,
sliced
1 1/2 tablespoons melted butter
1 1/4 dl (1/2 cup) breadcrumbs

Preheat the oven to 160°C (325°F). Grease a 2-liter (quart) terrine. Cover the bottom with half the fish forcemeat. Reduce the whipping cream over moderate heat (it burns easily) until 2 dl (3/4 cup) remains. Stir in the lobster meat and spoon over the fish forcemeat. Top with remaining fish forcemeat. Even the top with a rubber spatula, brush with melted butter and sprinkle with crumbs. Place the terrine on a towel (to keep it from moving) in an oven pan. Add hot water to reach halfway up the sides of the terrine. Cook in the oven 30-45 minutes. Slice and serve, allowing 1 slice per serving.

LOBSTER PUDDING

Serves 8

125 g (4 ounces, 1/2 cup) butter
2 dl (3/4 cup) flour
5 dl (2 cups) boiling milk
8 eggs, separated
salt
nutmeg
750 g (1 2/3 pounds) lobster meat
200 g (7 ounces, 3/4 cup) unsalted
butter
1 dl (1/3 cup) sherry

Preheat the oven to 160°C (325°F). Grease two large soufflé dishes or one large ovenproof dish and sprinkle with crumbs. Melt the butter and stir in the flour. Whisk in the boiling milk, a little at a time. Cool slightly. Beat in the egg yolks, one at a time. Season to taste with salt and nutmeg. Cube the lobster meat and add. Beat the egg whites until stiff but not dry and fold into the egg yolk mixture. Pour into the prepared dish, place on a towel (to keep it from moving) in an oven pan. Add hot water to reach

Toast ramekins filled with hot creamed shrimp.

halfway up the sides of the dishes and cook about 85 minutes. Melt the butter and mix with sieved lobster coral and sherry. Serve alongside the pudding.

GIANT MUSSELS WITH HERB DRESSING

1-2 giant mussels per person

Herb dressing:
2 dl (3/4 cup) olive oil
1 dl (1/3 cup) 7% vinegar
2 1/2 tablespoons minced onion
2 1/2 tablespoons minced green and/or
red pepper
2 1/2 tablespoons minced cucumber
1 1/2 tablespoons minced leek
1/4 teaspoon salt
1/8 teaspoon ground white pepper

Scrub the mussels and remove the beards. Steam until open, 5-8 minutes. Remove foot and gills. Chill the mussels before replacing in the shells. Combine all ingredients for the dressing. Drizzle a little dressing over the mussels. Garnish with blanched seaweed and lemon. Serve with melba toast.

HOT CREAMED SHRIMP ON TOAST

Serves 4

1 white bread
120 g (4 ounces, 1/2 cup) margarine
1 teaspoon flour
1 1/2 dl (2/3 cup) fish stock
1 egg yolk
3/4 dl (1/3 cup) whipping cream
1/4 teaspoon lemon juice
1/8 teaspoon pepper
1/8 teaspoon salt
1/8 teaspoon sugar
1/2 dl (3 1/2 tablespoons) sherry
5 dl (2 cups) shelled, cooked shrimp
chopped parsley

The bread should be at least one day old. Cut into about 3 cm (1 1/4") thick slices and cut with a glass or cookie cutter. Hollow out the insides of the slices almost to the bottom.

Melt all but 1 1/2 tablespoons of the margarine. Sauté the bread in the margarine. Place the fried bread on a serving platter. For the creamed shrimp, melt the remaining margarine. Stir in the flour and gradually whisk in the stock. Bring to a boil. Remove from the heat. Beat the egg yolk with the cream and add. Heat just to the boiling point, but do not allow to boil. Add lemon juice, salt, pepper, sugar and sherry. Stir in the shrimp.

Spoon into the toast rounds and sprinkle with chopped parsley.

OPEN-FACE SANDWICHES

The open-face sandwich has a long tradition in Norway. A slice of freshly-cut bread, thinly spread with butter, forms the basis for artfully arranged toppings and edible garnish.

Every element of the sandwich should be fresh. The ingredients should complement one another with respect both to taste and appearance.

1. Smoked salmon slices on a slice of white bread, with scrambled egg or hard-cooked egg wedges and dill.
2. Shelled shrimp or crabmeat on toast, with mayonnaise and lemon.
3. Sardines in tomato sauce on whole wheat bread, with hard-cooked egg slices and fresh dill.
4. Anchovy fillets on whole wheat bread with raw egg yolk placed in an onion ring sprinkled with chopped chives.
5. Roast reindeer meat on whole wheat bread with poached apple wedges and lingonberry preserves.
6. Sautéed minute steak on whole wheat bread with leek rings, tomato and parsley.
7. Cured ham on whole wheat bread with scrambled eggs.
8. Headcheese on whole wheat bread with pickled beets and pickled cucumbers.
9. Gamalost on whole wheat bread with butter and parsley.
10. Ship's plank with shrimp, eggs, cheese and boiled ham.

A selection of open-face sandwiches. Open-face sandwiches are often served for lunch. These are made with smoked salmon, sardines and eggs, shrimp, anchovies, "gamalost," headcheese, reindeer roast, roast beef and pressed veal.

PICKLED SALMON

Serves 10

1 kg (2 1/4 pounds) salmon fillet, skinless and boneless
1 1/4 dl (1/2 cup) salt
1 large onion, sliced
Brine:
1 liter (quart) water
6 dl (2 1/2 cups) 7% vinegar
750 g (1 2/3 pounds, 8 3/4 dl, 3 3/4
cups) sugar
1 tablespoon white peppercorns
1 tablespoon whole cloves
1 tablespoon mustard seed
3 bay leaves

Pack the salmon in salt and let rest 90
minutes.
Bring ingredients for the brine to a boil.
Cool.
Rinse the salmon, cut into 2 cm (3/4")
strips. Add to the brine with the onion.
Refrigerate at least 24 hours before
serving. Serves 10.

PICKLED REDFISH

Serves 4

1 pre-soaked salted redfish fillet
3 onions
6 dl (2 1/2 cups) brine for pickled
herring

Cut the fish into 2 cm (3/4") strips.
Peel and thinly slice the onion.
Layer fish and onion in a jar or bowl,
then pour over cold brine.
Note: Salted salmon or trout also can be
used in this recipe.

OYSTER TARTLETS

Serves 4

250 g (9 ounces) shucked oysters
1 dl (1/3 cup) breadcrumbs
1/4 teaspoon ground white pepper
1/4 teaspoon salt
2 tablespoons Madeira or sherry
4 puff pastry shells

Combine oysters with juice, breadcrumbs, salt, pepper and Madeira and

Puff pastry shells with a piquant oyster filling.

bring to a boil. Spoon into pastry shells
and serve immediately.

HERB-MARINATED MOOSE FILET

Serves 5

2 1/2 tablespoons gin
400 g (14 ounces) moose filet
2 tablespoons salt
4 tablespoons (1/4 cup) sugar
3-4 tablespoons freshly ground black
pepper
1 1/2 teaspoons chopped fresh basil
1 1/2 teaspoons chopped fresh
marjoram
1 1/2 teaspoons chopped fresh tarragon
1 1/2 teaspoons chopped fresh sage
2 bay leaves, crushed
chopped parsley
Pear aspic:
5 sheets (or 5 teaspoons powdered)
gelatin
4 pears

3 dl (1 1/4 cups) pear juice
1/2 dl (3 1/2 tablespoons) white wine

Marinate the moose filet with the gin in
a plastic bag 1 1/2-2 hours, turning several times.
Sprinkle the meat with salt, sugar and
pepper. Combine the herbs and sprinkle over the meat on all sides.
Marinate the meat in the plastic bag 4-6
days, depending upon the thickness of
the meat. Turn the bag regularly.
Soften the gelatin sheets in cold water
(or sprinkle the gelatin powder over 2
tablespoons of the pear juice) about 10
minutes. Peel and grate the pears.
Squeeze excess water from the gelatin
sheets (disregard for powdered gelatin) and melt the gelatin. Combine with
remaining ingredients and chill.
Serve the meat in thin slices with pear
jelly and a sweet mustard sauce.

Herb-marinated rosette of moose filet with pears and pear aspic.

SOUPS

FISH SOUPS

BROWN FISH SOUP

Serves 8

2 liters (quarts) fish stock made from 2
kg (4 1/2 pounds) mixed white fish
bones and trimmings
water
3-4 carrots
2-3 parsley roots
1/2 celeriac
1-2 onions
white peppercorns
whole cloves
Flour dumplings:
90 g (3 ounces, 1/3 cup) butter
2 dl (3/4 cup) flour
2 1/2 dl (1 cup) boiling water
2 eggs
salt
sugar
mace

Make the dumplings first:
Melt the butter, stir in the flour and add
boiling water. Cook the dough, stirring
vigorously, until it forms a ball. Cool,
then beat in the eggs, one at a time. Season with salt, sugar and mace.
Make small balls with a teaspoon and
simmer in lightly salted water about 6
minutes.
Cod, haddock and pollack make the
best stock, but bones from oily fish
such as mackerel, herring, salmon and
trout also can be used, but the flavor
will be more intense.
Cover the fish bones with 2 liters
(quarts) cold water (or to cover), adding 1 teaspoon salt per liter (quart)
water. Bring slowly to a boil and skim
well. Lower heat, add 1 carrot, 1 parsley
root, a chunk of celeriac and 1/4 onion,
sliced, along with a few peppercorns.
Simmer 30 minutes, then strain and
measure. There should be about 2 liters
(quarts) stock.
Season the stock, if desired. Shred the
remaining vegetables and add along
with the dumplings before serving.

SOUP WITH
FRESH FISH DUMPLINGS

Serves 10

500 g (1 1/4 pounds) smoked ham hock
4 tablespoons (1/4 cup) pearl barley
1 liter (quart) water
1/2 large rutabaga
1 onion
1 1/2 liters (quarts) fish stock
Fish dumplings:
750 g (1 2/3 pounds) pollack fillets
about 2 teaspoons salt
1 small onion
about 2 tablespoons barley flour or
regular flour
3-4 dl (1 1/4-1 1/2 cups) full fat milk
1/4 teaspoon ground white pepper
1/2 teaspoon grated nutmeg
750 g (1 2/3 pounds, about 4 large)
potatoes

Soak the ham hock and the barley separately in cold water overnight.
Place the hock and the barley in a soup
pot with the water. Bring to a boil, then
skim. Simmer until the barley is tender,
about 30 minutes.
Peel and cube the rutabaga and onion.
Add to the soup during the last 15 minutes, adding fish stock as needed.
Fish dumplings:
Grind the fish with the salt and onion 2
or 3 times. Add the flour and mix well
before gradually adding the milk.
Season, then cook a small dumpling to
check for seasoning.
Make large dumplings with wet hands
and a spoon.
Simmer in the soup 10-15 minutes. Peel
the potatoes and cut into wedges. Cook
in stock until tender, about 15 minutes,
then add to the soup with the dumplings. Remove the ham hock before
serving.
Serve with flatbread of freshly baked
whole wheat bread.

HALIBUT/REDFISH SOUP

Serves 8

1 dl (1/3 cup) pearl barley
1/2 large rutabaga
3 large carrots
1 large onion
500 g (18 ounces) small potatoes
1 3/4 liters (quarts) water
2 teaspoons salt
1 kg (2 1/4 pounds) halibut or redfish
fillets
1 teaspoon 7% vinegar
ground white pepper
1 tablespoon chopped parsley or chives

Soak the barley in cold water overnight.
Simmer in the soaking liquid about 30
minutes.
Clean and peel rutabaga, carrots and
the onion. Cut into (6 mm) 1/4" dice.

Clean and peel potatoes. They should remain whole.

Bring the water to a boil and add salt. Cook the potatoes about 15 minutes. Then add rutabaga and carrot cubes and the onion. Simmer until tender, about 10 minutes.

Cut the fish into large chunks and add. Simmer until just barely done, 8 minutes. The fish should not flake.

Season with vinegar and pepper. Sprinkle with parsley.

Serve with flatbread and butter.

FISH SOUP WITH TOMATOES

Serves 6

2 carrots
70 g (2 1/2 ounces, 1/3 cup) butter
1 dl (scant 1/2 cup) flour
1 1/2 liters (quarts) fish stock
2 dl (3/4 cup) tomato purée
2 dl (3/4 cup) elbow macaroni
1 tablespoon chopped parsley

Peel and slice the carrots. Sauté lightly in butter. Sprinkle with the flour and stir to coat well. Combine stock and tomato purée and add.

Simmer 30 minutes, then press through a sieve or purée in a food processor. Bring to a boil.

Prepare the macaroni according to package directions. Add to the soup just before serving. Sprinkle with parsley.

The soup also can be served with dumplings and cubed celeriac.

Fish soup with tomatoes.

SALMON SOUP

This recipe stems from a fish soup served during the last century, when trade with Russia flourished. The people of northern Norway bartered fish and pelts for grain, flour and cloth from the east. During this time, smoked salmon was a valuable trading commodity. It was salted or smoked for preservation. The leftovers—heads, backbones and tails were used fresh or salted in barrels. They appeared on many tables in northern Norway in the form of poached salmon heads and backs for dinner, on their own, or as ingredients in soup.

Serves 10

1 small bunch chives
2 1/2 dl (1 cup) spinach leaves
2 carrots
150 g (5 ounces, scant 2/3 cup) butter
2 3/4 liters (quarts) salmon stock
2 cloves garlic
2 tablespoons tomato paste
1/2 small bunch parsley
2 bay leaves
1 bunch fresh thyme
500 g (1 1/4 pounds) fresh salmon fillet
2 small dill pickles
3 tablespoons capers
salt
ground white pepper

Shred chives, spinach and carrots. Sauté lightly in butter in a pot. Add stock, garlic, tomato paste, parsley, bay leaves and thyme. Bring to a boil, then cut the salmon into large chunks and add. Lower the heat and simmer 4-5 minutes. Cut the pickles into thin strips and add with the capers and additional parsley, if necessary. Season with salt and pepper. Serve the soup hot with whipped sour cream and whole-grain rolls. Makes about 3 liters (quarts) soup.

Salmon soup.

GRANDMOTHER'S FISH SOUP

Serves 12

3 liters (quarts) fish stock
3 tablespoons butter
1 dl (1/3 cup) flour
5 dl (2 cups) buttermilk
4 apples
2 dl (3/4 cup) sour cream
2 carrots
1/4 leek
600 g (1 1/3 pounds) fish fillets
2 tablespoons chopped chives

Bring the stock to a boil.
Melt the butter and stir in the flour. Gradually add the boiling stock. Return to a boil and add the buttermilk. Simmer 30 minutes. Peel and core the apples. Add to the soup and simmer about 15 minutes. Strain and whisk in the sour cream. Slice the carrot and leek and cook each separately until tender, about 6 and 1 minute respectively. Add to the soup. Cut the fish into very thin slices and place in individual soup bowls or in a terrine. Reheat the soup almost to boiling and pour over the fish. Sprinkle with chives. Serve with flatbread.

POLLACK SOUP

Serves 6

1 liter (quart) fish stock
2 medium carrots
1 medium turnip
2 tablespoons butter
3 tablespoons flour
2 dl (3/4 cup) full fat milk
salt
1/4 teaspoon ground white pepper
1/4 teaspoon mace
1 egg yolk
1 dl (1/3 cup) sour cream
2 tablespoons chopped chives
2 tablespoons chopped dill
pickled purslane (optional)

The stock should be made from pollack, shallots and salt, skimmed well, simmered for 30 minutes, then strained. Clean the carrots and turnip and cut into strips. Cook in as little lightly salted water as possible until tender, about 5 minutes. Melt the butter and stir in the flour. Gradually add the milk, fish stock and vegetable cooking liquid, whisking until smooth. Simmer 5-10 minutes, then season. Stir the egg yolk into the sour cream and add, along with the chives, dill and purslane. Heat through, but do not allow the soup to boil after the sour cream has been added.

NORTH SEA FISH SOUP

Serves 4

2 1/2 tablespoons butter
4 tablespoons (1/4 cup) flour
8 dl (3 1/3 cups) fish stock
salt
pepper
1 small carrot
6 cm (2 1/2") leek
butter
12 peeled shrimp
12 mussels
*1 1/4 dl (1/2 cup) cooked ocean catfish
or monkfish*
1 dl (scant 1/2 cup) whipping cream
2 tablespoons sour heavy cream
2 teaspoons lumpfish caviar

Melt the butter and stir in the flour. Gradually add the stock. Simmer about 10 minutes, then season with salt and pepper. Clean the carrot and leek and cut into fine shreds. Sauté lightly in butter, then add to the soup.

Add shrimp, mussels, fish and cream. Heat until warm.
Divide the soup among four bowls. Spoon 1 1/2 teaspoons sour cream and 1/2 teaspoon caviar on top of each bowl of soup.

SHRIMP SOUP FROM HVALER

Serves 5

4 tablespoons (1/4 cup) diced carrot
2 tablespoons diced onion
3 tablespoons chopped parsley
*1 kg (2 1/4 pounds) whole cooked
shrimp in their shells*
1 dl (1/2 cup) white wine
salt
pepper
about 1 liter (quart) fish stock
1 dl (1/3 cup) rice
80 g (3 ounces, 1/3 cup) shrimp butter
2 tablespoons whipping cream

Sauté carrot, onion and parsley in butter. Peel about 120 g (4 ounces) shrimp and add to the vegetables. Add wine, salt, pepper and 1 1/4 dl (1/2 cup) fish stock. Simmer about 10 minutes.
Cook the rice in 3/4 liter (3 cups) fish stock until almost tender, about 20 minutes. Peel the remaining shrimp. Crush the shrimp shells with the cooked vegetables and shrimp. Add the rice with the stock and mash well. Sieve. Return the mixture to the pot. Add more stock, if necessary, to desired consistency.
Just before serving, add the shrimp butter (made from shrimp shells sautéed in butter, then cooked, strained and chilled) and cream.

North Sea fish soup with shellfish, shrimp and firm fish fillets.

HERRING BARLEY SOUP

Serves 8

2 dl (3/4 cup) pearl barley or green or yellow peas
6-8 salt herring fillets
1 1/2 liters (quarts) lamb stock
2 medium carrots, cubed
1/2 small rutabaga, cubed
small wedge cabbage, in small chunks
1 medium onion, cubed
1 large potato, cubed
salt

Soak the barley and herring separately in cold water overnight.

Drain the barley, cover with the lamb stock and bring to a boil. Lower heat, then simmer 30 minutes. Add the vegetables and potatoes.

Cut the herring into 1 cm (1/2") slices. Simmer carefully about 5 minutes in water, then transfer to the pot with the vegetables.

Season with salt and serve with flatbread.

COD TONGUE AND BARLEY SOUP

Serves 8

Cod tongues are a popular dish in the northern Norwegian kitchen. They are prepared in many ways - poached, sautéed and fried.

Cod tongues are a delicacy and have been an important source of income for young people in fishing villages.

1 dl (1/3 cup) pearl barley
1 1/2 liters (quarts) fish stock
1/4 small rutabaga, cubed
1 large carrot, cubed
1 medium parsley root, cubed
150 g (5 ounces, about 5) almond potatoes
20 cod tongues
salt
freshly ground black pepper
chopped parsley

Soak the barley in water overnight.
Bring the stock to a boil, skim, then add barley. Simmer 30 minutes. Add the vegetables and simmer 5 minutes.

Add the cod tongues and simmer until cooked, about 6 minutes.

Season with salt and pepper. Sprinkle with parsley just before serving.

Serve with whole-grain rolls and butter.

Cutting out cod tongues is a good source of income for young people in fishing villages.

VEGETABLE SOUPS

CAULIFLOWER SOUP

Serves 5

1 cauliflower, in florets
6 dl (2 1/2 cups) water
salt
1 tablespoon minced onion
2 1/2 tablespoons margarine
4 tablespoons (1/4 cup) flour
5 dl (2 cups) reduced cauliflower stock
5 dl (2 cups) light veal or chicken stock
1 dl (1/2 cup) whipping cream
freshly ground white pepper

Cook the prettiest florets in lightly-salted water until tender, about 10 minutes. Reserve for garnish. Strain and measure the cooking liquid. Reduce to 5 dl (2 cups).

Sauté onion until shiny in margarine along with the remaining cauliflower cut into small pieces. Stir in the flour.

Gradually add both kinds of stock. Bring to a boil, lower heat and simmer soup about 10 minutes. Strain. Stir in the cream, then season with salt and pepper. Just before serving, add the florets. Heat through.

YELLOW PEA SOUP

Serves 8

350 g (10 ounces, 4 dl, 1 2/3 cups) dried yellow peas
2 liters (quarts) water
1 onion, chopped
500 g (1 pound) lightly salted pork shoulder or belly, in 1 piece
bacon rind
2 teaspoons thyme
1 carrot, diced
1/5 leek, diced
salt
freshly ground white pepper

Soak the peas in cold water overnight. Rinse and drain the peas. Combine with the water, onion, pork, bacon rind and thyme. Bring to a boil and skim well. Simmer until peas and pork are done, about 1 hour.

Remove the meat and cut into 5 mm (1/4") cubes.

Remove the pea hulls with a whisk or slotted spoon.

Cook the carrot and leek in the soup 2-3 minutes, then add the meat. Season with salt and pepper. Serve hot.

CABBAGE SOUP

Serves 20

This dish was served at midday on Christmas Eve, and the meat was simmered 24 hours to make the stock.

1 meaty beef shank, 5 cm (2") slices
water
2 onions, quartered
2 carrots, in chunks
1/5 celeriac, sliced
1/5 leek, sliced
salt
10 black peppercorns
1 1/2 - 2 cabbages
Meatballs:
250 g (9 ounces) finely ground beef
1/4 teaspoon ginger
1/8 teaspoon pepper
3/4 teaspoon salt
2 tablespoons flour
1 1/2 dl (2/3 cup) light cream

Place the shank in a large pot, cover with 7 liters (quarts) water and bring to a boil. Skim well. Lower heat and add onions, carrots, celeriac, leek, salt and peppercorns. Simmer at least 6 hours, adding more water, if necessary. Strain the stock. It should measure 5 liters (quarts).

Core the cabbages and cut into 5 mm (1/4") dice. Add to the stock and simmer until tender, about 5 minutes.

For the meatballs, remove the meat (no membrane or gristle) from the shank and grind. There should be about 250 g (9 ounces). Combine with seasonings and flour. Beat in the cream. Form into 2 1/2 cm (1") balls and simmer in stock. Reheat the meatballs in the soup and serve with lukewarm sweet white bread.

Carrots and cabbage are among our most popular vegetables.

CARROT SOUP

Serves 5

500 g (1 pound) carrots
2 tablespoons minced onion
2 1/2 tablespoons butter
1 liter (quart) beef stock
3 tablespoons rice
salt
1 teaspoon sugar

Thinly slice the carrots. Cook with the onion in half the butter until tender, about 8 minutes.

Add stock and rice. Season with salt and sugar. Simmer 20 minutes, then sieve or purée in a food processor. Add more stock if the soup is too thick.

Reheat the soup with the remaining butter.

Serve with bread croutons fried in butter until golden.

POTATO SOUP

Serves 6

1 1/2 liters (quarts) water
2 1/4 teaspoons salt
500 g (1 1/4 pounds) potatoes, peeled and cut into chunks
2 leeks, in chunks
3 dl (1 1/4 cups) full fat milk
1 1/2 tablespoons butter

1 tablespoon sago or tapioca
1/4 teaspoon pepper

Combine water, salt, potatoes and leeks and simmer until potatoes are tender, 15-20 minutes. Sieve or purée in a mixer.

Return the pot and add remaining ingredients. Simmer until the sago is transparent, about 45 minutes. Quick-cooking tapioca requires about 15 minutes cooking time.

MILK-BASED SOUPS

DUMPLING SOUP

Serves 4

1 liter (quart) full fat milk
2 tablespoons flour
salt
Dumplings:
3 1/2 dl (1 1/2 cups) full fat milk
1/4 teaspoon salt
1 1/2 tablespoons butter
1/2 teaspoon sugar
3-4 almonds, ground or 1/2 teaspoon ground cardamom
1 - 1 1/4 dl (1/3-1/2 cup) flour
2 eggs

Mix 2 tablespoons milk with the flour.

Bring remaining milk to a boil and stir in the flour mixture.

Season with a pinch of salt. Serve the soup with dumplings, with cinnamon and sugar on the side.

Dumplings:

Combine milk, salt, butter, sugar and almonds and bring to a boil. Add the flour and cook, stirring constantly, until the mixture forms a ball. Cool.

When completely cold, beat in the eggs one at a time, beating well after each.

Form small balls with a teaspoon and simmer in the boiling milk 5-8 minutes. These egg dumplings also are good with all clear soups.

BUTTERMILK SOUP

Serves 14

4 tablespoons (1/4 cup) chopped blanched almonds
2 dl (3/4 cup) raisins
3 1/2 liters (quarts) buttermilk
1 1/4 dl (1/2 cup) sugar
1 1/2 dl (2/3 cup) flour

Add almonds and raisins to the milk. Combine sugar and flour and whisk gradually into the milk. Bring to a boil, stirring constantly, and cook until thickened.

OTHER SOUPS

MUTTON-BARLEY SOUP

Serves 6

4 tablespoons (1/4 cup) pearl barley
1 1/4 dl (1/2 cup) yellow peas
1 1/2 liters (quarts) cold water
125 g (4 ounces) salted mutton
1/4 large rutabaga
2 medium carrot
1 large potato
1/4 leek, chopped
salt
pepper

Soak barley and peas separately in cold water overnight.

Drain both, combine and cover with the cold water. Simmer barley and peas

about 90 minutes.

Add the meat and simmer 30 minutes. Remove the meat, cut into small dice and return to the pot.

Dice the vegetables and add. Simmer until tender, about 15 minutes. Season with salt and pepper.

The soup should be thick. Serve with flatbread.

MOCK TURTLE SOUP

Serves 4

1 calf's head
2 liters (quarts) water
salt
1 small red onion
1/2 celeriac
1 carrot
100 g (3 1/2 ounces, scant 1/2 cup) butter
1 slice bacon
1 tablespoon tomato paste
1 dl (scant 1/2 cup) flour
1 liter (quart) brown stock
pepper
1 dl (1/3 cup) white wine
soy sauce
3 hard-cooked eggs, in wedges
5 dl (2 cups) tiny fish balls (canned)

Scald and split the head. Wash well, then soak overnight in cold water, changing several times.

Clean the head. Place in 1 liter (quart) cold water and bring to a boil. Lower heat and simmer about 10 minutes.

Remove from the water, rinse and place in cold water with a little salt to cover. Bring to a boil, lower heat and

simmer around 45 minutes, until the head is white and firm, and the meat nearly falls off the bones.

Remove from the water and cut off the meat. Place the meat under a weight. Strain and skim the stock.

Clean and dice the vegetables. Sauté in 2 tablespoons butter with the bacon and tomato paste. Add the stock and simmer 2 hours.

Strain. There should be about 1 liter (quart) stock. Melt the remaining butter and stir in the flour. Gradually add the stock. Simmer until thickened, stirring constantly.

Cube meat and add to the soup with pepper and white wine. Add soy sauce for color. Divide hard-cooked egg wedges and tiny fish balls among four soup bowls. Pour over the soup.

THREE MEAT SOUP

Serves 8

400 g (14 ounces) smoked mutton
200 g (7 ounces) slab bacon
200 g (7 ounces) smoked pork sausage links
6 large potatoes
1 1/2 liters (quarts) water
5 dl (2 cups) buttermilk
2-3 tablespoons barley flour
flatbread

Cut the meat, bacon, sausage and potatoes into 1 cm (1/2") cubes.

Bring the water to a boil and add mutton and bacon. Simmer until almost tender, about 45 minutes. Skim well. Add the sausage and potato and simmer until the potato is tender, about 10 minutes.

Whisk together buttermilk and flour and whisk into the soup.

Crumble flatbread into soup bowls. Pour over soup.

Serve with a lump of butter, syrup and gamalost.

PORRIDGE

BARLEY FLOUR PORRIDGE

Serves 1

1 dl (1/3 cup) water
1 dl (1/3 cup) skim milk
2 dl (2/3 cup) barley flour
salt

Combine water and milk in a saucepan and bring to a boil.
Whisk the flour into the boiling liquid, and cook until thick and shiny.
Simmer 10-15 minutes. Season with salt.
Serve with syrup or sugar and butter.

VELVET PORRIDGE

Serves 4

1 liter (quart) full fat milk
75 g (2 3/4 ounces, 1/3 cup) butter
2 1/2 dl (1 cup) flour
1/2 teaspoon salt

Bring the milk to a boil.
Melt the butter, stir in the flour. Stir until smooth.
Gradually whisk in the boiling milk. Whisk until smooth.
Simmer 5-10 minutes. Season with salt.
Serve with sugar, cinnamon, butter and a glass of milk or juice.

OAT PORRIDGE

Serves 8

2 liters (quarts) water
7 dl (3 cups) quick-cooking oats
1 teaspoon salt

Bring the water to a boil, then add the oats.
Simmer 8-10 minutes. Season with salt.
Serve with milk, butter, sugar or syrup.

CARAMELIZED PORRIDGE

Serves 4

1 liter water
50 g (1 3/4 ounces, 1/4 cup) grated Norwegian brown blended goat milk cheese (Ski Queen) or cajeta (can be purchased in Mexican food stores)
3 dl (1 1/4 cups) barley flour
1 teaspoon salt
2 tablespoons butter

Bring the water and cheese or cajeta to a boil. Whisk in the flour and simmer, whisking constantly, until smooth and thick. Simmer 15 minutes, then stir in salt and butter.
Serve with bacon, sugar or syrup, brown goats' milk cheese or cajeta and milk.

POTATO PORRIDGE

Serves 4

1 kg (2 1/4 pounds, about 5 large) potatoes
5 dl (2 cups) potato water
1 tablespoon salt

1 1/2 dl (2/3 cup) barley flour

Peel and slice the potatoes and cook in water until tender, about 10 minutes. Drain and reserve 5 dl (2 cups) potato water. Mash the potatoes with salt and the potato water. Add flour and simmer 15 minutes.
Serve with bacon, butter and milk.

SEMOLINA PORRIDGE

Serves 4

1 liter (quart) full fat milk
1 1/4 dl (1/2 cup) semolina or cream of wheat
1 1/2 tablespoons butter
about 1 teaspoon salt

Bring the milk to a boil. Sprinkle the semolina over the milk and whisk until it comes to a boil. Simmer, covered, until the semolina is tender, about 15 minutes. Stir in the butter and season with salt. Serve with sugar.

BUTTERMILK PORRIDGE

Serves 5

6-8 dl (2 1/2 - 3 1/3 cups) barley or oat flour
2 liters (quarts) water
5 dl (2 cups) buttermilk
2 teaspoons salt

Whisk the flour into the water and bring to a boil. Add buttermilk and simmer about 15 minutes. Season with salt. Serve with cold buttermilk or warm full fat milk.

RICE PORRIDGE

Serves 5

4 dl (1 2/3 cups) water
1 3/4 dl (3/4 cup) round grain rice
1 liter (quart) full fat milk
1 teaspoon salt

Bring the water to a boil. Add the rice, lower the heat and simmer, covered, until the water is absorbed, 15-20 minutes.

Bring the milk to a boil, then add. Lower the heat, cover and simmer until the rice is tender, about 30 minutes. Season with salt.

Serve with butter, sugar, cinnamon and a glass of juice.

SOUR CREAM PORRIDGE

Sour cream porridge must be made from high fat (35%) natural sour cream, with no stabilizers or gelatin added. For the best results, use homemade sour cream. Heat 2 1/2 dl (1 cup) whipping cream to 35°C (95°F), almost body temperature, then whisk in 2 tablespoons buttermilk. Let stand at room temperature at least 8 hours, until thickened.

1.
Serves 8

1 liter (quart) 35% fat sour cream
2 1/2 dl (1 cup) semolina or cream of wheat
1 liter (quart) full fat milk
salt

Simmer the sour cream about 15 minutes. Stir in the semolina and bring to a boil. Remove the butterfat as it leaches out of the porridge.

Bring the milk to a boil and thin the porridge to the desired consistency. Bring to a boil and season with salt.

Serve with the melted butterfat, raisins, sugar and cinnamon.

2.
Serves 5

6 dl (2 1/2 cups) 35% fat sour cream
3 dl (1 1/4 cups) barley flour

Rice porridge.

1 liter (quart) full fat milk
1 teaspoon salt

Combine sour cream and barley flour (or a blend of barley and all-purpose flour) and simmer until the butterfat begins to leach out. Skim off the fat.

Cook until the porridge is reddish brown, 1-2 hours. Bring the milk to a boil and thin the porridge to the desired consistency. Season with salt.

Serve with the melted butterfat, sugar, cinnamon and milk or juice.

3.
Serves 8

1 liter (quart) full fat milk
1 1/4 dl (1/2 cup) semolina or cream of wheat
1 liter (quart) 35% fat sour cream
2 dl (3/4 cup) barley flour
1 dl (1/3 cup) flour

Combine milk and semolina and make porridge according to the directions on the package.

Combine sour cream and flour and sim-

mer until the butterfat begins to leach out. Skim off the fat.

Pour the semolina porridge onto a deep serving platter. Top with the sour cream porridge. Drizzle over the melted fat. Serve with buttermilk, dried meats and sausages, sugar and cinnamon.

4.
Serves 6

4 dl (1 2/3 cups) 35% fat sour cream
about 3 dl (1 1/4 cups) flour
about 1 1/4 liters (5 cups) full fat milk
3/4 teaspoon salt

Simmer sour cream, covered, about 15 minutes.

Sift over 1/3 of the flour. Simmer until the butterfat begins to leach out. Skim off the fat.

Sift over the remaining flour and bring to a boil. Bring the milk to a boil and thin the porridge to desired consistency. Whisk until smooth. Simmer about 10 minutes, and season with salt. Serve with the fat, sugar and cinnamon.

Sour cream porridge with dried meats was festive food in the olden days and is still considered that today.

5.
Serves 4

1 liter (quart) 35% fat sour cream
about 2 dl (3/4 cup) flour
salt

Simmer the sour cream about 15 minutes, then stir in the flour.
Simmer until the butterfat begins to leach out. Skim off the fat. The porridge will be lumpy. Whisk until smooth, then season with salt.
Since this porridge is not diluted with milk, it is very rich. Serve in small portions.
This porridge also can be used as a topping on other types of porridge, for example, rice porridge.

OTHER MILK DISHES

DRAVLE

Serves 5

2 liters (quarts) full fat milk
about 30 g (1 ounce, 1/4 cup) Norwegian brown blended goat milk cheese (Ski Queen), sliced
1 1/2 tablespoons sugar
2 dl (3/4 cup) buttermilk

Bring the milk, cheese and sugar to a boil, stirring constantly.
Reduce over high heat until half the original amount remains.
Remove 1 dl (scant 1/2 cup) of the reduced milk and reserve.
Add the buttermilk to the pot. Simmer until the curds separate and stiffen.
Chill. When cold, add the reserved caramelized milk.

FLATBREAD SOUP

flatbread
buttermilk
35% fat sour cream
sugar

Crush flatbread into a soup bowl.
Pour over buttermilk and top with a spoonful of sour cream.
Sprinkle with sugar.
This dish was eaten often during the summer.

GOMME

2 liters (quarts) full fat milk
5 dl (2 cups) buttermilk
1-2 tablespoons flour
1 dl (scant 1/2 cup) water
3/4 dl (1/3 cup) raisins
2 tablespoons grated orange peel or
1 1/2 teaspoons anise seed
1 teaspoon cinnamon

Bring the full fat milk to a boil, then stir in buttermilk.
Simmer until the mixture separates.
Simmer, uncovered, 3-4 hours, until the mixture is light brown. Stir occasionally.
Stir the flour into the water and whisk into the mixture to thicken. Stir in raisins, orange peel and cinnamon. Serve with a sprinkling of cinnamon-sugar.

MØLSE FROM OPPDAL

Serves 15

Mølse was used in early times, before sour cream porridge became popular.

10 liters (10 1/2 quarts) milk (preferably straight from the cow)
1 teaspoon rennet

Heat the milk to 32°C (90°F), then add the rennet.
After the milk separates, reduce over medium heat until golden.
Serve cold as soup for dinner.

FRESH CHEESE

2 liters (quarts) full fat milk
2 liters (quarts) buttermilk
whipped cream or sour cream

Heat the full fat milk to 37°C (98°F) and whisk in the buttermilk.
Set in a warm place until it separates, 24-48 hours, depending upon the temperature.
Carefully pour the mixture into a sieve lined with cheesecloth, to drain off the whey. Drain overnight.
The fresh cheese left in the sieve should be refrigerated until serving time and beaten just before serving. It can be enriched with a little whipped cream or sour cream.
Fresh cheese is good with berries.

BUTTERMILK PUDDING

1 liter (quart) full fat milk
1 dl (scant 1/2 cup) buttermilk

Heat the milk to 35°C (95°F). Stir in the buttermilk. Cover with cheesecloth and leave at room temperature about 24 hours to thicken. Refrigerate.
Serve with sugar.

Flatbread with buttermilk was summer food.

FISH AND SHELLFISH

FRESH FISH DISHES

Steaming fish has become more popular these last few years. A three-part steamer, with a pot for water, a perforated pan to set over the water for the fish, plus a lid, is the best equipment for the home kitchen. These can be purchased in stores specializing in products from the Far East. In restaurant kitchens, the steam program of a convection oven is used for this purpose.

STUFFED TROUT FILLET

Serves 4

400 g (14 ounces) skinless and boneless center-cut trout fillet
salt
freshly ground white pepper
leaves from 8 spinach plants, dipped for 30 seconds in boiling water
300 g (10 ounces) haddock mousse forcemeat (see below)

Mousse forcemeat:
200 g (7 ounces) skinless and boneless haddock fillet
1/4 medium onion
salt
pepper
nutmeg
1 egg white
1 1/2 dl (2/3 cup) light cream
Butter sauce:
4 shallots, minced
freshly ground white pepper
1 tablespoon butter

2 dl (3/4 cup) dry white wine
3 dl (1 1/4 cups) whipping cream
3 dl (1 1/4 cups) concentrated fish stock
600 g (1 1/3 pounds, 2 2/3 cups) unsalted butter, room temperature
lemon juice

Place the fish between two sheets of plastic wrap and pound lightly to even the thickness.

Remove the top sheet. Season with salt and pepper, then cover with blanched spinach leaves.

Make the fish forcemeat. Cut the fish into strips and place in a food processor along with the onion, salt, pepper, nutmeg and egg white. With the motor running, gradually add the cream and beat until light and fluffy.

Spoon a layer of fish forcemeat onto the spinach. Roll up the fish with the help of the plastic wrap. Be sure to keep the

Steamed trout stuffed with haddock mousse and spinach.

plastic wrap on the outside of the fish. Tie the ends well.

Steam in a three-part steamer on top of the stove, about 15 minutes.

Let the fish rest about 5 minutes before cutting into slices.

Butter sauce:

Sauté shallots and pepper in margarine. Add wine and reduce until the onion is almost dry. Add cream and fish stock and reduce until the mixture begins to thicken. Remove from the heat and beat in the butter in pats. Season with salt and lemon juice. Do not allow the sauce to boil after the butter is added.

Serve with a green salad and boiled potatoes.

MONKFISH STUFFED WITH SALMON

Serves 4

400 g (14 ounces) center-cut fillet of monkfish
200 g (7 ounces) salmon mousse force-meat (see previous recipe for method)
freshly ground white pepper
salt

Make a long hole in the center of the fish fillet with a thin sharp knife.

Using a pastry tube, pipe the forcemeat into the hole.

Season with salt and pepper, then pack in plastic wrap. Tie the ends well.

Steam in a three-part steamer on top of the stove, about 20 minutes.

Let the fish rest about 5 minutes before cutting into slices.

Serve with a butter sauce (see previous recipe), a green salad and boiled potatoes.

Steamed monkfish stuffed with salmon mousse.

Halibut stew. Soup or stew prepared with oily fish makes a hearty supper.

FISH STEWS

Stews have been part of the Norwegian diet since the days when all food was prepared over an open fire.

This method preserves all the flavors and nutrients in the different ingredients, since everything remains in the pot.

HALIBUT STEW

Serves 6

1 1/2 kg (3 pounds) halibut on the bone
500 g (1 pound) carrots
500 g (1 pound) rutabaga
1 small cabbage
1 large onion
8-10 large potatoes
salt
15 black peppercorns

Skin and bone the fish. Cut into slices. Make stock by placing the bones and trimmings in water to cover. Bring to a boil and skim well. Lower heat and cook 30 minutes. Strain and reserve.
Peel the vegetables and potatoes and cut into chunks. Cover with fish stock, add salt and pepper and simmer 6-8 minutes. Add the fish and simmer until cooked, 8-10 minutes. Season with salt and serve with flatbread.
Note: This dish also can be made with pre-soaked herring fillets. For a thicker stew, add oatmeal or pearl barley.

POLLACK AND POLLACK SOUP

Serves 6

1 1/2 kg (3 pounds) whole small pollack
1 1/2 liters (quarts) water
1 1/2 teaspoons salt
4-5 black peppercorns
1 bay leaf

Soup:
1 1/4 liters (quarts) fish stock
2 large carrots
2-3 stalks celery
2 dl (3/4 cup) full fat milk
3/4 dl (1/3 cup) flour
1 egg yolk
1 dl (1/2 cup) 35% fat sour cream
chopped chives or leek

Clean and wash the fish. Remove the eyes and gills and split the heads. Place the heads in cold water to cover. Bring to a boil and skim well. Add seasonings. Cut the fish into 2 cm (3/4") slices. Place them in water which has just reached the boiling point. Poach until the fish just pulls away from the bone when poked with a knife, 6-8 minutes. Remove the fish slices and reserve. Peel and wash the vegetables. Cut into 3 cm (1 1/4") shreds. Strain the fish stock and reduce slightly. Whisk the milk and flour together and add, stirring until thickened. Add the vegetables and simmer until almost tender, about 5 minutes. Whisk the egg yolk with the sour cream in a soup tureen. Whisk in the boiling soup. Sprinkle with chives. The fish can be boned and placed in the soup, or it can be served after the soup, with boiled potatoes, cooked carrots and melted butter or poached fish liver.

FISH AU GRATIN

Skinless and boneless cooked fish is used in this type of dish. Chunks of fish are mixed into a thick white sauce enriched with beaten egg, then the mixture is poured into a greased ovenproof dish and sprinkled with crumbs. It is usually baked in a water bath. Leftovers of cooked fresh, lightly salted or smoked fish can be prepared in this way.

FISH AU GRATIN

Serves 4

2 tablespoons margarine
3 1/2 tablespoons flour
2 dl (3/4 cup) full fat milk
salt
freshly ground white pepper
ground nutmeg
5 dl (2 cups) flaked cooked fish
2 eggs
1 1/2 dl (2/3 cup) breadcrumbs
1 tablespoon butter

Preheat the oven to 160° C.
Melt the margarine and add the flour. Gradually whisk in the milk and seasonings. Bring to a boil, whisking until thick. Stir in the fish. Beat the egg and stir into the mixture.
Grease a 1 liter (quart) ovenproof dish and sprinkle bottom and sides with breadcrumbs. Pour the fish mixture into the prepared dish. Smooth the top with a rubber spatula, sprinkle with breadcrumbs and dot with butter. Place a cloth towel in the bottom of an oven tray. Place the dish on the towel (to keep it from moving). Add water to reach halfway up the sides of the dish. Bake 25 minutes.
Serve with melted butter with chopped hard-cooked egg and coleslaw.

Fish au gratin uses up leftover fish. Serve with egg butter, boiled potatoes and cole slaw.

COLD COOKED FISH

Cold, cooked fish is a delicacy during the summer. The fish is prepared several hours before serving. All the ingredients, excluding the potatoes, can be cooked in advance, without hampering the quality.

COLD COOKED HALIBUT/ POLLACK/SALMON/TROUT

Allow per person:

180 g (6 ounces) cooked fish
1/2 dl (3 1/2 tablespoons) 35% sour cream
1 teaspoon lemon juice
sugar

or

1/2 dl (3 1/2 tablespoons) whipping cream
fresh grated horseradish
1 teaspoon 7% vinegar
sugar

The fish should be both skinless and boneless.
Beat the sour cream until thick (first it gets thinner, then it forms peaks). Season to taste with lemon juice and sugar.

or

Whip the cream to soft peaks, then add grated horseradish, vinegar and sugar to taste. The cream thickens quickly after the other ingredients are added.
Serve with a cucumber or lettuce salad with a vinegar or oil and vinegar dressing. Serve with hot boiled potatoes.

POACHED FISH

Poaching, along with frying, is one of the most popular ways to prepare fish. Fresh fish is poached in water containing 1/2 dl (3 1/2 tablespoons) salt and 1 teaspoon 7% vinegar per liter (quart) water. Vinegar keeps very fresh fish from falling apart and makes it stay white. It also can be used as a flavor enhancer.
Oily fish is cooked in water containing salt and vinegar with the addition of whole peppercorns and bay leaves.

POACHED HALIBUT/SALMON/ TROUT/MACKEREL/HERRING

halibut/salmon/trout slices

or

mackerel or herring in serving pieces
unsalted butter

Court bouillon:
water
salt (1/2 dl (3 1/2 tablespoons) per liter (quart) water)
lemon
black peppercorns (5 per liter (quart) water)
bay leaf (1 per liter (quart) water)

Bone the halibut, then cut into slices. Cut salmon and ocean trout into 2 cm (3/4") steaks across the bones. Cut mackerel and herring into 2-4 serving pieces across the bones.
Wash the fish and place in boiling court bouillon. Lower the heat and simmer about 10 minutes, until the flesh just pulls away from the bones when poked with a knife.
Place 1 tablespoon water in a saucepan. Stir in soft, unsalted butter and melt over low heat. Do not allow to boil.
Serve with lemon wedges, melted butter, a green salad and boiled potatoes.

POACHED COD

cod steaks, cut across the bone
cod roe
cod liver

Cooking liquid:
salt, 1/2 dl (3 1/2 tablespoons) per liter (quart) water
vinegar, 1 teaspoon 7% vinegar per liter (quart) water
Preparing cod liver:
1 dl (1/3 cup) water
cod liver
1/2 teaspoon salt
1/2 teaspoon freshly ground black pepper
1 tablespoon minced onion
1/2 bay leaf

Norwegians prefer winter cod, when it

swims to the Lofoten islands to spawn, from January to March. It should be cleaned without slitting the stomach, so that the slices are connected at the thin end. Run the fish slices under cold water a few minutes before cooking. Place in boiling water with salt and vinegar, lower the heat and poach 8-10 minutes. Do not allow the water to boil. Transfer the slices with a slotted spoon to a serving platter lined with a cotton napkin to absorb excess water. Serve with cod roe, cod liver and boiled potatoes. To prepare the roe, wash and press out any blood from the veins in the sac. Wrap in parchment paper or plastic wrap and simmer in fish stock 20-40 minutes, depending upon the size. To prepare the liver, remove all membrane and prominent veins. Cut into 12 mm (1/2") cubes. Place in a small saucepan with the water, salt, pepper, onion and bay leaf. Bring to a boil. Remove from the heat and skim well. Lower heat and simmer 2-3 minutes. Do not allow to boil.

There's plenty of fresh cod at fisherman's wharf in Bergen.

Cold poached trout, salmon or pollack, cucumber salad, sour cream with horseradish and hot boiled potatoes is the perfect meal on a warm summer day.

Poached cod with liver and roe is winter's culinary high point for many Norwegians.

HALIBUT IN CABBAGE

Serves 4

1 kg (2 1/4 pounds) halibut
1 kg (2 1/4 pounds) cabbage
1 tablespoon salt
1 tablespoon white peppercorns
3-4 dl (1 1/4 - 1 2/3 cups) water

Cut the fish into 2 cm (3/4") slices. Cut the cabbage into thin wedges. Layer fish and cabbage in a pot, sprinkling each layer with salt and pepper. Pour over the water. Simmer until the cabbage is cooked, about 15 minutes. Serve with boiled potatoes.

MACKEREL OR HERRING FRICASSEE

Serves 5

2 mackerel or 2-3 herrings
4-5 carrots
2-3 parsnips
1 tablespoon salt
1 1/2 liters (quarts) water
3 tablespoons butter
1 dl (1/3 cup) flour
1 1/2 liters (quarts) fish stock
salt
ground white pepper
3 dl (1 1/4 cups) whipping cream
1 tablespoon chopped parsley

Clean and rinse the fish. Cut into 2 cm (3/4") slices. Peel, wash and cut the vegetables into 1 cm (1/2") dice. Cook in salted water until tender, about 6 minutes. Keep warm. Poach the fish in the vegetable water 6-8 minutes. Remove the fish from the cooking water and keep warm. Strain the stock. Melt the butter, then add the flour. Gradually whisk in the stock. Simmer 10 minutes. Season with salt and pepper. Whisk in the cream and simmer 2-3 minutes. Arrange fish and vegetables on a platter. Nap with sauce and sprinkle with parsley. Serve with boiled potatoes.

MARINATED TROUT

Serves 6

800 g (1 3/4 pounds) boneless sea trout
fillet
fish heads and bones
Marinade:
1 large leek
3 large tomatoes
1 large cucumber
3 tablespoons chopped dill
juice of 1 lemon
1 1/2 tablespoons cognac
Sauce:
2 tablespoons butter
4 tablespoons (1/4 cup) flour
5 dl (2 cups) concentrated fish stock
fish marinade with vegetables
chopped dill
1/2 dl (3 1/2 tablespoons) 35% fat sour
cream

The whole fish should weigh 1 1/2 - 2 kg (3 - 4 1/2 pounds) for the fillets to be the desired thickness. Use a tweezers to remove the small bones down the center of the fillets. Shred the vegetables for the marinade. Place half the vegetables in a dish large enough to hold the fish in one layer. Sprinkle the fillet with chopped dill, lemon juice and cognac on both sides. Place on the bed of vegetables. Top with the remaining vegetables. Cover with plastic wrap and refrigerate 24 hours. Remove eyes and gills from the fish head. Place in a pan with the bones, cover with water and simmer 20 minutes. Strain and measure. If more than 5 dl (2 cups), reduce to that amount over high heat. Melt the butter and stir in the flour. Gradually add the stock, marinade with vegetables and dill. Just before serving, stir in the sour cream. Cut the fish fillet into 6 serving pieces. Poach in salted water according to the recipe about 10 minutes. Transfer the fish to a serving platter. Nap with the sauce. Garnish with lemon wedges and dill sprigs. Serve with boiled potatoes.

Fishing for trout in the mountains, for both recreation and filling the freezer.

Poached marinated trout on a mirror of sauce.

"Fish for a prince" is made from different kinds of fish. Side dishes vary from district to district.

FISH FOR A PRINCE

Serves 4

*600 g boneless and skinless cod or
halibut fillet
5 dl (2 cups) fish stock
1 1/2 tablespoons butter
2 1/2 tablespoons flour
1 egg yolk
1 dl (1/3 cup) whipping cream
salt
about 1 tablespoon lemon juice or sherry
1 1/4 dl (1/2 cup) peeled cooked shrimp
or lobster
8 asparagus spears, cooked
1 tablespoon chopped parsley*

Cut the fish into 4 serving pieces.
Poach in fish stock 8-10 minutes. Transfer the fish to a deep serving platter and
keep warm. Melt the butter and stir in
the flour. Gradually whisk in the stock.
Simmer until thickened. Beat the egg
yolk into the cream and whisk into the
sauce. Season with salt, lemon juice or
sherry. Nap the fish with the sauce.
Garnish with shrimp and asparagus.
Sprinkle with parsley.

TANANGER FISH

Serves 2

*2 teaspoons melted fat from boiled salted
mutton (or oil)
1 1/4 dl (1/2 cup) minced onion
3 dl (1 1/4 cups) flaked poached lightly
salted cod
1 dl (scant 1/2 cup) full fat milk
1/8 teaspoon pepper*

Melt the fat in a saucepan. Sauté the
onion in the fat until soft and shiny. Add
the fish with a little milk. Stir until almost
smooth, adding milk as needed. It should
have the texture of porridge. Serve with
boiled potatoes and vegetables.

VESTERÅLEN FISH

Serves 2

*1 1/2 tablespoons butter
2 1/2 tablespoons minced onion
120 g (4 ounces) skinless and boneless
ocean catfish fillet*

*This fish dish from Vesterålen in the Lofoten Islands is a modern one composed of ingredients
from that region.*

Crisp fried cod tongues are a seasonal delicacy.

120 g (4 ounces) skinless and boneless
salmon fillet
2 spears broccoli
1 dl (1/3 cup) white wine
salt
pepper
1 egg yolk
2 dl (3/4 cup) whipping cream
4 peeled cooked shrimp
4 peeled cooked mussels
2 mushrooms, sliced
lemon juice
chopped parsley

Grease a frying pan with the butter and add the onion. Roll up the fish fillets and place in the center of the pan. Place the broccoli alongside the fish. Add wine, salt and pepper. Cover with aluminum foil. Place over medium heat and steam 5 minutes. Fold back the foil and pour off some of the poaching liquid. Beat the egg yolk into the cream and add to the poaching liquid. Add shrimp, mussels and mushrooms to the pan and cook about 30 seconds. Pour the sauce back into the pan and reheat. Do not

allow to boil. Season with lemon juice and garnish with chopped parsley. Serve with boiled potatoes.

FRIED FISH

Frying has always been one of the most common methods to prepare fish in addition to poaching. Before frying, fish is either dipped into seasoned flour, a mixture of flour, salt and pepper, or it is breaded by dipping first in flour, then in lightly beaten egg or egg white and finally in breadcrumbs.

ARCTIC CHAR
STUFFED WITH BIRCH SHOOTS

Serves 3

100 g (4 ounces) fresh birch shoots
1 dl (1/3 cup) vegetable oil
4 whole Arctic char or brook trout,
about 250 g (9 ounces) each
salt
pepper

100 g (3 ounces, 1/3 cup) butter
1 dl (1/3 cup) chopped chives

Mince the birch shoots and marinate 24 hours in vegetable oil. Preheat the oven to 180°C (350°F) or heat the grill. Cut the heads off the fish. Slit the stomach and clean. Wash all blood from around the backbone. Salt and pepper the cavity. Beat the butter with the birch shoots and chives. Stuff the fish with the mixture. Pack each separately in aluminum foil. Bake or grill 15-20 minutes. Serve with a green salad and boiled potatoes.

FRIED COD TONGUES

200 g (7 ounces) cod tongues per person
flour seasoned with salt and pepper
lightly-beaten egg white
breadcrumbs
oil

Trim the tongues, soak in vinegar water until just ready to prepare, then dry well. Dip in seasoned flour, then in beaten egg white and finally in crumbs and fry in oil until golden, about 2 minutes per side. Drain on a napkin and serve with lemon wedges, deep-fried parsley, tartar sauce (mayonnaise with chopped onion, pickle, capers and anchovy) and boiled potatoes. Serve with a salad made of shredded carrot, apple and cabbage with a dressing of water, malt vinegar, salt and sugar.

SHARK SCHNITZEL

Serves 8

480 g (1 pound) shark fillet
8 large slices boiled ham
8 thick slices Jarlsberg cheese
flour seasoned with salt and pepper
lightly-beaten egg white
breadcrumbs
butter

Cut the fillet into 8 thin pieces. Pound lightly.
Cover almost half of each piece of fish with a slice of ham wrapped around a slice of cheese. Fold over the other half of the fish. Press the edges together.
Dip in seasoned flour, then in beaten egg white and finally in crumbs. Brown 2-3 minutes per side in butter, until the fish is cooked and the cheese begins to melt. Serve with browned butter, boiled potatoes and vegetables.

ARCTIC CHAR
IN RED CURRANT SAUCE

Serves 4

600 g (1 1/3 pounds) boneless and skin-less Arctic char or ocean trout fillet
flour seasoned with salt and pepper
butter
1 liter (quart) fish stock
2 dl (3/4 cup) red currant jelly
1 dl (1/3 cup) minced onion
2 branches fresh thyme (or 1/2 teaspoon dried)
1 1/2 dl (2/3 cup) 35% fat sour cream

Clean and dry the fish. Dip in seasoned flour and fry in butter, about 2 minutes per side. Remove from the pan. Deglaze

Arctic char is a farmed fish which has become popular in recent years. It can be prepared in many ways, one of which is sautéed with red currant sauce.

the pan with fish stock and add the jelly, onion and thyme. Reduce over medium heat until half the original amount remains. Stir in the sour cream. Return the fish to the pan and simmer until warm, about 2 minutes. Season sauce, if necessary. Serve with sautéed wild mushrooms sprinkled with chives or parsley, a branch of fresh red currants and boiled almond potatoes.

POLLACK WITH ONIONS

Serves 6

1 large onion
butter
1 kg (2 1/4 pounds) skinless and bone-less pollack fillets
flour seasoned with salt and pepper
6 dl (2 1/2 cups) whipping cream

Peel and slice the onion. Brown in butter and reserve. Cut the fish into serv-ing pieces. Dip in seasoned flour and fry in butter, 2-3 minutes per side. Arrange the fish and onion on a serving platter. Pour the cream into the frying pan. Boil about 1 minute. Nap the fish with the sauce. Serve with boiled al-mond potatoes and grated carrots.

POLLACK
WITH CABBAGE AND ONIONS

Serves 6

1 kg (2 1/4 pounds) skinless and bone-less pollack fillets
flour seasoned with salt and pepper
butter
1 small summer cabbage
2 large onions
7 1/2 dl (3 cups) water or fish stock

Preheat the oven to 180° C (350° F).
Cut the fish into serving pieces. Dip in

seasoned flour and fry in butter, 2-3 minutes per side. Cut out the core and blanch the whole cabbage 3 minutes in lightly salted water. Plunge immediately into cold water. Peel and slice the onion. Brown in butter. Shred the cabbage and stir into the onion. Layer fish and vegetables in a low, wide ovenproof dish. Deglaze the frying pan with water or stock and pour over the fish and vegetables. Bake about 20 minutes. Serve with boiled almond potatoes.

COD TONGUES IN SAUCE
◆

Serves 6

800 g (1 2/3 pounds) cod tongues
flour seasoned with salt and pepper
butter

Sauce:
3 tablespoons butter
1 1/4 dl (1/2 cup) minced onion
1 1/4 dl (1/2 cup) minced red bell pepper
3/4 dl (1/3 cup) flour
about 5 dl (2 cups) fish stock
1 dl (1/3 cup) 35% fat sour cream
1 dl (1/2 cup) whipping cream
soy sauce
salt
pepper

Wash and dry the tongues well.
Dip in seasoned flour and fry in butter, about 2 minutes per side. Transfer to a serving platter and keep warm.
Sauté onion and paprika in the same butter. Stir in the flour. Gradually whisk

in the fish stock, sour cream and whipping cream.
Boil 5 minutes, until thickened. Add a few drops soy sauce for color, if desired, and season with salt and pepper. Nap the tongues with the sauce and serve with boiled potatoes and cole slaw.

Fried pollack is a tasty dish often served in coastal districts.

"Boknafisk" with milk soup. In earlier days, salty fish dishes, or those with a strong fish flavor, were served with a milk soup.

DRIED FISH DISHES

Dried fish is air-dried, neither salted nor seasoned, but with the moisture removed. There are two main types of dried fish: One is "raw-cut," in which the fish is halved lengthwise. Half the backbone is removed, and the two fillets hang together at the tail end. The other is "stockfish," in which headless fish is slit open at the stomach only. Fish are tied two and two, bound at the tail, and hung together. Dried fish is cut into pieces with a saw and then soaked in cold water for 2-3 days or more. When the fish has returned to normal size, the skins and bones are removed and it is cut into 3-4 cm (1 1/2") pieces. 1 kg (2 1/4 pounds) dried fish makes 2 1/2 - 3 kg (5 - 6 1 1/2 pounds) soaked fish = about 2 kg (4 1/2 pounds) cleaned, boneless, skinless fish. Drying removes about 70% of the water, but all the nutrients remain. 1 kg (2 1/4 pounds) dried fish has the same nutritional value as 5 kg (11 pounds) fresh fish.

BOKNA FISH

Bokna fish is fresh or lightly salted fish which has been hung in the fresh air to dry for a few days. It also can be salted fish, which often does not withstand extended storage, which is soaked and then dried.

This method of preparation was common to coastal districts.

BOKNA FISH

salted cod, pollack or redfish
water

Soak the fish in cold water 48 hours. Hang to dry in a cool and airy place about 14 days, until half-dried.
Cut the fish into serving pieces and poach about 10 minutes.
Serve with fried pork belly, boiled or creamed rutabagas, boiled potatoes and a milk soup.

BOKNA POLLACK

Serves 4

1 - 1 1/2 kg (2 1/4 - 3 pounds) fresh pollack

Wash the fish. Do not scale. Slit the stomach and clean. Wash all blood from around the backbone. Hang to dry in a cool and airy place 14 days, until half-dried.
Scale and cut into serving pieces.
Poach in lightly salted water about 10 minutes.
Serve with bacon fat, boiled carrots and boiled potatoes.

BOKNA HERRING
(plump herring)

fresh herring
salt
water

Cut off the heads. Fillet the fish along the backbone, leaving the two fillets connected together across the stomach. Clean and rinse in cold water.
Make a slit just above the tail and draw the tail through the hole. This spreads out the fish and it dries easier.
Cover with salt a few hours, then hang to dry in a cool and airy place, until half-dried, about 1 week.
Poach about 10 minutes.
Serve with boiled rutabaga, cold butter, boiled potatoes, flatbread and milk soup with barley.

POACHED DRIED FISH

Serves 10

2 kg (4 1/2 pounds) dried fish
3 liters (quarts) water
1 dl (1/3 cup) salt
Potato dumplings:
500 g (1 pound) boiled potatoes
1 egg
1 tablespoon sugar
1/2 teaspoon cinnamon
all-purpose flour or barley flour
1 liter (quart) full fat milk

Soak the fish in cold water 2-3 days, changing water frequently. Cut into serving pieces and steam about 10 minutes. Season with salt. Serve with creamed dried peas, fried bacon, boiled potatoes and milk soup with potato dumplings.
Potato dumplings: Grind the potatoes once. Add the remaining ingredients to make a firm dough. Bring the milk to a boil. Roll finger-thick sausages, then cut into 4 cm (1 3/4") lengths. Poach the dumplings 5-10 minutes in the milk.

Opposite page: Cod from the Lofoten islands is dried on racks.

"Lutefisk" and poached cod are among the most popular festive dishes in Norway. The best time for lutefisk is during the dark days before Christmas.

LUTEFISK

750 g (1 2/3 pounds) lutefisk per person
water
salt (1/2 dl (3 1/2 tablespoons) per liter
(quart) water)

Cut the fish into oversized serving pieces (to allow for shrinkage) and soak in cold water 30 minutes before poaching. Bring the water to a boil. Add salt. Place the fish in the boiling water. When the water returns to a boil, lower the heat, skim and then simmer 5-10 minutes, depending upon the thickness. Serve on a cloth napkin with bacon fat, mashed yellow peas, boiled potatoes, cold butter, mustard sauce, flatbread or lefse.

DRIED FISH SALAD

Serves 4

Dressing:
1 tablespoon 5% vinegar
3 tablespoons olive oil
salt
pepper
mustard
6 dl (2 1/2 cups) flaked, cooked, cold reconstituted dried fish
1 small lettuce, separated into leaves and torn
2 hard-cooked eggs, in wedges
8-10 green olives, sliced

Whisk dressing ingredients together in a large bowl. Add fish and lettuce and coat with the dressing.
Garnish with egg wedges and sprinkle with olives.
Serve tomato wedges sprinkled with chopped onion alongside the salad.

SALT FISH DISHES

Before refrigeration, fish was often salted, because then it could keep indefinitely. Today, fish is salted because we enjoy the dishes made with salt fish. Now we salt the fish until it has the right taste and salt content, then we freeze it until we plan to use it.

Old pollack gets its reddish color and its special flavor after many years' preservation in salt.

SPICED HERRING

40 herring
strong vinegar water, 1 part 7% vinegar to 2 parts water
1 3/4 dl (1 3/4 cup) sugar
2 teaspoons pepper
350 g (12 ounces, 2 3/4 dl, 1 1/4 cups) salt
2 teaspoons ground allspice
7   leaves

W.. the herring. Dry and soak in vinegar water 24 hours. Drain the herring and dry well. Combine the remaining ingredients and layer with the herring. Cover and store in the refrigerator 6 weeks to mature.

Spiced herring needs to be soaked in cold water before use.

OLD POLLACK FROM SALTEN (RED POLLACK)

1-3 year old salt pollack

Old pollack is supposed to be reddish brown, because it is not bled before preservation and the blood leaches out into the soaking water.
Cut the fish into serving pieces and soak 4-5 hours in cold water, changing several times. Place the fish in a pot with cold water to cover and bring to a boil. Drain, then cover with cold water and bring to a boil again. Simmer 10

minutes. Serve with creamed carrots, rutabagas or dried peas, fried bacon, boiled potatoes and flatbread.

KUBBESILD

2 large herring fillets per person
salt
Breste:
6 dl (2 1/2 cups) skim milk
1 dl (scant 1/2 cup) buttermilk

Wash the herring. Layer with salt in a barrel, backbone down. Store in a cool place 72 hours. Check for saltiness.
Wash the salt off the herring.
Smoke 24 hours. Use juniper wood for smoking.
Hang to dry in an airy place about 6 days.
Breste:
Combine skim milk and buttermilk and wait until it curdles.
Fillet the herring. Serve with boiled potatoes, butter, flatbread and breste.

LIGHTLY-SALTED FISH

300 g (10 ounces) lightly-salted cod, cusk or redfish per person

Fish which is not too salty does not need to be soaked before cooking.
Cut the fish into serving pieces. Red-fish is usually sold with the head, which is cooked and served with the fish. The head of the redfish is a delicacy.
Place the fish in a pot and cover with cold water. Bring to a boil. Lower heat and simmer about 10 minutes, until the backbone loosens.
Serve with fried bacon or egg-butter, creamed carrots, boiled potatoes and flatbread.

PERSE COD

Serves 6

1 1/2 kg (3 pounds) cod
salt
water

Fresh cod weighing 4-5 kg (9-11 pounds) is best in this dish.
Use the part of the fish in front of the anal hole. Use the tail for another dish.
Clean, fillet and wash the fish.
Sprinkle the fillets generously with salt, especially the thicker pieces. Press the fillets down with a weight for about 3 hours.
Remove the skin and cut into serving pieces.
Bring water to a boil in a large pot. Add the fish. Return to a boil, lower the heat and simmer about 8 minutes.
Transfer the fish to a serving platter and serve with boiled potatoes and melted butter with chopped egg.

KLIPPFISH DISHES

Klippfish is dried salted fish. It is mainly an export product, which is shipped out of Norway's west coast ports, Ålesund and Kristiansund.

BACALAO

Serves 8

600 g (1 1/3 pounds) skinless, boneless, soaked klippfish
750 g (1 2/3 pounds, 4 large) potatoes, peeled
1 large onion
2 dl (scant 1 cup) water
2 dl (3/4 cup) oil
1 1/2 dl (2/3 cup) tomato purée
1/4 fresh red chili pepper or 1 small dried chili

Soak the fish 24 hours.
Cut the fish into 4 cm (1 3/4") squares.
Slice the potatoes and onion.
Combine remaining ingredients in a large, wide pot.
Bring to a boil, then layer the fish, then the onions and finally the potatoes.
Cover and simmer until the potatoes are tender, 1 1/2 - 2 hours.

"Perse" cod is an old Bergen specialty made from the front part of the fish.

Bacalao is the Spanish and Portuguese word for dried salted fish. In Norway, bacalao is a stew made from dried salted fish, tomatoes, potatoes, oil and seasonings. It is most popular in the salt fish ports of Kristiansund and Ålesund.

KLIPPFISH CASSEROLE

Serves 4

250 g (9 ounces) skinless, boneless
klippfish
1 1/2 tablespoons butter
2 tablespoons flour
2 tablespoons breadcrumbs
4 teaspoons salt
2 teaspoons mace
cayenne pepper
7 1/2 dl (3 cups) whipping cream
9 eggs, separated

Soak the fish in cold water 24 hours.
Place in a pot, cover with water and simmer 10 minutes.
Preheat the oven to 160°C (325°F).
Grease and flour a 2 liter (quart) ovenproof dish.
Clean and chop the fish. Beat in the butter, then the flour, breadcrumbs, salt
and seasonings. Gradually add the
cream and egg yolks. Beat the egg
whites until stiff but not dry and fold
into the fish mixture.
Pour into the prepared dish. Place a
cloth towel in the bottom of an oven
tray. Place the dish on the towel (to
keep it from moving) and add water to
reach halfway up the sides of the dish.
Bake 30-45 minutes.
Unmold onto a serving platter and
serve with cole slaw, egg-butter and
boiled potatoes.

SMOKED FISH DISHES

SMOKED TAIL ENDS

Serves 4

1 1/2 kg (3 pounds) tail ends of cod
salt
butter
1 dl (1/2 cup) 35% fat sour cream
1 dl (1/2 cup) buttermilk or yogurt.

Clean, fillet and wash the fish.
Sprinkle generously with salt on both
sides and marinate in the refrigerator 2-
3 hours. Rinse the salt off the fish and

hand to dry in an airy place overnight.
Lightly smoke the fish 2-4 hours.
Remove the skin, but leave the fillets
whole. Brown the fish in butter on both
sides. Lower the heat and add the sour
cream and buttermilk. Braise over low
heat 2-3 minutes.
Serve with the sauce, boiled carrots
and boiled potatoes.

GROUND FISH DISHES

In Norwegian cooking, forcemeat
dishes are an important group, both
with fish and meat.
Forcemeat demands top-quality raw
materials, which is especially true for
fish forcemeat. Dishes prepared from
ground fish usually are made in large
batches when the fish is freshest and
then frozen, while earlier, these dishes
were canned.

FISH AND POTATO DUMPLINGS

Serves 6

1 kg (2 1/4 pounds) fresh pollack or
haddock
1 liter (quart) potatoes, in chunks
2 tablespoons salt
2 large onions, quartered
1 dl (scant 1/2 cup) full fat milk

3 tablespoons potato starch
1 tablespoon flour
150 g (5 ounces) bacon, in large cubes
Cooking liquid:
fish stock or
salt water (1/2 teaspoon salt per liter
(quart) water)
bacon rind

Grind fish once with potatoes, salt and
onions. Gradually add milk. Add both
flours, stirring until well-blended. Form
into about 20 large dumplings, filling
each with a bacon chunk. Simmer in the
cooking liquid about 20 minutes. Serve
with boiled carrots, fried bacon cubes,
mashed rutabagas and boiled potatoes.

SMOKED HERRING DUMPLINGS

Serves 4

4 smoked herring
2 hard-cooked eggs
salt
pepper
about 1 tablespoon butter
1 tablespoon chopped chives

Clean and chop the herring. Chop the
egg and add with salt and pepper. Bind
with about 1 tablespoon soft butter.
Make small, round balls and sauté in
butter 2-4 minutes. Sprinkle with
chives.

Smoked tail ends is an old Bergen specialty made from the back part of the cod.

FORCEMEAT FOR FISH MOUSSE

1 kg (2 1/4 pounds) boneless, skinless fish fillets (salmon, trout, flounder, whiting or other white fish)
2-3 teaspoons salt
1 teaspoon freshly ground white pepper
4-5 egg whites
about 9 dl (3 3/4 cups) whipping cream

Grind the fish once, then transfer it to a food processor. Season with salt and pepper.
Add the egg whites, one at a time. Gradually add the cream.
Let the prepared fish mousse rest in the refrigerator 1-2 hours before using.
This forcemeat can be used as stuffing fish, for hot fish mousse or for small individual timbales.

FRIED FISH CAKES

Serves 6

1 kg (2 1/4 pounds) skinless, boneless haddock fillets
1 1/2 teaspoons salt
1 1/2 teaspoons potato starch
1/2 teaspoon ground nutmeg
2 dl (3/4 cup) full fat milk
150 g (5 ounces) bacon cubes
flour
butter
1 liter (quart) prepared brown gravy

Ground the fish with the salt 3 times. During the last grinding, add the potato starch.
Add the nutmeg and gradually add the milk, stirring well.
Form into 12 oval cakes and fill each with bacon.
Dip in flour and fry on three sides in butter over medium heat.
Simmer in brown gravy until done, about 3 minutes. Serve in the gravy.
Serve with boiled potatoes and vegetables.

Fish sausages are another dish made with ground fish, one of the many varieties of sausage in the Norwegian kitchen.

FISH CAKES

Serves 6

750 g (1 2/3 pounds) skinless, boneless haddock fillets
1 tablespoon salt
2 tablespoons potato starch
1/4 teaspoon ground nutmeg
1/4 teaspoon freshly ground white pepper
about 5 dl (2 cups) milk/fish stock
butter

Grind the fish once, then transfer to a food processor. If not using a food processor, grind 5 times, the last time with salt before adding the other ingredients. Add salt, potato starch, nutmeg and pepper to the fish. Gradually add the milk or stock. Process until smooth. Fill the forcemeat into a pastry tube without a tip. Pipe directly into a medium hot skillet with browned butter. Make medium-sized round cakes. Fry about 2 minutes per side.
Serve with fried onions, browned butter, cole slaw and boiled potatoes, or serve in brown gravy with boiled or creamed vegetables and boiled potatoes.

FISH SAUSAGE

Serves 6

750 g (1 2/3 pounds) skinless, boneless fish fillets
250 g (9 ounces) pork fat
salt
1 onion, quartered
1 teaspoon ground white pepper
1 teaspoon ground allspice
1 teaspoon ground ginger
5 m (yards) lamb sausage casings

Grind the fish twice, the fat once, separately, then once with the onion.
Combine with the seasonings. Fill the casings and tie at 10 cm (4") intervals. Simmer 15 minutes.
Serve hot with bacon, boiled root vegetables and boiled potatoes. Makes about 45 small sausages.

HITRA DUMPLINGS

Serves 10

*1 kg (2 1/4 pounds) skinless, boneless
haddock fillets
1 onion, quartered
2 1/4 teaspoons salt
3 tablespoons potato starch
3/4 - 1 liter (3-4 cups) full fat milk
150 g (5 ounces) pork or mutton fat,
cubed
1 liter (quart) fish stock*

Make fish forcemeat following the
directions for fish cakes.
Form into about 20 large dumplings,
filling each with a cube of fat.
Simmer in fish stock about 20 minutes.

FISH DUMPLINGS
STUFFED WITH LIVER

Serves 10

*1 kg (2 1/4 pounds) skinless, boneless
haddock fillets
salt
ground white pepper
1 large onion, quartered
1 1/2 tablespoons potato starch
5-7 dl (2-3 cups) cold milk
Liver forcemeat:
250 g (8 ounces) cod liver
1 dl (1/3 cup) barley flour
1 dl (1/3 cup) flour
2 tablespoons buttermilk
1 1/2 teaspoons salt
about 1 tablespoon light corn syrup or
sugar
1 teaspoon ground white pepper
1/2 teaspoon caraway seeds
1 liter (quart) fish stock*

Fish forcemeat:
Grind the fish once with salt and onion.
Transfer to a food processor. Add
potato starch and gradually add the
milk. Process until smooth.
Liver forcemeat:
Clean the liver, removing all membrane
and veins. Mash with a fork.
Add remaining ingredients. The mixture should be thick.
Form into about 20 large dumplings,
filling each with a small spoonful of the
liver mixture. The liver mixture must
be completely covered with fish forcemeat.
Simmer in fish stock 15-20 minutes.
Serve with fried bacon, boiled carrots
and leeks and boiled potatoes.

Fish dumplings stuffed with liver come from Romsdal in western Norway. They combine the rich fish dumpling traditions from Nordmøre and the fish liver dishes of Sunnmøre.

All along our coastline are many good fishing spots, where cod, pollack, mackerel and haddock are just waiting to be caught.

KRISTIANSUND DUMPLINGS

Serves 4-6

*750 g (1 2/3 pounds) skinless, boneless
pollack fillets
30 g (1 ounce) suet
1 onion, quartered
1/2 tablespoon salt
750 g (1 2/3 pounds, 4 large) potatoes
5-6 tablespoons (3/4 dl, 1/3 cup) barley
flour
1/4 teaspoon ground ginger
1/4 teaspoon freshly ground white
pepper
150 g (5 ounces) bacon cubes
dried beef shank*

Grind the fish with suet, onion and salt.
Grind the potatoes. Combine fish, potatoes, flour and seasonings. Form into
about 10 large dumplings, filling each
with a bacon cube. Simmer in salted
water with a dried beef shank about 45
minutes. Serve with melted butter,
chives, fried bacon, boiled rutabaga,
carrots and potatoes.

KVITSØY DUMPLINGS
IN FISH SOUP

Serves 5

*600 g (1 1/3 pounds) skinless, boneless
haddock fillets
3 dl (1 1/4 cups) full fat milk
1 tablespoon flour
1 tablespoon potato flour
1 egg
1 tablespoon salt
ground white pepper
1 teaspoon ground ginger
1 teaspoon ground nutmeg
butter
Soup:
1 liter (quart) fish stock
60 g (4 tablespoons, 1/4 cup) butter
1 dl (scant 1/2 cup) flour
3 dl (1 1/4 cups) whipping cream
1 carrot, julienned
small chunk rutabaga, julienned
small chunk celeriac, julienned
1/2 leek, julienned
chopped parsley*

Cut the fish into small pieces.

Place in a food processor along with the
remaining ingredients (except for the
butter) and process until smooth.
Form 8-10 "tennis balls" of the mixture,
filling each with a small pat of butter.
Place in the cold fish stock and bring to
a boil. Lower the heat and simmer 10-15
minutes. Remove from the stock and
reserve. Knead the butter and flour
together and whisk gradually into the
fish stock to thicken. Add the cream
and the vegetables. Reheat the dumplings in the soup. Just before serving,
sprinkle with chopped parsley.

Serve with boiled potatoes, melted butter and flatbread.

*Fish dumplings with fish soup is a tasty main dish from Kvitsøy, in Rogaland, on the south-
west coast.*

SALMON SAUSAGES

Serves 10

500 g (1 1/4 pounds) skinless, boneless salmon fillet
500 g (1 pound) skinless, boneless smoked salmon
3 tablespoons potato starch
3 dl (1 1/4 cups) full fat milk
Sage sauce:
65 g (4 1/2 tablespoons, 1/4 cup) butter
1 1/4 dl (1/2 cup) flour
2 tablespoons dried sage
1 1/2 liters (quarts) boiling water
salt
5 egg yolks
250 g (8 ounces, 1 cup) butter
lemon juice

Make forcemeat of both salmons, potato starch and milk. Spoon the mixture onto a clean kitchen towel to make a thick sausage. Tie both ends.
Simmer in lightly-salted water about 20 minutes. Cut into slices and serve with sage sauce, boiled carrots and boiled potatoes.
Sage sauce:
Melt butter and add flour and sage. Gradually add boiling water and season with salt. Mix the egg yolks lightly and whisk into the sauce. Do not allow to boil. Beat in the unsalted butter in pats. Add lemon juice to taste.

Salmon sausages are a newer creation.

MACKEREL CAKES

Serves 2

250 g (9 ounces) scraped mackerel fillet
1 teaspoon salt
2 tablespoons finely chopped suet
1 teaspoon potato starch
1 teaspoon minced onion or chives
3/4-1 dl (1/3 cup) mackerel stock
butter

Grind the mackerel twice with the salt and suet. Transfer to a food processor and add potato starch and onion. Process until stiff. With the motor running, gradually add the stock. The mixture should not be too loose.
Form into burgers and fry in browned butter 2-3 minutes per side.

Serve with pan juices, mashed rutabagas and boiled potatoes.

POLLACK BALLS

Serves 4

500 g (1 pound) skinless, boneless pollack fillet
1 tablespoon potato starch
about 1 1/4 teaspoons salt
about 3 dl (1 1/4 cups) full fat milk
1/4 teaspoon nutmeg
5 dl (2 cups) fish stock

Grind the fish 3-4 times, the last time with the potato starch, nutmeg and salt. Gradually add milk, stirring constantly. Make a tiny ball and cook to check the taste and texture.
Make 8-10 smooth, round balls with a wet hand and spoon.
Simmer in fish stock about 5 minutes. Store in the refrigerator in the stock.
Serve with white sauce flavored with shrimp or curry, cole slaw and boiled potatoes.

ROE PATTIES

Serves 4-5

2 large cod roe, about 750 g (1 2/3 pounds)
1 1/2 teaspoons salt
1 teaspoon pepper
about 4 dl (1 2/3 cups) full fat milk
1 dl (1/2 cup) flour
butter
brown gravy

Clean and dry the roe. Scrape the roe out of the sacs.
Add the remaining ingredients to form a medium-firm mass.
Form into 6-8 patties and fry in browned butter, about 3 minutes per side. Simmer 2-3 minutes in brown gravy.
Serve in the gravy with creamed cabbage and boiled potatoes.

SALT FISH DUMPLINGS

Serves 6

1 kg (2 1/4 pounds) pre-soaked boneless and skinless salted pollack or cod fillets
750 g (1 2/3 pounds, 4 large) peeled potatoes
2 cold boiled potatoes
1 small onion
4 tablespoons (1/4 cup) barley flour
1 tablespoon light corn syrup
about 1 dl (1/3 cup) full fat milk
150 g (5 ounces) fresh pork fat, cubed

Grind fish, potatoes and onion once. Work in the flour, syrup and milk. The forcemeat should be quite loose. Make a small sample ball to check for seasoning. Make 14-16 dumplings with wet hands. Place a cube of fat in the center of each. Place in boiling water and simmer about 45 minutes. Serve with fried pork, boiled rutabagas, potatoes.

HERRINGBURGERS

Serves 4

750 g (1 2/3 pounds) fresh herring
200 g (7 ounces, 1 large) boiled potato
3/4 teaspoon salt
2 1/4 teaspoons potato starch
5 dl (2 cups) fish stock
margarine or butter

Clean, fillet, wash and dry the herring. Grind the fish once, then grind with the potatoes.
Stir in salt and potato starch. Gradually add fish stock.
Form round burgers and fry in margarine 3 minutes per side.
Serve with fried onions, browned butter and vegetables.

TROUT PATÉ WITH CHIVE SAUCE

Serves 4

150 g (5 ounces) smoked boneless, skinless trout fillet
100 g (4 ounces) fresh boneless, skinless trout fillet
1 teaspoon cold butter
1/4 teaspoon salt
1/2 teaspoon ground white pepper
1/2 dl (3 1/2 tablespoons) whipping cream
4 lettuce leaves
4 dill sprigs
4 lemon slices
Chive sauce:
4 ss (1/4 cup) 20% fat sour cream
1 tablespoon chopped chives

Cut 4 thin slices of the smoked trout and reserve. Grind remaining smoked trout with the fresh and press through a sieve. Beat with butter, salt and pepper.

Trout paté with smoked trout and chive sauce.

Gradually add the cream. Spoon into a pastry tube and pipe onto 4 individual plates. Arrange the sliced smoked trout around the mound of paté. Combine sour cream and chives. Place a lettuce leaf on each plate. Garnish with dill and lemon and a spoonful of sauce. Serve with melba toast.

SHELLFISH AND OTHER SEAFOOD DISHES

SQUID

SQUID OMELET

Serves 4

500 g (1 pound) squid
flour seasoned with salt and pepper
butter
small wedge cabbage
1 small onion or leek
small chunk celeriac
2 medium carrots
1/4 small rutabaga
1 tablespoon soy sauce
4 eggs
4 ss (1/4 cup) full fat milk

Clean the squid. Flay and cut into 1x5 cm (1/2x2") strips.
Dip in seasoned flour and fry on both sides in browned butter. Reserve.
Shred the cabbage, onion and celeriac. Grate the carrots and rutabaga. Sauté in butter. Add soy sauce and sauté 3 minutes more. Remove from the heat and add the squid.
Whisk together eggs, milk, salt and pepper. Pour over the squid mixture. Stir until set.
Serve with toast and butter.

FRIED SQUID

As above, but do not add eggs and milk.

Fried Squid

SQUIDBURGERS

Serves 6

1 kg (2 1/4 pounds) cleaned and flayed squid
2 eggs
1/2 dl (3 1/2 tablespoons) vegetable oil
2 dl (3/4 cup) full fat milk
1/2 medium onion, chopped
1 dl (1/3 cup) chopped parsley
2 tablespoons potato starch
1 tablespoon salt
1 teaspoon pepper
1/4 teaspoon ground nutmeg
breadcrumbs
butter

Grind the squid once.
In a large bowl, combine with the next 10 ingredients, adding as much breadcrumbs as necessary to hold the mixture together.
Form into 1 cm (1/2") thick patties and fry about 3 minutes per side in butter.
Serve with a green salad and tomatoes, onion and mayonnaise.

SHELLFISH ON ITS OWN

Serve lobster, crab or shrimp cold.
Per portion:
4-500 g (1 pound) lobster, 1 stuffed
crabshell, 1 liter (quart) shrimp with
shells
3 slices toast
butter
2-4 lemon wedges
2 tablespoons mayonnaise

1. Halve lobster lengthwise. Remove the stomach, which is located at the front of the head, and remove the black vein. Crack the claws so that the meat easily can be removed with a lobster fork. Serve on a cloth napkin with toast, butter, lemon and mayonnaise.

2. Remove all the crabmeat from 1 crab and pack in the shell, placing the claws on top. Serve on a napkin with toast, butter, lemon and mayonnaise.

3. Serve shrimp in the shell. Place in a large glass bowl or on a platter garnished with parsley and lemon wedges. Serve with toast, butter and mayonnaise.

Live crabs can be bought directly from the fisherman.

A seafood table with poached lobster, crab, ocean crayfish, shrimp, mussels, clams and oysters.

SEAFOOD SANDWICH FILLINGS

CURRIED FISH

Serves 8

1 kg (2 1/4 pounds) boneless, skinless pollack fillets
flour seasoned with salt and pepper
butter
500 g (1 lb, 2-3 large) onions
2 teaspoons salt
1 liter (quart) water
1/2 dl (3 1/2 tablespoons) 35% vinegar concentrate
5 dl (2 cups) sugar
3 tablespoons curry powder

Dip the fish in seasoned flour and fry in butter 4-5 minutes. Cool. Slice the onion and boil 2 minutes in salted water. Cool. Combine cold fish and onion. Combine onion water, vinegar concentrate, sugar and curry powder and pour over the fish. Refrigerate 24 hours before serving. Serve on bread with mayonnaise.

POLLACK SALMON

500 g (1 pound) skinless, boneless pollack fillets
salt
2 tablespoons instant smoke flavor
2 teaspoons lobster coloring
1 liter (quart) water
vegetable oil

Dry salt the fish on a tray and refrigerate 48-72 hours.
Rinse off the salt and dry well. Cut across the grain of the fish into thin slices.
Combine smoke flavor, lobster color and water. Add the fish and soak overnight.
Remove the fish with a slotted spoon, place on a rack and drain well.
Place the fish slices in jars. Pour over oil. If the fish is to be stored for a long time, it should be covered with paraffin, rather than oil, which gets stale more quickly.

COD ROE CAVIAR

1.
1 kg (2 1/4 pounds) cod roe
2 tablespoons salt
1/2 teaspoon saltpeter

1 tablespoon sugar
1 tablespoon instant smoke flavor
1 teaspoon pepper
2 dl (3/4 cup) + 1-2 tablespoons vegetable oil

Scrape the roe from the membrane and stir with salt and saltpeter several minutes. Refrigerate overnight.
Add sugar, instant smoke and pepper. Carefully stir in the first amount of oil. Pour into jars. Top with a spoonful of oil. Refrigerate 8 days to mature before using.

2.
250 g (8 ounces) cooked cod roe
1 dl (1/3 cup) melted butter
1 dl (1/3 cup) whipping cream
salt
3-4 drops instant smoke flavor

Peel the membrane off the roe and stir until smooth. Add butter and cream until easily spreadable.
Season with salt and instant smoke.
Use as a sandwich filling.

Curried fish, pollack salmon and cod roe caviar are popular homemade sandwich fillings.

MEAT AND GAME

MEAT DISHES

ROUND STEAK

Serves 4

750 g (1 2/3 pounds) bottom round or eye of round
flour seasoned with salt and pepper
3 tablespoons margarine
1 medium onion
beef stock or water
salt
freshly ground black pepper

Cut the meat into 12 mm (1/2") slices. Dip in seasoned flour and sauté in browned margarine. Transfer to a pot. Slice the onion and sauté. Add to the meat.
Add stock or water just to cover.
Cover and simmer until meat is tender, about 1 hour. Season with salt and pepper.
Serve with mashed or boiled potatoes and vegetables.

BEEFSTEAK

Serves 1

180 g (6-7 ounces) boneless strip loin
salt
pepper
butter

Pound the beef lightly. Sprinkle with salt and pepper.
Brown in browned butter in a hot skillet. Turn the steak when droplets of juice begin to appear on the raw side. The steak is "medium" when juice begins to appear on top of the cooked side. Let rest 2-3 minutes before serving.
Serve with pan juices, boiled potatoes, fried onions and peas.

Round steak with onions and vegetables.

A good selection of fresh meat is available in most places.

BEEF HASH

Serves 6

500 g (1 pound) boneless beef chuck or round
1 kg (2 pounds) potatoes
1 small onion
salt
pepper
90 g (3 ounces, 1/3 cup) butter or margarine
4-5 dl (2 cups) beef stock

Cut meat, potatoes and onion into 1 cm (1/2") cubes. Sprinkle with salt and pepper and brown in butter. Bring the stock to a boil and add. Simmer until the meat is tender, about 45 minutes. The potatoes will boil to pieces and thicken the dish. Season with salt and pepper.

BROWN HASH

Serves 4

5-6 dl (2-2 1/2 cups) brown gravy
water
2 medium carrots
1 small onion
3 medium potatoes
2 1/2 dl (1 cup) leftover roast beef cubes

Thin the gravy with a little water. Cut the carrots, onions and potatoes into 1 cm (1/2") cubes and cook in the gravy until the potatoes are tender, 6-8 minutes. Cut the beef into 1 cm (1/2") cubes and add. Heat until warm. Season with salt and pepper. Serve with flatbread.

MUTTON STEW

Serves 4

1 tablespoon butter
700 g (1 1/2 pounds) boneless lamb shoulder meat, sliced or in chunks
1/4 medium cabbage, in thin wedges
1/4 small rutabaga, sliced
1 large carrot, in chunks
15 cm (6" length) leek, in chunks
salt
2 teaspoons grated fresh ginger
1 teaspoon ground black pepper
2 dl (3/4 cup) water
2 1/2 tablespoons butter
3/4 dl (1/3 cup) flour
vinegar
sugar

Melt the butter in the bottom of a pot. Add the meat, then the vegetables. Sprinkle with salt, ginger and pepper. Pour over water to cover. Bring to a boil and skim well. Lower heat and simmer, shaking the pot now and then so the meat won't stick, until the meat is tender, 60-75 minutes. Melt the butter and stir in the flour. Gradually add cooking liquid. Season with salt, pepper, vinegar and sugar. Arrange meat and vegetables on a platter. Serve with sauce and boiled potatoes.

BOILED BEEF WITH SOUP, DUMPLINGS AND ONION SAUCE

Serves 6-8

1 1/2 liters (quarts) water
2 teaspoons salt

1 kg (2 1/4 pounds) boneless beef chuck, short ribs or brisket
1 leek
1 large onion
2-3 carrots
1/2 small celeriac
1 medium parsley root
medium wedge cabbage
salt
pepper
Dumplings:
60 g (2 ounces, 4 tablespoons, 1/4 cup) margarine
1 dl (1/3 cup) flour
1 dl (1/3 cup) water
1 egg
salt
cardamom
Onion sauce:
1 onion, minced
2 1/2 tablespoons margarine
2 tablespoons flour
5 1/2 dl (2 1/3 cups) beef stock
salt
freshly ground white pepper
2 teaspoons 7% vinegar
3-4 teaspoons sugar
1/2 dl (3 1/2 tablespoons) whipping cream

Bring the water and salt to a boil. Add the meat. Bring to a boil and skim well. Add the green part of a leek, half an onion, one carrot and the washed peelings from the celeriac. Simmer until the meat is tender, about 1 1/2 hours. Season with salt and pepper. Cut the remaining vegetables into chunks and cook each separately in stock. Strain the stock and measure out 5 1/2 dl (2-1/3 cups) for the sauce. Cut the meat into small chunks. Serve the stock on its own or with vegetables and dumplings served with the meat on the side.
Dumplings:
Melt the margarine and stir in the flour. Gradually add the water and cook until the mixture forms a ball. Cool slightly, then beat in the egg, beating until smooth. Season with salt and cardamom. Form dumplings with a wet teaspoon and place in simmering (90°C, 195°F) broth and cook minutes.
Onion sauce:
Sauté the onion in margarine. Stir in the flour. Gradually add stock to desired

Boiled beef with soup is a typical Sunday dinner.

consistency. Bring to a boil. Season with salt, pepper, vinegar and sugar. Just before serving, stir in the cream. Arrange the sliced meat on a platter with the vegetables. Serve with onion sauce and boiled potatoes.

STUFFED PORK LOIN

Serves 6

1 1/2 kg (3 pounds) fresh pork loin, on the bone
about 30 pitted prunes
1 teaspoon prepared mustard
salt
pepper
1 liter (quart) beef stock or bouillon
4 tablespoons (1/4 cup) flour
soy sauce

Preheat the oven to 180°C (350°F). Press a pointed knife through the center of the meat. Fill the hole with prunes. Spread the mustard over the meat, then sprinkle with salt and pepper. Stick a meat thermometer into the thickest part, making sure that it does not touch bone. Roast, basting frequently with stock, until the internal temperature is 80°C (175°F), about 1 hour. Cut the meat from the bones and cut into 8 mm (3/4") slices. Deglaze the roasting pan with stock. Reduce to about 6 dl. Thicken, if desired, with flour stirred into a small amount of cold water, and adjust the color with soy sauce. Strain. Serve with boiled potatoes, sauerkraut, poached prunes and fried apple slices.

ROAST LEG OF PORK

A fresh leg of pork or pork shoulder can be prepared in the same way.

LAMB AND CABBAGE STEW

Serves 10-12

3 kg (6 1/2 pounds) sliced lamb shoulder, neck or breast on the bone
3 kg (6 1/2 pounds) cabbage, in large wedges
salt
1 tablespoon black peppercorns
1 liter (quart) boiling water
1 1/2 dl (2/3 cup) flour
1 1/4 dl (1/2 cup) cold water

In a wide, heavy pot, layer the meat with the cabbage, sprinkling each layer with salt and peppercorns. Add boiling water.
Bring to a boil and simmer until the meat is tender, about 1 1/2 hours.
Season with salt and pepper. The stock should be quite peppery. Stir the flour into the cold water, then stir into the pot to thicken. Bring to a boil.
Serve with boiled potatoes.

Stuffed pork loin is party food.

In the late fall, lamb and cabbage stew is a popular Sunday dinner dish.

Yellow pea soup with salt meat or dried peas, salt meat and bacon are typical sailor's dishes which were eaten on specific days of the week.

YELLOW PEA SOUP WITH SALT PORK

Serves 8

350-400 g (12-14 ounces, 4 dl, 1 2/3 cups) dried yellow peas
water
1 kg (2 1/4 pounds) lightly salted pork belly
2-3 carrots, in chunks
1/2 small rutabaga, in chunks

Soak the peas in water overnight.
If the meat is especially salty, soak overnight.
Drain the peas, cover with cold water and bring to a boil. Skim, lower the heat and cook until tender and the hulls float to the top, about 1 hour.
Cover the meat with cold water and bring to a boil. Skim, lower the heat and simmer until tender, about 1 hour.
Cook the vegetables until tender in the meat stock, about 10-15 minutes. Add stock to the peas to make a medium thick soup. Season with salt, if necessary.
Serve the soup in a terrine, with the meat and vegetables and boiled potatoes alongside. Serve the stock in a gravyboat.

BEEF TENDERLOIN

Serves 6-8

1 kg (2 1/4 pounds) beef tenderloin
salt
freshly ground black pepper
3 tablespoons butter
3-4 dl (1 1/2 cups) beef stock
2 tablespoons flour

Tie the meat. Sprinkle with salt and pepper. Brown on all sides in butter. Add stock and simmer, covered, 15-20 minutes, turning several times. The meat should have a rosy center. Let the meat rest 5 minutes before slicing.
Thicken the pan juices with flour stirred into a small amount of cold water, if desired.
Serve with boiled potatoes, brown gravy and vegetables.

LAMB IN TOMATO SAUCE

Serves 4-6

1 1/2 kg (3 pounds) lamb neck or shoulder slices
1 liter (quart) boiling water
salt
60 g (4 tablespoons, 1/4 cup) margarine
1 1/4 dl (1/2 cup) flour
1 dl (1/3 cup) tomato paste
5 dl (2 cups) lamb stock
1 dl (scant 1/2 cup) whipping cream
cayenne pepper
1 tablespoon chopped parsley

Place the meat in a pot and pour over boiling water just to cover. Add salt. Bring to a boil and skim well. Lower heat and simmer until tender, 45-60 minutes.
Remove the meat and reserve. Strain and measure the cooking liquid. Reduce, if necessary, to 5 dl (2 cups).
Melt the margarine and stir in the flour and tomato paste. Gradually add stock and cream. Bring to a boil and simmer 5 minutes. Season with salt and cayenne pepper.
Arrange the meat on a serving platter. Pour over the sauce. Sprinkle with parsley. Served with boiled potatoes and vegetables.

Whole roast tenderloin of beef is typical restaurant food, served with potatoes, vegetables and a good sauce.

MUTTON VEGETABLE SOUP WITH MEATBALLS

Serves 10

1 kg (2 1/4 pounds) boneless lamb stew
meat
2 1/2 liters (quarts) water
1 bay leaf
salt
ground black pepper
1/2 onion, in chunks
1/4 small celeriac, in batons
10 cm (4") leek, sliced
1 carrot, in batons
Meatballs:
500 g (1 pound) finely ground lamb
2 teaspoons salt
1 1/2 teaspoons potato starch
3/8 teaspoon ground ginger
1/8 teaspoon ground nutmeg
freshly ground white pepper
3 1/2 dl (1 1/2 cups) 10% fat cream
500 g (1 pound) carrots
1 tablespoon chopped parsley
Potato-oat cakes:
1 kg (2 1/4 pounds, about 5 large)
boiled potatoes (not too dry)
500 g (18 ounces, 1 liter, 4 cups)
coarsely milled oat flour
barley flour
sugar
milk

Cover the meat with water and bring to a boil. Skim well. Add salt, pepper and vegetables. Cover and simmer until meat is tender, about 1 hour.
Cut the meat into 1 cm (1/2") cubes. Strain the cooking liquid.
Combine ground lamb with seasonings and cream. Make small meatballs with a teaspoon. Simmer in the cooking liquid about 5 minutes. Peel the carrots and cut into batons. Cook in lightly-salted water until tender, about 6-8 minutes. Heat the stock. Add the lamb cubes, meatballs and carrots. Serve in soup bowls with boiled potatoes, chopped parsley and potato-oat cakes.
Potato-oat cakes:
Grind the potatoes and combine with the oat flour to make a stiff dough.
Divide the dough into pieces. Roll out in barley flour.

Use a special rolling pin which makes small holes in the dough.
Cook on a griddle.
Cook on one side only. When the cake is almost done, brush the uncooked side with a mixture of milk and sugar. Cut into pieces before the cake is completely cooked.

SOUP FROM MELDAL

Serves 6

1 1/2 kg (3 pounds) boneless stew meat
(pork, beef and/or lamb)
3 liters (quarts) water
3-4 teaspoons salt
4 black peppercorns
1 chunk fresh ginger
1 teaspoon chopped onion
5 dl (2 cups) carrot in matchstick pieces
5 dl (2 cups) cabbage squares
5 dl (2 cups) rutabaga cubes
Meatballs:
250 g (8 ounces) finely-ground meatloaf
mixture
Dumplings:
2 dl (3/4 cup) 10% fat cream
1 1/2 tablespoons sugar
2 dl (3/4 cup) flour
2 eggs
1/8 teaspoon ground nutmeg

Simmer the meat in the water with salt and pepper until tender, about 60-90 minutes. Remove from the stock and slice across the grain. Moisten with stock.
Cook the vegetables in the stock until tender, 8-10 minutes.
Make small meatballs with a teaspoon. Simmer in the stock together with the vegetables about 5 minutes.
Dumplings:
Bring the cream and sugar to a boil. Add flour, stirring until the mixture forms a ball. Remove from the heat and beat in the eggs one at a time. Season with nutmeg. Make small dumplings and simmer in the stock together with the vegetables and meatballs about 5 minutes.
Serve the soup with the vegetables, meatballs and dumplings. Arrange the meat on a platter and serve with boiled potatoes and flatbread.

These two kinds of soup are often served at parties in Trøndelag, the region around Trondheim.

Veal brisket with mashed potatoes.

CHRISTMAS MEAT

Serves 6

1 kg (2 1/4 pounds, 6 medium) veal chops
1 teaspoon salt
1 liter (quart) water
1 1/2 dl (2/3 cup) cracker crumbs
salt
1 teaspoon ground black pepper
butter
1 teaspoon dark corn syrup
4-5 tablespoons 35% fat sour cream

Trim excess fat from the meat and rinse. Cover the meat with salted water and bring to a boil. Lower heat and simmer 5 minutes. Dry the chops, then dip in cracker crumbs mixed with salt and pepper. Brown in butter. Add syrup and sour cream. Cover and simmer over low heat until tender, about 30 minutes. Shake the pan occasionally to prevent the meat from sticking. Serve with boiled potatoes and vegetables.

VEAL BRISKET

Serves 4-6

1 1/2 kg (3 pounds) boneless veal breast
3-4 tablespoons flour
salt
black pepper
80 g (2 2/3 ounces, 1/3 cup) butter
7-8 dl (3 cups) boiling water
1/2 bay leaf
1 teaspoon dried thyme
20 tiny onions, peeled
carrots, in chunks

Remove veins and glands from the veal. Wash and dry. Cut into serving pieces. Dip in flour mixed with salt and pepper, then brown in butter.
Transfer the meat to a pot. Add boiling water to cover. Add seasonings. Cover and simmer until tender, about 90 minutes. After 75 minutes, add onions and carrots and cook until tender. Season, if necessary. Serve in the cooking liquid with mashed potatoes.

MOCK CHICKEN LEGS

Serves 6-8

1 1/2 kg (3 pounds) boneless veal round steak
salt
ground black pepper
2 tablespoons chopped parsley
120 g (4 ounces, 1/2 cup) butter
butter
4 dl (1 2/3 cups) whipping cream

Remove all fat and membrane from the meat and cut across the grain into 1 cm (1/2") slices.
Pound the meat into rectangular pieces of equal size. Sprinkle with salt and pepper. Combine parsley and butter and spread over the meat. Roll up and tie with string.
Brown in butter. Add cream and simmer until tender, 30-40 minutes. Remove string before serving. Serve with boiled potatoes and vegetables.

CREAMED VEAL IN ASPIC

Serves 8-10

1 calf's head or 1/2 - 3/4 kg (1 - 1 1/2 pounds) veal
500 g (1 pound) veal shoulder meat
1 - 1 1/2 liters (quarts) full fat milk
salt

The head should be flayed, split lengthwise, cleaned and soaked in water.
Simmer the head with the meat in as little water as possible until tender, about 45 minutes. Additional shoulder meat can be substituted for the veal, but it contains less gelatin.
Remove all the meat from the bones and grind once.
Bring the milk to a boil and combine with the meat. If not using the heat, add the smaller amount of milk. Season with salt and simmer about 10 minutes. Pour the mixture into a mold and chill overnight.
Unmold and serve cold with hot boiled potatoes and flatbread.

LIGHTLY SALTED AND SMOKED LEG OF LAMB

Serves 6-8

1 lightly salted leg of lamb
2 tablespoons butter
2 teaspoons flour
3 dl (1 1/4 cups) whipping cream
300 g (10 ounces, 1 1/4 cups) unsalted butter

Preheat the oven to 125°C (250°F).
Wrap the leg of lamb in aluminum foil. Insert a meat thermometer into the thickest muscle. Roast until the internal temperature is 71-74°C (160-165°F). Count on 3 - 3 1/2 hours.
Cut across the grain into thin slices.
Melt the butter and stir in the flour. Gradually add the cream. Bring to a boil. Remove from the heat and beat in the butter in pats. Do not allow the sauce to boil after the butter has been added.
Serve with boiled potatoes and mashed rutabagas.

BACON-POTATO DUMPLINGS

Serves 4-6

225 g (8 ounces) bacon, diced
2 tablespoons minced onion
pepper
750 g (1 2/3 pounds, about 4 large) boiled potatoes
1-2 eggs
3/4 liter (3 cups) full fat milk
3 3/4 dl (1 1/2 cups) flour
1 teaspoon salt
3 liters (quarts) water
1 tablespoon salt

Fry the bacon and onion. Sprinkle with pepper.
Mash the potatoes. Beat the egg and milk together and add. Sift over the flour and salt and mix to a semi-firm dough.
Make the dumplings immediately, or the dough will become soft. Roll the dough into a long sausage. Cut out pieces of equal size and make round cakes with an indentation in the center. Place a spoonful of the bacon-onion mixture there, then press the dough over the filling. Roll until completely round. Flatten slightly.
Simmer in lightly-salted water about 10 minutes.
Serve with bacon fat and mashed boiled rutabagas.

LAMB CASSEROLE

Serves 4-6

8 large potatoes, peeled and sliced
1 large onion, thinly sliced
1 bunch parsley, chopped
5 tomatoes, sliced
1 1/2 teaspoons salt
1 1/2 teaspoons pepper
4 dl (1 2/3 cups) water
1 kg (2 1/4 pounds) boneless lamb stew meat

Layer in the following order in an oven tray or large ovenproof dish: Potatoes, onion, parsley and tomatoes. Sprinkle with half the salt and pepper.
Add water, then place the meat on the vegetables. Sprinkle with remaining salt and pepper.
Cover with aluminum foil and place in a cold oven. Turn the oven to 150°C (300°F). Roast 2 3/4 hours. Remove the foil, increase the temperature to 200°C (400°F), and roast 15 minutes more.

Poached lightly salted and smoked leg of lamb with rutabaga purée.

LAMB CHOPS WITH CARROT SAUCE

◆

Serves 4

1 liter (quart) light lamb stock
1 large carrot
salt
pepper
1 teaspoon rosemary
12 single lamb chops, about 70 g (2 1/2 ounces) each
butter

Reduce the lamb stock until 4 dl (1 3/4 cups) remains. Boil the carrot until tender. Mash and sieve. Thicken the stock with the carrot purée. Season with salt, pepper and rosemary.

Sprinkle the chops with salt, pepper and rosemary and sauté in browned butter.

Serve with boiled almond potatoes and creamed green beans.

LEG OF LAMB

◆

Serves 6-8

2 1/2 kg (5 pounds) leg of lamb
1 bunch parsley, chopped
salt
freshly ground black pepper
2 teaspoons rosemary

5 dl (2 cups) lamb stock
4 tablespoons (1/4 cup) flour
soy sauce

Preheat the oven to 175°C (350°F). Bone the leg of lamb. Sprinkle the meaty side with parsley, salt, pepper and rosemary. Roll up and tie with cotton string. Insert a meat thermometer into the thickest part.

Roast until the meat reaches an internal temperature of 75°C (165°F), about 90 minutes. During roasting, baste often with stock. Deglaze the pan with the remaining stock. Thicken with flour stirred into a little water, if desired. Season with salt and pepper and add soy sauce for color.

Serve with boiled potatoes, braised onions, brussels sprouts, carrots, baked apple halves filled with jelly and gravy.

Core the apples and halve lengthwise. Brush with lemon juice and bake in the oven until tender, about 15 minutes. Spoon jelly into the indentations.

SADDLE OF LAMB

◆

Bone the saddle. Score the fat. Tie with cotton string, so that it retains its shape. Prepare according to the above recipe. The saddle takes about 45-60 minutes to cook.

Lamb chops with carrot sauce.

Boned roast saddle of lamb.

LIGHTLY SALTED AND SMOKED LAMB TONGUES

Serves 4-5

4 lightly salted and smoked lamb
tongues
water
1-2 bay leaves
5-8 black peppercorns

Wash the tongues.
Bring the water to a boil and add the seasonings. Add the tongues. Skim well. Simmer over low heat until tender, about 30 minutes. Remove and flay while still warm. Return to the cooking liquid. Serve with mashed potatoes, boiled carrots, rutabaga batons and natural juices.

ROAST BEEF

Serves 4

800 g (1 3/4 pounds) sirloin or top
round roast
2 teaspoons salt

1 teaspoon pepper
butter
6-8 dl (2 1/2 - 3 cups) beef stock
4 tablespoons (1/4 cup) flour

Preheat the oven to 160°C (325°F).
Trim and tie the meat, making it as uniform in thickness as possible.
Rub with salt and pepper, then brown on all sides in butter.
Place the roast in a pot slightly larger than the meat. Insert a meat thermometer into the thickest part. Add stock just to cover. Bring to a boil, cover and place the pot in the oven. Roast until the internal temperature reaches 60°C (140°F), about 45 minutes. Remove the meat from the oven. Wrap in aluminum foil and let rest 10 minutes.
Strain the stock and thicken, if desired, with flour stirred into a small amount of cold water. Boil 3-4 minutes, then strain. Thinly slice the meat against the grain. Serve with boiled potatoes and vegetables.

ORKDAL SOUP

Serves 4

1 kg (2 1/4 pounds) sliced lamb
shoulder or breast
3 liters (quarts) water
1 1/2 teaspoons salt
2-3 dl (3/4 - 1 1/4 cups) rice
500 g (1 pound) carrots
500 g (1 pound, about 1/2 small)
cabbage, in thin wedges
1 tablespoon minced onion

Place the meat in cold water and bring to a boil. Skim well. Add salt. Simmer until the meat is tender, 45-60 minutes. Rinse the rice and add to the meat stock with whole carrots, cabbage wedges and onion. Simmer until the rice is done, about 20 minutes.
Arrange the meat and vegetables on a serving platter. Serve with soup and boiled potatoes.

Roast beef is served both rare and well done.

Opposite page:
Roast dried ribs of mutton is Christmas
dinner in many parts of western Norway.

ROAST RIBS OF MUTTON

Serves 5

2 - 2 1/2 kg dried mutton ribs
birch twigs
1 large rutabaga, peeled and sliced

Cut the meat between the ribs into serving pieces. Soak in cold water overnight.
Peel the bark off the birch twigs and arrange in the bottom of a pot, or use a rack. Arrange the meat on the twigs. Add water to just under the meat. Cover and steam about 2 hours.
After 1 hour, add the rutabaga and cook until tender.
Preheat the oven to 250°C (500°F). Grill the meat in a hot oven until crispy. Mash the rutabaga.
Serve with boiled potatoes, boiled rutabagas or rutabaga purée, and pan juices.

POTTED MUTTON

Serves 4

8-10 mutton chops
1 1/2 liters (quarts) water
1 tablespoon salt
1 teaspoon black peppercorns
1 teaspoon whole cloves
1 teaspoon allspice berries
1-2 bay leaves
Per liter stock:
10-12 sheets (3-4 tablespoons powdered)
gelatin
about 3 tablespoons 7% vinegar

Place the chops in a wide, high pot. Add water just to cover. Add seasonings. Bring to a boil, then skim. Lower the heat, cover and simmer until tender, about 45 minutes. Arrange the chops on a serving platter. Strain the cooking liquid. Chill, then remove the hardened fat. Measure the stock and heat. Soak the gelatin sheets in cold water (or sprinkle powdered gelatin over 1 dl (1/2 cup) of the stock) 5 minutes to soften. Squeeze the sheets to remove excess water (disregard for powdered gelatin). Melt the gelatin in the stock. Season with vinegar. Pour over the meat and chill.

To serve, garnish with lemon slices, tomatoes and radish roses. Serve with boiled potatoes and cream or tomato sauce.

PRIMSOLL

Serves 8-10

200 g (7 ounces) bacon or smoked
mutton sausage
2 liters (quarts) boiling water
1 1/2 tablespoons flour
1/2 dl (3 1/2 tablespoons) water
about 1 1/2 dl (2/3 cup) thin slices of
brown goat milk cheese (Ski Queen)
flatbread
brown goat milk cheese
sour cream

Cut the meat into small cubes and add to the boiling water. Simmer 20 minutes. Combine flour and water and stir into the meat. Add the cheese and simmer until melted.
Spread flatbread with cheese and sour cream.
Break the flatbread into small pieces and place in a soup bowl. Ladle the soup over.

RØROS STEW

Serves 10-12

500 g (1 pound) dried mutton
250 g (8 ounces, 2 1/2 dl, 1 cup) dried
yellow peas
250 g (8 ounces, 3 dl, 1 1/4 cups) pearl
barley
500 g (1 1/4 pounds) meaty beef short
ribs
2 liters (quarts) water
500 g (1 pound) cooked mutton flank
500 g (1 1/4 pounds) lightly salted pork
belly
500 g (1 pound) raw pork link sausage
2 liters (quarts) stock
3 carrots
500 g (1 1/4 pounds) raw pork link
sausage

Soak the dried mutton in cold water 36 hours. Soak the peas and barley separately in cold water overnight. Cut the soaked mutton and short ribs into serv-

ing pieces. Bring 2 liters (quarts) water to a boil. Add both kinds of mutton. Return to a boil and skim. Lower the heat and simmer about 15 minutes. Add the salt pork and beef, return to a boil and skim. Simmer until tender, about 1 hour. Add the sausages for the last 15 minutes. Remove the meat from the pot and reserve. Drain the peas and the

This meat dish with soup comes from Røros in central Norway.

barley. Boil in the meat stock until tender, about 1 hour. Peel the carrots. Wash, cut into 1 cm (1/2") cubes and cook in lightly-salted water until tender, about 8 minutes.

Meatballs:
Bring water to a boil. Sprinkle with salt. Make a hole in the other raw sausage. Press out small meatballs directly into the water. Simmer about 5 minutes. Add to the pot with the carrot cubes.

To serve, use both plates and soup bowls. Slice the meat, cut the sausages into chunks and arrange on a platter with boiled, sliced rutabagas. Serve soup, meat and boiled almond potatoes at the same time. Serve with beer and aquavit.

SMOKED PORK LOIN

Serves 6

boiling water
1 kg (2 1/4 pounds) lightly-salted and smoked pork loin
1 1/4 dl (1/2 cup) sugar
3 tablespoons margarine
3/4 dl (1/3 cup) flour

Pour boiling water over the pork loin until covered. Insert a meat thermometer into the thickest part. Simmer until the internal temperature reaches 65°C (160°F), about 1 hour.
Preheat the oven to 250°C (450°F).
Transfer the meat to an oven tray. Sprinkle with sugar and roast until the sugar turns to caramel, about 5 minutes. Remove from the oven, wrap in aluminum foil and let rest 10 minutes.
Melt the margarine and stir in the flour. Gradually add cooking liquid and simmer 5 minutes. Season with salt and pepper.
Bone and slice the meat. Serve with boiled potatoes, sauerkraut and poached prunes.

SALT MEAT HASH

Serves 10-12

450 g (1 pound) salt mutton
150 g (5 ounces) bacon, in one piece
300 g (10 ounces) fresh mutton
1 1/2 kg (3 pounds) potatoes
750 g (1 2/3 pounds) carrots
1/2 medium celeriac
1/2 large rutabaga
1 leek
8 dl (3 1/3 cups) salt meat stock
salt
freshly ground white pepper

Soak the salt mutton in cold water overnight.
Simmer all the meat in water until almost tender, about 1 hour. Remove from the stock and let cool. Cut the potatoes and vegetables into 8 mm (1/2") cubes and cook in the salt meat stock until tender, about 10 minutes.
Cut the meat into 8 mm (1/2") cubes and add. Season with salt and pepper and serve with flatbread.

SMALAHOVE

Serve 1/2 head per person

sheep heads
water
Brine:
6 liters (quarts) water
1 1/2 kg (3 pounds) salt
2 dl (scant 1 cup) sugar
2 1/4 teaspoons saltpeter
Mashed rutabagas:
1 kg (2 1/4 pounds) rutabagas
2 large potatoes
3 dl (1 1/4 cups) water
100 g (3 1/2 ounces, scant 1/2 cup) butter
1-2 teaspoons sugar
salt
ground white pepper
ground nutmeg
sugar
1-2 dl (1/2 cup) salt mutton stock
1/2 dl (3 1/2 tablespoons) whipping cream

Smoked pork loin with sauerkraut, apples, prunes and carrots.

Singe the head. Do not flay. Split lengthwise and soak in cold water at least 24 hours, changing the water several times.

Make the brine by combining the ingredients and bringing to a boil. Dry the head well, then soak in brine up to 72 hours.

Smoke, then dry. Simmer the head in water until tender, about 50 minutes. Serve with boiled potatoes and mashed rutabagas.

Mashed rutabagas:

Peel, wash and slice rutabaga and potatoes. Cook in water until tender, about 15 minutes.

Grind the rutabaga and potatoes. Transfer to the bowl of an electric mixer. Add butter, salt and seasonings and mix well. Stir in stock and cream. Add more seasoning, if necessary.

Smalahove, smoked mutton heads, is a dish from western Norway with many fan clubs all over the country.

This beef dish has been party food in many parts of Norway for years.

for color. Simmer 5 minutes, then strain over the meat. Serve with boiled potatoes and vegetables.

CORNED BRISKET OF BEEF

Serves 6

1-2 tablespoons salt
1 teaspoon sugar
1 1/4 kg (2 1/2 pounds) boneless beef brisket
Brine:
2 liters (quarts) water
2 1/4 dl (scant 1 cup) salt
2 tablespoons sugar
1 1/2 liters (quarts) water

Combine salt and sugar and rub into the meat. Refrigerate 2 hours.
Combine the ingredients for the brine and bring to a boil. Cool. Place the meat in the brine and soak 2 days at about 10°C (50°F). Bring the water to a boil. Rinse the meat and add. Simmer until thoroughly cooked and tender, about 2 hours. Slice and serve with a thin gravy made from the stock, boiled potatoes and creamed green beans.

SAUERBRATEN

This roast is tenderized in a sour liquid. The most common method is to soak in buttermilk, but a brine also can be used. The flavor of the meat will therefore be slightly sour.

Serves 6

1 kg (2 1/4 pounds) boneless rump or top round beef roast
1 liter (quart) buttermilk
salt
pepper
2 tablespoons butter
1 large onion, in wedges
3 dl (1 1/4 cups) water
3 dl (1 1/4 cups) milk
1 bay leaf
10 black peppercorns
1/2 teaspoon salt
1 1/2 - 2 dl (3/4 cup) 35% fat sour cream
pan juices
2 tablespoons flour

SMALL FOOD

Serves 8-10

3 1/2 dl (1 1/4 cups) dried yellow peas
2 kg (4 1/2 pounds) boneless beef stew meat
water
salt
1 bouquet garni (bay leaf, parsley stalks, peppercorns)
3 large carrots, cubed
2 liters (quarts) cubed potatoes
stock
ham hock

Soak the peas in cold water overnight. Simmer the meat in water to cover with salt and bouquet garni until tender, 60-90 minutes. Cool.
Cut the meat into 2 cm (1/2") cubes.
Cook carrots and potatoes separately in stock until tender, 6-8 minutes. Simmer the peas with the ham hock about 1 hour.
Combine meat and vegetables. Serve with rolls or lefse. Count on 5 dl (2 cups) per serving.

SOUSED BEEF

Serves 6

1 kg (2 1/4 pounds) boneless beef chuck or arm
4 tablespoons (1/4 cup) flour
salt
pepper
butter
3 onions, in wedges
5 dl (2 cups) boiling water
10 black peppercorns
2 bay leaves
flour
soy sauce

Cut the meat into 4 cm (1 1/2") cubes. Shake in flour seasoned with salt and pepper. Brown in butter in a heavy skillet, then transfer to a pot.
Brown the onion in the same skillet and add to the meat.
Deglaze the pan with boiling water and strain over the meat. Add peppercorns and bay leaves. Add additional boiling water to just cover the meat. Simmer, covered, until tender, about 1 hour.
Remove the meat and keep warm. Thicken the stock with flour stirred into a small amount of cold water, if desired. Count on 1 dl (1/2 cup) flour per liter (quart) liquid. Add soy sauce

Wash the meat and dry with paper towels. Place in a container slightly larger than the piece of meat. Pour over buttermilk to cover. Place a weight on the meat, so that it won't float. The meat also can be marinated in a plastic bag. Cover the container with plastic wrap or a lit and chill. The meat can marinate up to 6 days. Turn the meat occasionally. Rinse off the meat. Dry thoroughly, then season with salt and pepper and brown in butter in a heavy pot.

Brown the onion with the meat.

Bring water and milk to a boil and pour over the meat. Add bay leaf, peppercorns and salt.

Bring to a boil, cover and lower the heat. Simmer about 1 hour, until an instant thermometer indicates an internal temperature of 60-65°C (140-150°F). Turn the meat after 30 minutes and add the sour cream during the last 15 minutes. Remove the meat and wrap in foil to keep warm.

Thicken the pan juices with flour stirred into a small amount of cold water. Simmer 5 minutes, then strain. Season with salt and pepper. Cut the meat across the grain in thin slices. Serve with boiled potatoes, cauliflower, carrots, peas and lingonberry compote.

PORK CHOPS

pork chops
flour
salt
pepper
butter
Sauerkraut:
2 kg (4 1/2 pounds) cabbage
2 tablespoons caraway seed
2 teaspoons salt
1 liter (quart) water
2-3 tablespoons sugar
1-2 tablespoons vinegar
butter or bacon fat

Dip the chops in a mixture of flour, salt and pepper, then brown in browned butter on one side until droplets of juice appear on the surface of the raw side. Turn and brown on the other side until juices begin to break through the surface, 6-8 minutes total. Let rest 2-3 minutes before serving.

Serve with pan juices, boiled potatoes and sauerkraut.

Sauerkraut:

Shred the cabbage and layer in a pot with caraway seed. Add remaining ingredients and bring to a boil.

Simmer about 4 hours, until it begins to brown.

Season with salt, vinegar and sugar, if necessary. It should be slightly sweet.

Sauerbraten is a popular dish in Rogaland.

Roast pork ribs is traditional Christmas fare in many parts of Norway, especially the eastern regions.

PORK RIBS

Serves 4

*1 kg (2 1/4 pounds) fresh pork belly
with bones and rind
salt
pepper
2 tablespoons dry mustard
butter
flour*

Have your butcher crack the bones at 5-6 cm (2-3") intervals. Score the rind and rub with a mixture of salt, pepper and mustard, preferably 2 days before preparing. Preheat the oven to 200°C (400°F). Place the ribs, rind up, on a rack over an oven tray. Add water to a depth of 1 cm (1/2") in the tray, to prevent the juices from burning. Cover with aluminum foil and bake 15 minutes. Lower the heat to 175°C (350°F), remove the foil and bake until an instant thermometer indicates an internal temperature of 70°C (160°F), about 60-75 minutes. Remove the rind as it becomes crisp. Remove the meat from the oven. Increase the temperature to 270°C (550°F). Cut the meat into serving pieces. Return to the oven for 3-4 minutes just before serving. Thicken pan juices with flour stirred into a small amount of cold water, if desired. Count on 3 1/2 tablespoons

flour per 5 dl (2 cups) pan juices. Serve the meat with crispy rind, pork sausage patties, fried sausages, boiled potatoes, pickled red cabbage and baked apples with currant jelly.

GROUND MEAT DISHES

BONELESS BIRDS

Serves 6

*1 kg (2 1/4 pounds) lean beef, ground twice
2 teaspoons salt
2 tablespoons potato starch
4 teaspoons flour
2 tablespoons breadcrumbs
1 teaspoon freshly ground black pepper
1 teaspoon ground ginger
1/2 teaspoon ground nutmeg
1 onion, minced
5 dl (2 cups) milk
150 g (5 ounces) beef marrow cubes
1 teaspoon ground cloves
1 teaspoon ground ginger
butter
1 liter (quart) brown gravy*

Combine the meat with the dry ingredients in a mixer bowl and beat in the milk. Form oval cakes, about 80 g (3

ounces) each. Press a cube of marrow sprinkled with cloves and ginger into each cake. Fry in butter on all sides, then simmer in brown gravy until thoroughly cooked, about 5 minutes. Serve with boiled potatoes and creamed vegetables.

MEATLOAF

Serves 4

*500 g (1 pound) beef stew meat
1 teaspoon salt
4 teaspoons potato starch
50 g + 65 g (1 3/4 ounces + 2 1/4 ounces) fresh pork fat
3 1/2 dl (1 1/2 cups) skim milk
1/8 teaspoon pepper
1/8 teaspoon ground ginger
1/8 teaspoon nutmeg
margarine
3 dl (1 1/4 cups) stock
3 dl (1 1/4 cups) full fat milk
Sauce:
2 1/2 tablespoons margarine
3/4 dl (1/3 cup) flour
5 dl (2 cups) pan juices
5 dl (2 cups) 35% fat sour cream
salt*

Grind the meat with salt and potato starch 4 times, the last 2 with the first amount of fresh pork fat and spices. Cut the remaining fat into strips. Preheat the oven to 175°C (350°F). Layer on a wet cutting board: 1/3 of the meat mixture in a 1 1/2 cm (3/4") thick layer, half the fat laid lengthwise about 1 cm (1/2") apart, half the remaining amount of meat, the rest of the fat and the rest of the meat. Smooth the top of the meat loaf. Brown the meatloaf on all sides in margarine. Use 2 spatulas to transfer the meat from the cutting board. Then bake 30-40 minutes. Deglaze the frying pan with stock and milk and pour over the meatloaf in the oven. Remove the meatloaf from the oven. Strain and measure the cooking juices. If they measure more than 5 dl (2 cups), reduce to that amount over high heat. For the sauce, melt the margarine and stir in the flour. Gradually add the cooking juices and bring to a boil. Simmer 5 minutes. Stir in the sour cream, bring to a boil and season with salt. Slice the meatloaf and serve with boiled potatoes, vegetables and sauce.

Boneless birds are a ground meat variation on a dish originally made with veal slices.

BEEF AND CABBAGE CASSEROLE

Serves 5-6

1 1/2 kg (3 pounds) cabbage
5 dl (2 cups) clear stock flavored with pepper
750 g (1 2/3 pounds) ground beef
1 1/2 teaspoons salt
1/2 teaspoon pepper
2 tablespoons flour
2 tablespoons potato starch
1 egg
butter
3 dl (1 1/4 cups) water
flour

Cut the cabbage into 3 cm (1 1/4") cubes. Place in a pot and add the stock. Combine the ground beef with salt, pepper, flour, potato starch and egg. Form 2 loaves. Brown on all sides in butter, then place on the bed of cabbage.

Deglaze the pan with water and pour over the meat.

Bring to a boil, lower the heat and simmer until the cabbage turns light brown, about 45 minutes.

Thicken with flour stirred into a small amount of cold water, if desired. Count on 3 1/2 tablespoons flour per 5 dl (2 cups) liquid. Serve with boiled potatoes and lingonberry compote.

Meatloaf is a tasty ground meat dish.

NORWEGIAN BURGERS

Serves 3-4

500 g (1 pound) lean beef stew meat
2 tablespoons potato starch
1/2 onion, minced
salt
1/2 teaspoon pepper
about 3 1/2 dl (1 1/2 cups) milk
butter

Grind the meat twice, then mix with the dry ingredients. Gradually add the milk.

Form flat round cakes, about 90 g (3 ounces) each, and fry on both sides in butter. Serve with fried onions, boiled potatoes and vegetables.

Norwegian burgers are a popular dish served for both dinner and lunch.

ORGAN MEAT SAUSAGES

Serves 6

*1 kg (2 1/4 pounds) mixed beef heart,
lungs and stew meat
1 1/2 dl (2/3 cup) potato starch
1 tablespoon salt
1 teaspoon pepper
1 teaspoon ground ginger
3-4 dl (1 1/4 - 1 2/3 cups) cold stock
5 meters (yards) rinsed lamb sausage
casing*

Soak the meat in cold water 24 hours.
Drain well.
Grind the meat once, then add the
remaining ingredients.
Stuff the sausages and tie at 10 cm (4")
intervals.
Simmer the sausage in lightly-salted
water about 15 minutes.
Makes about 45 small sausages.

MEATBALLS

Serves 6-8

*1 kg (2 1/4 pounds) boneless beef chuck
1 teaspoon salt
1 teaspoon pepper
1 dl (1/3 cup) potato starch
3 tablespoons minced onion
about 5 dl (2 cups) milk*

Grind the meat 2 or 3 times, then mix
with the dry ingredients. Gradually add
the milk.
Form the mixture into 4 cm (1 1/2")
meatballs and simmer in water or stock
until thoroughly cooked, 6-8 minutes.
Serve with a light brown gravy, boiled
potatoes and vegetables.

MEAT CAKES

Serves 3-4

*500 g (1 pound) boneless beef chuck
1 tablespoon potato starch
1 teaspoon salt
1 1/2 teaspoons ground ginger
1/2 teaspoon pepper
2 dl (3/4 cup) stock
butter
5 dl (2 cups) brown gravy*

Grind the meat three times, then mix
with the dry ingredients. Gradually add
the stock. Form round cakes and brown
on all sides in butter. Simmer in brown
gravy until thoroughly cooked, 5-8 minutes. Serve with boiled potatoes,
creamed peas and lingonberry compote.

MEAT PUDDING

Same meat mixture as for meatballs.
Preheat the oven to 160°C (325°F).
Prepare the meat according to the recipe for meatballs, but spoon the mixture
into a greased 1 - 1 1/2 liter (quart) loaf
pan. Rap the pan against the kitchen
counter so the mixture will not develop
air tunnels. Place a cloth towel in the
bottom of an oven tray. Place the loaf
pan on the towel (to keep it from moving). Add water to reach halfway up the
sides of the pan. Bake about 50 minutes, until set. Slice and serve with
brown gravy, boiled potatoes and
creamed vegetables.
Creamed vegetables:
Cube cabbage, rutabaga and carrots.
Leave string beans whole. Cook the
vegetables until tender in lightly salted
water. Drain. Stir thick bechamel sauce
into the cooked vegetables. The mixture should not be thin and soupy. It
should be almost as thick as porridge.

CABBAGE ROLLS

Serves 4

*16 medium cabbage leaves
boiling water
1 teaspoon salt per liter (quart) water
500 g (1 pound) ground beef
1 1/4 teaspoons salt
4 teaspoons potato starch
3-4 dl (1 1/2 cups) full fat milk
1/2 teaspoon pepper
1/2 teaspoon ground ginger
1/4 teaspoon nutmeg
5 dl (2 cups) boiling, lightly-salted water*

Parboil the cabbage in lightly-salted
boiling water until soft, about 2 minutes. Drain well. Cut out the thick stem
part. Preheat the oven to 160°C
(325°F). Mix the ground beef with salt
and potato starch. Gradually add milk
and season with spices. Place a spoonful of the meat mixture onto each cabbage leaf. Wrap the leaf around the
meat to form a small package. Place the
cabbage rolls, seam side down, in a
greased ovenproof dish. Pour over the
water and place the dish in a water bath
(see previous recipe). Bake about 30
minutes.
Serve with brown gravy, boiled potatoes and cooked carrots.

Cabbage rolls.

BEEF AND ONIONS

Serves 2-3

3 onions, minced
2-3 tablespoons butter
300 g (10 ounces) lean ground beef
100 g (4 ounces) ground pork
2 tablespoons breadcrumbs
salt
1/4 teaspoon freshly ground white
pepper
2 dl (3/4 cup) water
2 dl (3/4 cup) whipping cream

Sauté the onion in butter until golden, then transfer to a pot.
Mix the ground beef and pork with the dry ingredients. Gradually add the water.
Form large flat burgers. Brown quickly on both sides, then add to the pot with the onions.
Deglaze the pan with cream, then strain over the meat. Simmer 5 minutes.
Serve with boiled potatoes, vegetables and lingonberry compote.

PORK PATTIES

Serves 6-8

750 g (1 2/3 pounds) ground pork
250 g (8 ounces) ground beef
1 tablespoon potato starch
2 teaspoons salt
1 teaspoon pepper
1 teaspoon ground ginger
about 2 dl (3/4 cup) full fat milk
butter

Mix the ground pork and beef with the dry ingredients. Mix well. Gradually add the milk.
Form into oval cakes and fry on all sides in butter, about 6 minutes total.
Serve with pan drippings, boiled potatoes and sauerkraut.

MIXED MEAT LOAF

Serves 12

1 kg (2 1/4 pounds) lamb organ meats
(lungs, diaphragm, heart, esophagus)

100-200 g (3 1/2 - 7 ounces) suet or
fresh pork fat
500 g (1 pound) boneless lamb stew
meat
2 teaspoons salt per kg (1 teaspoon per
pound) meat mixture
1 teaspoon freshly ground black pepper
3/4 teaspoon ground allspice
1-2 onions, minced
2-4 dl (3/4 - 1 1/2 cups) stock or water

Wash the organ meats and drain well.
Blanch 5 minutes in boiling water.
Preheat the oven to 150° C (300° F).
Clean the organ meats, removing membrane and connective tissue. Cut into small pieces and grind with the suet and stew meat. Season with salt, pepper, allspice and onion. Gradually add stock or water.
Spoon the mixture into a greased 1-1 1/2 liter (quart) ovenproof dish.
Bake in a water bath (see recipe for meat pudding) until thoroughly cooked, about 45 minutes.

Pork patties are served with pork ribs at Christmas.

SOUR SAUSAGE FROM RØROS

1 beef head and other trimmings
1 kg (2 1/4 pounds) pearl barley
3/4-1 kg (1 1/2 - 2 pounds) suet
salt
4 teaspoons pepper
4 teaspoons ground ginger
15 meters (yards) rinsed lamb sausage
casings

Soak the head and barley separately in
cold water at least 24 hours.
Simmer the meat until it nearly falls off
the bones, about 2 hours. Remove all
meat and grind.
Cook the barley in the meat broth until
tender, about 30 minutes. Add the suet
during the last 10 minutes.
Combine ground meat, seasonings,
barley and suet, mixing well.
Stuff the sausages and tie at 15 cm (6")
intervals.
Dip the sausages in boiling water to
cook the casings, about 3 minutes.
Hang the sausages in a warm room,
about 20°C (60°F), 3-4 days to turn
sour. Then refrigerate.
Fry in a hot skillet without added fat.
The sausages are supposed to fry in
their own fat until they are crispy and
golden.
Serve with boiled potatoes and mashed
rutabagas. Makes about 90 sausages.

VOSS SAUSAGES

Serves 20

2 1/2 kg (5 pounds) mutton, from the
shoulder, neck and flank
500 g (1 pound) fresh pork fat
4 tablespoons (1/4 cup) salt
2 dl (3/4 cup) potato starch
8-9 dl (7 1/2 - 8 cups) stock or water
2 tablespoons sugar
1/2 tablespoon pepper
1/4 teaspoon nutmeg
1/4 teaspoon ground ginger
4 meters (yards) rinsed beef casings

Bone the meat and cut into strips.
Remove the rind from the pork fat and
cut into strips.
Crack the bones, cover with water and
make stock. Strain and chill.

Sour sausage from Røros.

Sausages from Voss.

Grind meat and fat once. Add the salt and refrigerate 12 hours.

Whisk the potato starch, sugar and seasonings into the cold stock. Gradually add to the meat mixture. Do not overwork the meat.

Rinse the sausage casings well, then stuff with the mixture, tying at 40 cm (16") intervals.

Smoke 3-4 hours.

Simmer in lightly-salted water about 20 minutes.

Serve with boiled potatoes and mashed rutabagas, preferably alongside pinnekjøtt, steamed, dried ribs of mutton.

Cold Voss sausages are good as sandwich filling and add an extra flavor to soups and stews. Makes 9-10 large sausages.

GAME DISHES

GAME SWISS STEAK

Serves 4

750 g (1 2/3 pounds) reindeer or moose
top round steak
50 g (1 3/4 ounces) fresh pork fat
1 1/2 tablespoons flour
1 teaspoon salt
3 tablespoons butter
3 dl (1 1/4 cups) full fat milk
2 dl (3/4 cup) water
1/2 dl (3 1/2 tablespoons) 35% fat sour
cream
3/4 teaspoon pepper

Trim and rinse the meat. Dry with paper towels and remove all membrane. Cut the meat into 1 1/2 cm (3/4") slices. Cut the fat into thin strips. Thread the fat through the pieces of meat with a larding needle.

Combine flour and salt and dip the meat into the mixture. Sauté in butter, then transfer to a pot.

Bring the milk and water to a boil. Deglaze the pan with the liquid, then strain over the meat.

Simmer until meat is tender and the sauce has thickened, 45-60 minutes. Stir in the sour cream and season with salt and pepper.

Serve with boiled potatoes, vegetables and lingonberry compote.

VENISON ROAST

Serves 4

750 g (1 2/3 pounds) rump roast of
reindeer, deer or moose
salt
3/4 teaspoon pepper
8 juniper berries, crushed
2 tablespoons butter
3 dl (1 1/4 cups) water
3 dl (1 1/4 cups) full fat milk
1 dl (1/2 cup) 35% fat sour cream
Sauce:
6 dl (2 1/2 cups) pan juices
1 dl (1/2 cup) whipping cream or 35%
fat sour cream
1 dl (1/3 cup) cold milk
3 tablespoons flour
soy sauce
1 slice brown goat milk cheese (Ski
Queen)

Wild reindeer grazing.

Reindeer roast with vegetables.

salt
1 dl (1/2 cup) red currant jelly
2 tablespoons whipping cream or sour cream

Tie the roast. Season on all sides with salt, pepper and crushed juniper berries. Brown on all sides in browned butter. Transfer to a pot. Bring water, milk and sour cream to a boil and add. Deglaze the pan with 2 tablespoons water and pour over the meat. Simmer until an instant thermometer indicates an internal temperature of 75°C (165°F), 45-60 minutes, depending upon the thickness. Turn the roast several times while simmering. Remove the roast and wrap in foil. Strain and measure the pan juices. Reduce or add stock, if necessary, to make 6 dl (2 1/2 cups). Stir in cream or sour cream. Combine milk and flour and whisk into the pan juices to thicken. Season with cheese, salt, pepper and jelly. Temper with cream or sour cream. Serve with boiled potatoes, gravy and vegetables.

MOOSE VEGETABLE SOUP

Serves 10-12

2 kg (4 1/2 pounds) boneless moose meat
lightly salted water
1 carrot, sliced
1 onion, in wedges
8 black peppercorns
4 large carrots
1/2 medium rutabaga
2 teaspoons salt

Cut the meat into serving pieces. Cover with lightly salted water and bring to a boil. Skim well and add carrot, onion and peppercorns. Simmer until tender, about 1 hour. Peel the vegetables and cut into chunks. Add during the last 20 minutes cooking time. Season with salt. Serve in soup bowls with boiled potatoes and flatbread.

FINN STEAK

Serves 6

500 g (1 pound) reindeer suet
750 g (1 2/3 pounds) boneless reindeer meat

3-4 tablespoons oatmeal
1 teaspoon salt
1/4 teaspoon pepper

Cut the suet into small cubes. Melt in a pot. Cube the meat and cook in the fat about 30 minutes. The meat should be just about covered with the fat. Add remaining ingredients and simmer until the oatmeal is cooked, about 10 minutes. Serve in soup bowls with boiled potatoes and bread.

REINDEER PORRIDGE

Serves 6

140 g (5 ounces) reindeer heart
140 g (5 ounces) reindeer kidney
140 g (5 ounces) reindeer tongue
140 g (5 ounces) reindeer liver
70 g (2 1/2 ounces) reindeer fat
140 g (5 ounces) boneless reindeer meat
3 1/2 dl (1 1/2 cups) oatmeal
1-2 teaspoons salt
1 teaspoon pepper

Coarsely grind all the meat. Cook the meat with the oatmeal in a small amount of water 25 minutes. Season with salt and pepper. The water should be completely evaporated, so the dish

The moose is the king of our forests.

has the consistency of porridge. Serve with boiled potatoes and vegetables.

BOILED REINDEER WITH MARROW BONES, TONGUE AND BOUILLON

Serves 4

2 reindeer tongues
1 1/4 kg (2 1/2 pounds) sliced reindeer shoulder or brisket
2 teaspoons salt
1 teaspoon freshly ground white pepper
4 marrow bones

Lightly salt the tongues 24 hours. Place the meat and the tongues in cold water to cover and bring to a boil. Skim, lower heat and season with salt. Simmer until tender, about 60-80 minutes. Remove the meat and tongues from the pot. Season the stock with salt and pepper. Cook the bones in the stock about 10 minutes. Slice the tongues and serve with the meat and marrow bones. Serve with boiled potatoes, rutabagas and bouillon. An onion sauce or light stock-based sauce is good with this dish. See page 36 about Sami culture.

SHAVED REINDEER WITH BEER

Serves 2-3

500 g (1 pound) shaved reindeer meat
2-3 tablespoons butter
1/2 teaspoon salt
1 1/2 - 2 1/2 dl (2/3 - 1 cup) bock beer
2 tablespoons whipping cream
2 teaspoons cornstarch
1/2 teaspoon pepper

To make this dish, reindeer meat is shaved while half-frozen for extra thin slices. Brown in butter in a hot skillet. Fry small portions at a time and deglaze the pan with water after each portion. Transfer to a pot.
Season with salt and add beer. Simmer until meat is tender, about 15 minutes. Add sour cream.
Thicken with cornstarch stirred into a little water, if desired, and season with

Opposite page:
Boiled reindeer with marrow bones, tongue and bouillon is festive fare among the Sami people.

salt and pepper. Serve with mashed potatoes and lingonberry compote.

SADDLE OF ROEDEER

Serves 4-6

2 kg (4 1/2 pounds) roedeer saddle
100 g (4 ounces) slab bacon, diced
1/2 medium onion, chopped
200 g (8 ounces) mushrooms
3 tablespoons chopped parsley
2 teaspoons salt
1/2 teaspoon ground black pepper
butter
5 dl (2 cups) stock
3 tablespoons flour

Remove the tiny filets from the underside of the saddle. Bone the saddle, cutting as closely to the ribs as possible toward the backbone. Carefully cut out the backbone without making any holes in the meat. Cover the bones with water and bring to a boil. Skim well. Simmer 1 hour. Strain and measure the stock. If more than 5 dl (2 cups), reduce to that amount over high heat.

Sauté the bacon in its own fat. Add onion and mushrooms and brown lightly. Combine with the parsley.

Preheat the oven to 200°C (400°F).

Lay the meat flat, skin side down. Spread the bacon mixture over the meat. Sprinkle with salt and pepper. Place the 2 small filets on the meat. Cover the filling first with 1 thin flank section, then with the other. Tie with cotton string. Try to maintain the cut's original shape. Brown in butter on all sides. Sprinkle with salt and pepper. Roast until an instant thermometer indicates an internal temperature of 60°C (140°F), 30-40 minutes. Baste with stock while roasting. Allow the meat to rest 5 minutes before carving into slices. Thicken the pan juices with flour stirred into a small amount of cold water, if desired. Serve with potatoes, sautéed mushrooms and vegetables.

ROAST HARE

Serves 4

saddle and thighs of 1 hare
100 g (4 ounces) fresh pork fat, in thin slices
butter
200 g (8 ounces) mushrooms
1 1/2 tablespoons flour
2 dl (3/4 cup) cream
salt
pepper
nutmeg
cloves
lemon juice
soy sauce

Roast saddle of roedeer is one of nature's delicacies.

Stuffed turkey breast.

Preheat the oven to 180°C (350°F). Bard the meat with the fat. Sprinkle with salt and pepper and brown on all sides in butter. Transfer to an oven tray. Scatter the mushrooms around the meat. Roast 15-20 minutes. Remove the mushrooms. Wrap the meat in foil and let rest 5 minutes. Pour all but 2 tablespoons pan juices into a cup and reserve. Sprinkle the flour over the roasting pan and brown. Add pan juices and cream, scraping up all bits stuck to the bottom. Bring to a boil and season with spices. Add color with soy sauce, if desired. Remove the barding fat and carve into serving pieces. Serve with boiled or mashed potatoes, vegetables and lingonberry compote.

HARE/RABBIT STEW

Serves 4

4 carrots, in chunks
2 leeks, in chunks
4 tablespoons (1/4 cup) butter
1 1/4 kg (2 1/2 pounds) hare or rabbit, in serving pieces
salt
4 bay leaves
1/4 teaspoon ground cloves
1/4 teaspoon nutmeg
1/4 teaspoon ground ginger
1/4 teaspoon rosemary

7 dl (3 cups) red wine
400 g (14 ounces) mushrooms
3 tablespoons cornstarch
juice of 1 lemon

Sauté the vegetables in butter in a pot. Add the meat. Sprinkle with seasonings, then add wine. Bring to a boil. Preheat the oven to 150°C (300°F). Quarter the mushrooms and sauté in butter, then add to the meat. Bring the pot with the meat to a boil, then bake 25 minutes. Remove the meat from the pot, thicken the pan juices with cornstarch stirred into water. Season to taste with lemon juice.

Serve with boiled almond potatoes, vegetables and lingonberry compote.

POULTRY DISHES

STEAMED CHICKEN BREAST

Serves 1-2

2 boneless chicken breasts
1 1/2 tablespoons butter
salt
freshly ground white pepper

Remove the skin from the breasts. Butter a deep plate, top with the breasts and sprinkle with salt and pepper. Place

another plate over the chicken. Steam over boiling water until tender, about 30 minutes.

STUFFED TURKEY BREAST

Serves 5-6

1 turkey breast, about 700 g (1 2/3 pounds)
200 g (7 ounces) boneless turkey thigh meat
1 1/2 teaspoons chopped onion
salt
1 1/2 teaspoons potato starch
1 egg
1 1/2 dl (2/3 cup) 10% fat cream
1 teaspoon chopped fresh basil
1 teaspoon chopped fresh thyme
1 teaspoon chopped fresh tarragon
1 egg white
freshly ground white pepper
Sauce:
2 tablespoons butter
3 1/2 tablespoons flour
5 dl (2 cups) turkey stock
1/2 dl (3 1/2 tablespoons) Madeira

Preheat the oven to 120°C (250°F). Remove the skin from the turkey breast and cut horizontally almost all the way through, so the breast can be opened like a book. Cover with plastic wrap on both sides and pound lightly. Combine thigh meat, onion and salt in a food processor. With the motor running, add potato starch, egg, cream and fresh herbs. Lightly beat the egg white and brush over the breast. Sprinkle with salt and pepper. Spread the ground turkey filling over the breast, fold and tie with cotton string. Sprinkle with salt and pepper and brown in butter. Transfer to an oven tray and roast until an instant thermometer indicates an internal temperature of 70°C (160°F), about 60 minutes. Remove the turkey breast from the pan and pack in foil. Let rest 5 minutes before carving. Melt the butter and stir in the flour. Deglaze the pan with turkey or chicken stock and gradually whisk into the butter-flour mixture. Add Madeira just before serving. Season with salt and pepper, if necessary. Serve with butter-steamed spring onions, red onions and tiny spring turnips which have been sliced and sautéed in butter.

Chicken fricassee.

POACHED HEN WITH HERB BUTTER

Serves 4

*1 stewing hen, about 1 1/2 kg
(3 pounds)
7 1/2 dl chicken stock
2 egg yolks
salt
100 g (3 1/2 ounces, scant 1/2 cup)
clarified butter
breadcrumbs
butter
Herb butter:
125 g (4 ounces, 1/2 cup) butter
2 egg yolks
3 tablespoons chopped fresh herbs
(chives, parsley, basil)
1 teaspoon mustard
salt
pepper*

Clean the hen and poach until tender in the stock, about 90 minutes. Cool. Remove skin and quarter the chicken. Beat the eggs with a few grains salt until creamy. Beat in the clarified butter. Dip the chicken pieces in the egg yolk mixture, then coat with crumbs. Fry until golden in butter. For the herb butter, beat the butter until fluffy. Beat in the egg yolks and herbs. Season with mustard, salt and pepper. Serve with deep-fried parsley and herb butter.

CHICKEN FRICASSEE

Serves 4

*1 stewing hen, about 1 1/2 kg
(3 pounds)
lightly salted water
3 tablespoons butter
3 tablespoons flour
salt
1 teaspoon ground white pepper
2 teaspoons curry powder
grated rind of 1 orange
2 dl (3/4 cup) whipping cream
1 small bunch parsley, chopped*

Poach the hen in lightly salted water about 90 minutes. Cool. Remove skin and bone and cut the meat into bite-sized pieces. Melt the butter and stir in the flour. Gradually add the cooking liquid. Season with salt, pepper, curry powder and orange rind. Simmer 5 minutes. Add the cream and simmer until slightly thickened, 5 minutes more. Stir in parsley. Serve the chicken in the sauce with boiled potatoes, peas, carrot cubes and cauliflower.

LIGHTLY SALTED DUCK

Serves 4

*Brine:
3 liters (quarts) water
2 1/4 dl (scant 1 cup) salt
3/4 dl (1/3 cup) sugar
1 bay leaf
5 black peppercorns
1 duck
Stock:
2 liters (quarts) water
2 carrots
1/2 onion
1 bay leaf
5 black peppercorns
1 bunch parsley
5-6 juniper berries
Gravy:
2 1/2 tablespoons butter
4 tablespoons (1/4 cup) flour
5 dl (2 cups) stock*

Bring all ingredients for the brine to a boil. Cool.
Clean the duck. Dry thoroughly, both inside and out, then place in the brine, which should cover completely. Soak 48 hours at about 10°C (50°F).
Rinse with cold water, then place in a pot with the water. Bring to a boil and skim well. Add vegetables and herbs. Lower heat and simmer until the duck is tender, 70-90 minutes.
Melt the butter and stir in the flour. Gradually whisk in the stock. Bring to a boil, then simmer 5 minutes. Season, if necessary.
Carve the duck and serve with boiled potatoes, vegetables and gravy.

FRIED CHICKEN

Serves 2

*1 chicken
salt
freshly ground black pepper
water
1 tablespoon diced carrot
2 slices onion
5 black peppercorns
1 1/2 tablespoons butter
3 tablespoons flour*

Fried chicken with vegetables.

Cut the thighs and breasts from the carcass. Divide the thighs in two and sprinkle breasts and thighs with salt and pepper. Chop the carcass and place in a small pot. Add cold water to cover. Bring to a boil and skim well. Add carrot, onion and peppercorns. Simmer 1 hour. Strain and measure. If more than 4 dl (1 2/3 cups), reduce over high heat to that amount.

Preheat the oven to 180°C (350°F).

Brown thighs and breasts in butter, then transfer to a greased ovenproof dish. Roast 10-15 minutes.

Melt the butter and stir in the flour. Gradually whisk in the stock. Simmer 5 minutes. Season with salt and pepper. Strain.

Serve with boiled or fried potatoes, gravy and a salad.

DUCK STEW

Serves 8

2 ducks
salt
1 teaspoon ground black pepper
1/2 carrot
1/2 stalk celery
2 slices onion
1 liter (quart) stock
2 tablespoons butter
3/4 dl (1/3 cup) flour
1 shallot, chopped
2 1/2 dl (1 cup) red wine
20 tiny onions
butter
40 carrot balls
lemon juice

Preheat the oven to 180°C (350°F). Clean the ducks. Reserve the giblets for the gravy. Dry thoroughly, both inside and out. Rub with salt and pepper. Roast the ducks 1 hour. While the ducks are roasting, make the stock. Place the necks, hearts and gizzards (but not the livers, which will not be used in this dish) in water to cover. Bring to a boil and skim. Add carrot, celery and onion and simmer 45 minutes. Strain and measure. Reduce or add water to make 1 liter (quart). Melt the butter and stir in the flour. Gradually add the stock. Add the shallot and wine and bring to a boil. Cut the ducks into serving pieces and add to the sauce. Lower the heat and simmer until tender, 30-40 minutes. While the ducks are cooking, brown the onions in butter and boil the carrots 3 minutes in lightly salted water. Add to the stew about 5 minutes before it is ready to serve. Season with lemon juice, salt and pepper. Serve with mashed potatoes.

Pigeon in mushroom sauce.

PIGEONS IN MUSHROOM SAUCE

Serves 6-8

6 pigeons
125 g (4 ounces) pork fat, in 6 thin slices
butter
salt
7 1/2 dl (3 cups) boiling milk
bouillon powder
3 tablespoons butter
3/4 dl (1/3 cup) flour
1 dl (1/2 cup) red wine reduced to 3 tablespoons
1 dl (1/2 cup) whipping cream
200 g (8 ounces) mushrooms

Clean the pigeons and place a slice of pork fat over each breast. Bind with cotton string. Clean the giblets and soak in water 30 minutes. Brown the pigeons in butter, one at a time. Then brown the giblets. Return the pigeons to the pan, add salt and gradually add boiling milk. Add a little more butter and season with bouillon powder. Simmer about 20 minutes, basting often. Strain the cooking liquid. Slice the mushrooms and sauté in butter. Melt the butter and stir in the flour. Gradually whisk in the stock. Bring to a boil and simmer 10 minutes. Add red wine, cream, mushrooms and their liquid. Halve the pigeons lengthwise. Serve with boiled potatoes, vegetables and gravy.

PIGEON STEW

Serves 5

4 pigeons
salt
1 onion
150 g (5 ounces) fresh pork belly
4 tablespoons (1/4 cup) flour
1 liter (quart) stock
1 bay leaf
2 black peppercorns
1 clove
pinch nutmeg
3 slices lemon
cornstarch

Flay and wash the pigeons. Halve lengthwise, sprinkle with salt and refrigerate 30 minutes. Place the giblets (but not the livers) in a pot with water to

The mating game of the wood grouse is one of the first signs of spring.

cover. Bring to a boil and skim well. Simmer 30 minutes. Strain and measure. Reduce or add water to make 1 liter (quart). Dice the onion and the pork and fry without extra fat in a pot. Add the flour and stir until slightly browned. Gradually add the stock, seasonings and lemon slices.

Dry the pigeons and add. Simmer until tender, about 30 minutes.

Transfer the birds to a deep serving platter. Strain the sauce, then thicken with cornstarch stirred into a little cold water, if desired. Pour over the pigeons.

POACHED GROUSE

Serves 6

1 wood grouse, about 4 kg (8 1/2 pounds)
1 kg (2 1/4 pounds) salt pork, in 1 piece
water
salt
1 bouquet garni
black peppercorns
3 large carrots
about 1 small celeriac
Soup:
120 g (4 ounces, 1/2 cup) margarine

2 dl (3/4 cup) flour
about 3 liters (quarts) stock from the bird and vegetables
1 dl (scant 1/2 cup) whipping cream
1 tablespoon vinegar
1 tablespoon sugar

Clean the bird well. Place the bird and its giblets (but not the liver, which will not be used in this dish) and the salt pork in a pot with boiling, unsalted water. Return to a boil and skim well. Add the salt, bouquet garni, peppercorns and root vegetables. Lower the heat and simmer. Remove the vegetables when tender, after about 15 minutes, the pork after about 1 hour, and the bird after about 2 hours. Strain and measure the stock. Reduce or add water to make 3 liters (quarts). Carve out the breasts and slice. Slice the legs. Arrange on a dome of boiled rice, if desired. Serve with boiled potatoes and steamed vegetables. To make the soup, melt the margarine and stir in the flour. Gradually whisk in the stock. Simmer 5 minutes. Add cream and season with vinegar and sugar. Garnish the soup with poached apple wedges and prunes. Serve the soup with the grouse.

Poached grouse with soup.

Ptarmigan in cream sauce is the traditional method of preparation.

PTARMIGAN IN CREAM SAUCE

Serves 2

1 ptarmigan
1 thin slice fresh pork fat
salt
ground black pepper
2 teaspoons butter
1 dl (1/3 cup) full fat milk
1 dl (1/2 cup) stock
flour
1 dl (1/2 cup) 35% fat sour cream
1 tablespoon red currant jelly

Flay the ptarmigan. Rinse well, especially in the cavity along the backbone.
Cover the breast with pork fat and bind with cotton string.
Rub with salt and pepper and brown on all sides in butter.
Preheat the oven to 150°C (300°F).
Place the ptarmigan in a pot slightly larger than the bird. Combine milk and stock, bring to a boil and pour over the bird. Return to a boil. Cover and place in the oven. Roast 35-40 minutes.
Remove the bird from the cooking liquid. Let it rest 5 minutes before dividing lengthwise. Remove rib- and backbones.
Strain the pan juices and thicken with flour stirred into a little cold water, if desired. Season the sauce with sour cream, salt, pepper and jelly.
Serve in the sauce with boiled potatoes, brussels sprouts with bacon and poached pear with currant jelly.

BRAISED AUK/SEABIRD

Serves 2

1 auk/seabird
1 dl (scant 1/2 cup) 7% vinegar
4 dl (1 2/3 cups) water
50-60 g (2 ounces) fresh pork fat, in thin slices
salt
pepper
3 tablespoons butter
5 dl (2 cups) stock
flour
1 dl (1/2 cup) whipping cream

All sea birds should be flayed immedi-

Roast ptarmigan breast is a more modern method of preparation.

ately and fat and giblets removed, to reduce fishiness.
Soak the bird in vinegar water overnight. Rinse and dry well .
Place pork fat slices over the breast and bind with cotton string. Rub with salt and pepper and brown in butter.
Bring the stock to a boil and add the bird, which should be completely covered. Simmer until tender, about 10-15 minutes. Remove from the cooking liquid. Thicken with flour stirred into a little cold water, if desired. Add cream, simmer 5 minutes and season with salt and pepper. Strain.
Carve out the breasts and slice on the diagonal. Serve with boiled potatoes, vegetables, sauce and lingonberry compote.

ROAST PTARMIGAN BREAST

Serves 1

1 ptarmigan
salt
pepper
butter
70 g (2 1/2 ounces) mushrooms, sliced
1/2 dl (3 1/2 tablespoons) whipping cream
1 1/2 tablespoons unsalted butter
1/2 dl (3 1/2 tablespoons) 35% fat sour cream
1 tablespoon red currant jelly

Preheat the oven to 200°C (400°F).
Carve the breasts from the carcass.
Reserve the rest for another use.
Rub with salt and pepper and brown in butter. Roast 5-6 minutes (for medium).
Remove from the oven and let rest a few minutes before carving.
Deglaze the pan with cream. Beat in the unsalted butter. Stir in sour cream and red currant jelly. Season with salt and pepper. Strain.
Sauté the mushrooms in butter.
Spoon sauce onto a plate. Pile the mushrooms in the center. Slice the breasts and arrange on the mushrooms. Serve with boiled potatoes and red currant jelly.

ROAST HAZEL GROUSE

Serves 2

1 hazel grouse, about 300 g (10 ounces)
1 slice fresh pork fat
salt
pepper
butter
2 dl (3/4 cup) full fat milk
flour
1 dl (1/3 cup) 35% fat sour cream
1 tablespoon red currant jelly

Pluck the bird carefully, to keep the skin from tearing.

Place the pork fat under the skin, directly on the breast meat, covering the entire breast. Tie with cotton string. Rub with salt and pepper. Preheat the oven to 150°C (300°F). Brown on all sides in butter until golden. Bring the milk to a boil in a pot slightly larger than the bird. Add the bird and cover. Place in the oven and roast 10 minutes.

Remove from the pot, halve lengthwise and remove ribs and backbone.

Thicken sauce with flour, if desired. Stir in sour cream and currant jelly. Season with salt and pepper. Strain.

Serve the grouse in the sauce with boiled potatoes, vegetables and red currant jelly.

BLOOD DISHES

BLOOD PANCAKES

Blood pancakes, blood pudding and blood sausage are usually prepared during the slaughtering season.

Serves 4-6

1/2 dl (3 1/2 tablespoons) rye flour
1/2 dl (3 1/2 tablespoons) flour
2 teaspoons sugar
salt
pepper
ground cloves
2 dl (3/4 cup) blood
1/2 dl (3 1/2 tablespoons) full fat milk
salt
butter

Combine the dry ingredients. Strain the blood and mix with the milk. Whisk into the dry ingredients. Melt the butter in a non-stick pan. Add enough batter just to cover the bottom of the pan with a thin layer. Cook over low heat on both sides. Serve with jam or syrup.

BLOOD PUDDING

Serves 16

500 g (18 ounces, 6 dl, 2 1/2 cups) rice
2 1/2 liters (quarts) full fat milk
2 liters (quarts) blood
250 g (9 ounces, 6 dl, 2 1/2 cups) cracker or dry bread crumbs
250 g (9 ounces, 4 1/4 dl, 1 3/4 cups) raisins
100 g (3 1/2 ounces) suet, in small dice

500 g (18 ounces, 8 1/4 dl, 3 1/2 cups) flour
1 dl (scant 1/2 cup) sugar
1 dl (1/3 cup) light corn syrup
1/2 teaspoon ground cloves
1/2 teaspoon ground black pepper
2 tablespoons salt

Preheat the oven to 180°C (350°F). Make porridge of the rice and milk (see directions on page 84). Stir in the remaining ingredients. Pour into greased loaf pans and bake about 1 hour.

BLOOD SAUSAGE

2 liters (quarts) pearl barley
1 dl (6 tablespoons) salt
6 liters (quarts) blood
1 1/4 kg (2 1/2 pounds) pork fat, in small dice
5 dl (2 cups) boiling milk
250 g (3 dl, 1 1/4 cups) sugar
500 g (18 ounces, 8 1/2 dl, 3 1/2 cups) raisins
100 g (3 1/2 ounces, 2 1/2 dl, 1 cup) chopped almonds
cracker or dry bread crumbs
cinnamon
pepper
ground cloves
thyme
canvas sausage bags

Stir the barley and salt into the blood. Refrigerate overnight. Melt the fat in the milk, add the grain-blood mixture and heat. Beat until it thickens, but do not allow it to boil. Cool, then add remaining ingredients. Make a small patty of the mixture and fry. Taste for seasoning. If the mixture is too thick, add more milk or stock. If it is too thin, add more crumbs. Stuff into canvas sausage bags and tie. Simmer in water about 30 minutes. Serve with melted butter and applesauce.

SANDWICH FILLINGS

MUTTON ROLL

1 mutton flank
500 g (1 pound) lamb or mutton neck meat
salt
freshly ground black pepper
1 onion, minced

Cut the flank into as large a rectangle as possible. Cut long strips of neck meat which are almost as long as the flank. Layer meat strips, sprinkling each with salt and pepper, on one half of the flank. Do not use more meat than can be covered by the other half of the flank. Fold the other half of the flank over the pile of meat strips. Sew the roll together with a needle and cotton thread. Pack in salt about 14 days. Simmer 45 minutes, then place under a weight. Cool completely before slicing.

LIVER PATÉ

1 kg (2 1/4 pounds) pork liver
1 kg (2 1/4 pounds) fresh pork belly
2 large onions
10 anchovy fillets in brine
2 bay leaves
3 eggs
4 tablespoons (1/4 cup) flour
1 1/2 teaspoons salt
1/2 teaspoon ground cloves or allspice
1 teaspoon ground ginger
up to 1 liter (quart) warm milk
thin slices of pork fat

Preheat the oven to 160°C (325°F). Grind the liver with the pork belly, onions, anchovies and bay leaves 5 times. Add eggs, flour, salt and spices. Add enough milk to make a medium-thick mixture. Line 3 1-liter loaf pans with slices of pork fat. Pour in the liver mixture. Place a cloth towel in the bottom of an oven tray. Place the loaf pans on the towel (to keep them from moving). Add water to reach halfway up the sides of the pan. Bake about 1 hour.

HEADCHEESE

1 pig's head
lightly-salted water
water
5 teaspoons salt
1 teaspoon pepper
1 teaspoon ground cloves
1 teaspoon ground allspice
1 teaspoon ground ginger
7 teaspoons powdered gelatin

Split the head and soak in cold water 24 hours. Change water often. Simmer the head in water until a instant thermometer indicates an internal temperature of 75°C (170°F), about 2 hours. Cool.

Remove the rind carefully, so that it doesn't tear. Remove the fat and meat and cut into pieces of similar thickness. Keep separate. Cover the bottom and sides of a headcheese-press or a bowl with a clean linen towel.

Place a layer of rind in the bottom, hairside against the cloth.

Top with a thin layer of fat. Combine seasonings and gelatin powder and sprinkle some over the fat. Layer meat, seasonings and gelatin powder until the container is full. End with a layer of fat and then top with rind, hairside up.

Straighten out the cloth on top. Cover with a lid with clamps or tie down.

Poach the headcheese in the cooking liquid about 1 hour. Do not allow to boil. Remove from the cooking liquid. Press the lid down and cool.

Remove the headcheese from the press or bowl. Trim and soak 2 days in a light salt brine (225 g (8 ounces) salt per liter (quart) water) flavored with black pepper and bay leaves.

Headcheese, mutton roll and liver paté are sandwich fillings traditionally made during the Christmas season.

VEGETABLE AND GRAIN DISHES

PICKLED PUMPKIN

1 kg (2 1/4 pounds) pumpkin
1 kg (2 1/4 pounds) sugar
2 1/2 dl (1 cup) 7% vinegar
25 g (1 ounce) fresh ginger

Peel the pumpkin and cut the flesh into 8 mm (1/3") cubes.
Parboil 1-2 minutes. Drain and dry on a cloth.
Bring sugar, vinegar and ginger to a boil. If this syrup seems too thin, reduce slightly.
Pour over the pumpkin.
Pour into clean jars.

RUTABAGA SALAD

Serves 4

1/2 small rutabaga
2 apples
1/4 leek
3 tablespoons oil
1 tablespoon vinegar
1/4 teaspoon salt
1/4 teaspoon pepper

Peel and grate the rutabaga, cube the apples and slice the leek. Layer in a bowl.
Shake remaining ingredients in a jar and pour over.

FRIED RUTABAGA

rutabaga
flour
salt
pepper
butter

Peel the rutabaga and cut into thick slices.
Boil until almost tender, about 10 minutes, then drain on a rack. They should be dry.
Dip in flour mixed with salt and pepper and fry in butter. Serve as a vegetarian main dish with boiled potatoes, flatbread and milk soup.

BARLEY CAKES

Serves 4

3 dl (1 1/4 cups) pearl barley
3 onions, minced
2 eggs
salt
nutmeg
ground allspice
1 dl (scant 1/2 cup) whipping cream
1 1/4 dl (1/2 cup) ground nuts or breadcrumbs

Soak the barley in cold water overnight.
Cook until tender, about 20 minutes. Cool.
Combine with remaining ingredients.
Form small patties and fry on both sides in butter. Serve with brown gravy, fried onions and cole slaw.

POTATO DUMPLINGS AND DIP

Serves 4-5

750 g (1 2/3 pounds, about 4 large) potatoes
350 g (10 ounces, about 2 medium) boiled potatoes
4 dl (1 2/3 cups) barley flour
1 1/2 teaspoons salt
Dip:
30 g (1 ounce) brown goat milk cheese (Ski Queen)
2 tablespoons sugar
4 teaspoons flour
1 1/2 dl (2/3 cup) water
40 g (1 1/2 ounces) fat bacon or fresh fat pork belly

Peel and grate the raw potatoes. Mash the boiled potatoes. Sprinkle the raw potatoes with some of the flour immediately, so that they do not discolor.
Add salt and remaining flour and mix well.
Make oval or round balls with a wet serving spoon.
Place a few at a time in boiling water—the water should always be boiling—and cook about 30 minutes.
Serve warm with dip.

Dip:
Combine all ingredients except for the bacon. Bring to a boil, stirring constantly. Simmer 10 minutes. Melt the bacon or pork and pour it over the mixture. Serve in a sauce boat.

Opposite page:
Pickled pumpkin, rutabaga salad,
fried rutabaga and barley cakes.

POTATO-BACON CASSEROLE

Serves 6

1 kg (2 1/4 pounds, about 5 large) potatoes
1 teaspoon salt
1 dl (scant 1/2 cup) barley flour
about 2 dl (3/4 cup) full fat milk
about 400 g (14 ounces) bacon, thinly sliced

Preheat the oven to 175°C (350°F). Wash and peel the potatoes. Grate. Combine with salt and flour. Stir in the milk. The mixture should be fairly loose. Pour into a greased 1 1/2 - 2 liter ovenproof dish. Smooth the top with a rubber spatula. Top with bacon slices. Bake on the lowest oven shelf about 45 minutes.

POTATO DUMPLINGS

Serves 4

600 g (1 1/3 pounds, 3 large) potatoes
3 boiled potatoes
2-3 dl (about 1 cup) barley flour
stock from salt pork and smoked mutton

Wash and peel the raw potatoes. Grate. Mash the boiled potatoes. Combine the potatoes with the flour. Make round balls with a wet serving spoon. Simmer 30-40 minutes in stock from salt pork and smoked mutton. Serve with boiled salt mutton, fried bacon and, if desired, boiled potatoes.

STUFFED POTATO DUMPLINGS

Serves 4

1 kg (2 1/4 pounds, about 5) potatoes
about 2 dl (3/4 cup) barley flour
about 2 dl (3/4 cup) whole wheat flour
1 teaspoon salt
100 g (3 1/2 ounces) salt pork or suet, cubed

Follow the directions for Raw Potato Dumplings below, but make the dumplings a little larger and stuff with salt pork or suet. Serve with the same side dishes.

POTATO-MEAT STEW

Serves 6

2 1/4 kg (4 1/2 pounds) potatoes
750 g (1 2/3 pounds) dried mutton
500 g (18 ounces, 5-6 large) carrots, cubed
1 1/4 liters (5 cups) skim milk
70 g (2 1/2 ounces, 4 1/2 tablespoons) butter
salt
chopped parsley

Boil the potatoes in their skins until tender, 20-30 minutes, peel and grind.

Simmer the meat in water to cover about 60 minutes. Add the carrots during the last 10 minutes. Cube the meat. Return the ground potatoes to the pot, add the butter and pour over the milk. Bring to a boil, stirring constantly. Add meat and carrots. Season with salt. Serve in small bowls. Sprinkle with parsley and serve with flatbread.

MASHED POTATOES

Serves 4-6

800 g (1 3/4 pounds, about 4 large) potatoes
2 1/2 tablespoons butter
salt
1 teaspoon ground white pepper
1/2 teaspoon ground nutmeg
3 dl (1 1/4 cups) full fat milk

Peel, slice and boil the potatoes until tender. Drain.
Grind the potatoes, then transfer to an electric mixer bowl. Add butter and seasonings. Mix well. Bring the milk to a boil and add gradually to desired consistency. Season to taste.

RAW POTATO DUMPLINGS

Serves 4-5

1 kg (2 1/4 pounds, about 5 large) potatoes
about 2 dl (3/4 cup) barley flour
about 2 dl (1 cup) whole wheat flour
1 teaspoon salt
Cooking liquid:
3 liters (quarts) water
1 tablespoon salt

Peel and grate the potatoes.
Try to squeeze out as much liquid as possible from the potatoes. Then stir in flour and salt.
Bring water and salt to a boil.
Make large, oval balls with a wet serving spoon and drop into the boiling water. When all the dumplings are in the water, lower the heat and simmer about 45 minutes. Serve with fried fresh pork belly, boiled salt mutton, smoked sausages, boiled carrots and rutabagas.

Freshly picked fruit and vegetables from local producers add color to any market. And they taste fantastic.

Opposite page: Potato dumplings, with an assortment of names, are popular in many places in Norway, and are usually served on specific days of the week.

DESSERTS

DESSERT SOUPS

BERRY SOUP WITH BARLEY

Serves 6

3/4 dl (1/3 cup) pearl parley
1 1/2 liters (quarts) water
1 dl (1/3 cup) berry juice concentrate
(can be purchased in health food stores)
1 dl (1/3 cup) sugar
a few grains salt

Soak the barley in water overnight.
Simmer 30 minutes in the soaking water.
Flavor with juice, sugar and salt.

EVERYDAY SOUP

Serves 6

3 dl (1 1/4 cups) blueberry, raspberry or strawberry preserves
raisins
1 liter (quart) water
sugar
1 1/2 tablespoons potato starch
1 1/2 tablespoons cold water

Bring preserves, raisins and water to a boil. Sweeten to taste with sugar and return to a boil.
Remove from the heat and thicken with potato starch stirred into water.
Serve cold.

MILK SOUP WITH DUMPLINGS

Serves 6

1 1/2 liters (6 1/4 cups) full fat milk
Dumplings:
1 egg
2 tablespoons sugar
1 1/2 dl (2/3 cup) milk
6-7 dl (2 1/2 - 3 cups) flour

Bring the milk to a boil. Combine ingredients for the dumplings. The dough should be stiff. Let rest 10 minutes. Dip a spoon in the boiling milk, then use it to form dumplings of the dough. Drop into the milk, which should remain at a simmer at all times. The dumplings float to the top when cooked. Remove as ready. Serve the milk soup with dumplings with cinnamon-sugar after a meal of herring and potatoes.

OATMEAL-FRUIT SOUP

Serves 5

1 dl (1/3 cup) oatmeal
1 liter (quart) water
prunes
2 tablespoons sugar
up to 1 dl (1/3 cup) berry juice concentrate (can be purchased in health food stores)

Cook the oatmeal in half the water about 5 minutes. Cook the prunes in half the water about 5 minutes. Combine and add berry juice concentrate to taste. Chill before serving.

TAPIOCA SOUP

Serves 3

5 dl (2 cups) water
1 dl (scant 1/2 cup) quick-cooking tapioca
2 dl (3/4 cup) raisins
20 prunes
1 cinnamon stick
berry juice concentrate (can be purchased in health food stores)
sugar

Combine water, tapioca, raisins, prunes and cinnamon. Cook until tapioca is transparent and the fruit is soft, 8-10 minutes. Sweeten with berry juice concentrate and sugar.

TAPIOCA BEER

Serves 6

5 dl (2 cups) pilsner beer
5 dl (2 cups) water
4 tablespoons (1/4 cup) quick-cooking tapioca
1/2 dl (3 1/2 tablespoons) sugar
1 dl (scant 1/2 cup) whipping cream

Bring beer and water to a boil. Add tapioca and cook until transparent, 8-10 minutes.
Sweeten with sugar.
Whip the cream and whisk into the soup just before serving.

RHUBARB SOUP

Serves 16

1 kg (2 1/4 pounds) rhubarb
4 liters (1 gallon) water
1 cinnamon stick (optional)
3 1/2 dl (1 1/2 cups) sugar
1 dl (scant 1/2 cup) potato starch
3 tablespoons cold water

Wash and peel the rhubarb. Cut into 4 cm (1 1/2") lengths.
Bring the water and cinnamon bark to a boil. Add the rhubarb and simmer 5 minutes. Remove the cinnamon. The rhubarb falls apart easily if overcooked. Stir with a whisk and remove any rhubarb which sticks to the whisk.
Sweeten with sugar. Stir potato starch and water together and stir into the soup. Cook until thickened.
Chill before serving.

Rhubarb soup is a popular May dessert.

Rhubarb sprinkled with sugar is often the first spring dessert with Norwegian fruit.

LEMON SOUP

Serves 8

1 dl (scant 1/2 cup) quick-cooking
tapioca
3/4 dl (1/3 cup) raisins
1 1/2 liters (quarts) water
1 1/2 lemons, sliced
1 3/4 dl (3/4 cup) sugar
1 1/2 tablespoons whipping cream

Combine tapioca, raisins, water and
lemon and bring to a boil. Cook until
tapioca is transparent, 8-10 minutes.
Pour the cream into a soup terrine.
Whisk in the hot soup.

HOT CHOCOLATE
WITH SNOWBALLS

Serves 6-8

125 g (4 ounces) semi-sweet chocolate
2 liters (quarts) full fat milk
1 tablespoon butter
1-2 tablespoons sugar
2 1/2 teaspoons rice flour or cornstarch
1 tablespoon cold water
Snowballs:
2 egg whites
salt
2 tablespoons sugar
boiling water

Break the chocolate into small squares
and melt in 1 dl (1/2 cup) of the milk
with the butter. Add sugar and remaining milk and heat just to the boiling
point.
Thicken with rice flour stirred into cold
water.
Beat the egg white with a few grains salt
until stiff but not dry. Fold in the sugar.
Form 6-8 balls and poach in the water
until set, turning once, about 5 minutes.
Remove with a slotted spoon and drain.
Serve the balls in the chocolate.

Trondheim soup and hot chocolate with snowballs.

TRONDHEIM SOUP

Serves 6

1 1/4 liters (quarts) water
4 tablespoons (1/4 cup) parboiled rice
3/4 dl (1/3 cup) raisins
1 cinnamon stick
1 tablespoon flour
2 1/2 dl (1 cup) whipping cream

4 tablespoons (1/4 cup) sugar
salt

Combine water, rice, raisins and cinnamon and bring to a boil. Simmer until
rice is tender, about 20 minutes.
Whisk the flour into the cream and add.
Bring to a boil. Simmer 1-2 minutes,
until thickened.
Stir in the sugar and a few grains salt.

Fresh berries with sugar and cream are a favorite dessert.

DESSERT CAKES

VEILED COUNTRY LASS

Serves 4

3-4 dl (1 1/2 cups) sweet rusk or
graham cracker crumbs
3 tablespoons sugar
about 2 tablespoons butter
2 1/2 dl (1 cup) whipping cream
3-4 dl (1 1/2 cups) applesauce

Brown the crumbs and sugar lightly in
butter. Cool. Whip the cream.
Layer crumbs, applesauce and cream in
a glass bowl.

Veiled country lass (applesauce-crumb pudding).

Norwegian apples are of excellent quality, thanks to healthy trees and long, light summer days.

Apricot bavarian cream.

TRIFLE

Serves 4

250 g (8 ounces) almond macaroons
2 tablespoons sliced almonds
2 1/2 dl (1 cup) sherry or Madeira
Vanilla cream:
5 tablespoons (1/3 cup) cornstarch

3 egg yolks
5 tablespoons (1/3 cup) confectioner's sugar
2 teaspoons vanilla sugar (1 teaspoon vanilla extract)
5 dl (2 cups) full fat milk
2 dl (3/4 cup) whipping cream

Crush the macaroons and soak with the almonds in sherry 1 hour. Drain. Whisk together cornstarch, egg yolks, sugar, vanilla sugar (but not extract) and 1 dl (1/2 cup) milk. Bring the remaining milk to a boil. Whisk the egg yolk mixture into the boiling milk. Return to the boil. Cool. Stir in vanilla extract. Whip the cream. Layer macaroons and almonds, vanilla cream and whipped cream in a glass bowl.

Nesselrode Bavarian cream.

4 eggs
4 dl (1 2/3 cups) whipping cream

Soak the apricots in the water overnight. Cook until tender in the soaking water with 3 tablespoons of the sugar, 5-8 minutes. Mash. Remove 3 tablespoons and reserve for the sauce.

Soak the gelatin sheets in cold water (or sprinkle powdered gelatin over 3 tablespoons apricot liquid) 5 minutes to soften. Squeeze excess water from the sheets (disregard for powdered gelatin). Melt the gelatin over low heat. Stir into the hot apricot mixture. Beat the eggs with the remaining sugar until light and lemon-colored. Lightly whip the cream. Fold the egg mixture and the cream into the apricot mixture. Pour into a rinsed 2-liter (quart) mold. Refrigerate at least 3 hours.

Unmold and serve with a sauce made from the reserved apricot purée mixed with 3 tablespoons water.

JELLIED DESSERTS

APRICOT BAVARIAN CREAM

Serves 10

250 g (8 ounces) dried apricots
7 1/2 dl (3 cups) water
1 1/4 dl (1/2 cup) sugar
8 sheets (8 teaspoons powdered) gelatin

NESSELRODE BAVARIAN CREAM

Serves 4

1 1/2 dl (2/3 cup) raisins
5 sheets (5 teaspoons powdered) gelatin
2 eggs
1 dl (scant 1/2 cup) sugar
2 1/2 dl (1 cup) whipping cream

1 tablespoon dark rum
3 1/2 tablespoons grated semi-sweet chocolate

If the raisins are dry, cover with boiling water and soak 10 minutes. Drain well. Soak the gelatin sheets in cold water (or sprinkle the powdered gelatin over 2 tablespoons of the cream) 5 minutes to soften. Squeeze excess water from the sheets (disregard for powdered gelatin). Melt the gelatin over low heat. Cool slightly. Beat the eggs and sugar until light and lemon-colored. Beat in the rum. Whip the cream. Fold the cream and the melted gelatin into the egg mixture. Fold in raisins and chocolate. Pour into a rinsed 1-liter (quart) mold. Refrigerate at least 3 hours. To serve, unmold and decorate with whipped cream and chocolate.

BUTTERMILK MOLD

Serves 4-5

3 1/2 dl (1 1/2 cups) buttermilk
1 dl (scant 1/2 cup) sugar
lemon juice
6 sheets (2 tablespoons powdered) gelatin
1 1/2 dl (2/3 cup) whipping cream

Whisk buttermilk and sugar. Add lemon juice to taste. Soak the gelatin sheets in cold water (or sprinkle the powdered gelatin over 2 tablespoons water) 5 minutes to soften. Squeeze excess water from the sheets (disregard for powdered gelatin). Melt the gelatin over low heat. Stir into the buttermilk mixture. Refrigerate until it becomes syrupy. Whip the cream and fold into the slightly-stiffened mixture. Pour into a rinsed 1-liter (quart) mold and refrigerate at least 3 hours. Unmold and serve with a berry juice sauce.

LINGONBERRY BAVARIAN CREAM

Serves 4-5

5 sheets (5 teaspoons powdered) gelatin
2 1/2 dl (1 cup) full fat milk
3 egg yolks
1 dl (scant 1/2 cup) sugar
3 1/2 dl (1 1/2 cups) whipping cream
3 1/2 dl (1 1/2 cups) lingonberries
3 tablespoons sugar

Soak the gelatin sheets in cold water (or sprinkle the powdered gelatin over 3 tablespoons of the milk) 5 minutes to soften. Squeeze excess water from the

Buttermilk molded dessert.

sheets (disregard for powdered gelatin). Melt the gelatin over low heat. Bring the milk to a boil. Beat the egg yolks with 1 dl (scant 1/2 cup) sugar until light and lemon-colored. Whisk in the boiling milk. Stir in the melted gelatin. Refrigerate until syrupy. Combine berries with the remaining sugar. Lightly whip the cream. Fold in the berries. Fold this mixture carefully into the slightly stiffened mixture. Pour the mixture into a rinsed 1-liter (quart) mold. Refrigerate at least 3 hours. Unmold and garnish with whipped cream and fresh lingonberries.

FRUIT PUDDINGS AND COMPOTES

LINGONBERRY PUDDING

Serves 10-12

1 liter (quart) lingonberries
5 dl (2 cups) water
5 3/4 dl (2 1/2 cups) sugar
2 dl (3/4 cup) rye flour

Bring the berries and 1 dl (1/2 cup) of the water to a boil. Add sugar and simmer 10 minutes. Whisk the flour into the remaining water and whisk into the

berry mixture. Simmer about 10 minutes. Serve warm with light cream.

RHUBARB CREAM PUDDING

Serves 8

500 g (1 pound) rhubarb
1 1/2 dl (2/3 cup) confectioner's sugar
Cream Pudding:
4 sheets (4 teaspoons powdered) gelatin
4 dl (1 2/3 cups) whipping cream
1/2 vanilla bean, split lengthwise
4 egg yolks
3 tablespoons confectioner's sugar
4 egg whites

Preheat the oven to 175° C (350° F).
Clean the rhubarb, cut into 5 cm (2") lengths and place in an ovenproof dish. Sprinkle with confectioner's sugar, cover with foil or a lid and bake until tender, 20-25 minutes. Soak the gelatin sheets in cold water (or sprinkle the powdered gelatin over 2 tablespoons of the cream) 5 minutes to soften. Squeeze excess water from the sheets (disregard for powdered gelatin). Melt the gelatin over low heat. Bring the cream and vanilla bean to a boil. Beat the egg yolks with the sugar until light and lemon-colored. Whisk in the boiling cream. Stir in the gelatin. Remove

Lingonberry Bavarian cream.

the vanilla bean. Chill until syrupy. Beat the egg whites until stiff but not dry. Fold into the slightly-stiffened egg yolk mixture. Spoon the rhubarb into a glass bowl. Top with the cream mixture. Refrigerate at least 3 hours. Decorate with whipped cream.

PRUNE COMPOTE

Serves 6

about 30 pitted prunes
8 dl (3 1/4 cups) water
1 1/2 dl (2/3 cup) sugar
3 tablespoons potato starch
2 tablespoons cold water
sugar

Bring prunes, water and sugar to a boil and simmer until prunes are tender, about 15 minutes. Remove from the heat. Stir the potato starch into cold water and add. Simmer until thickened. Chill. Sprinkle with sugar to prevent a skin from forming.

JELLY/JUICE

FRUIT/BERRY GELATIN

Serves 6

1 liter (quart) ready-to-drink berry juice
15 sheets (5 tablespoons powdered)
gelatin
juice of 1 lemon

Soak the gelatin sheets in cold water (or sprinkle the powdered gelatin over 1 dl (1/2 cup) of the juice) 5 minutes to soften. Heat 1 1/2 dl (2/3 cup) of the berry juice. Squeeze excess water from

Gelatin desserts have always been children's favorites, often served at birthday parties.

Prune compote was once a wedding dessert.

Strawberry and raspberry ice cream, along with all other flavors, are Norway's most popular dessert.

the sheets (disregard for powdered gelatin). Melt the gelatin in the juice, stirring until dissolved. Strain into the remaining juice. Add lemon juice for balance. Pour into a 1-liter (quart) mold and refrigerate at least 3 hours. Serve with whipped cream or vanilla sauce.

RED OR BLACK CURRANT JELLY

1 kg (2 1/4 pounds, about 10 cups) red or black currants
5 dl (2 cups) water
500 g (18 ounces, 6 dl, 2 1/2 cups) sugar per liter (quart) juice

Bring the berries and water to a boil. Simmer 5 minutes, then strain in a juice press. Bring the juice and sugar to a boil. Skim. Lower heat and simmer 1 hour. Pour into hot, sterilized jars. Cool, then refrigerate. Use with meat dishes.

ICE CREAM DESSERTS

STRAWBERRY OR RASPBERRY ICE CREAM

Serves 8

5 dl (2 cups) whipping cream
1-2 dl (1/2-3/4 cups) strawberry or raspberry jam
1 3/4 dl (3/4 cup) sugar
1 tablespoon sherry
500 g (1 pound, 4 cups) fresh berries

Whip the cream. Fold in the jam, sugar and sherry. Carefully fold the berries into the cream. Pour into a 2- liter (quart) ice cream mold with a lid and freeze.

SPIKED BERRY ICE CREAM

Serves 4-5

1 dl (1/2 cup) your choice of berries
2 tablespoons gin
3 dl (1 1/4 cups) whipping cream
2 eggs
1/2 dl (3 1/2 tablespoons) confectioner's sugar
3 1/2 dl (1 1/2 cups) berry jam

Soak the berries in gin. Whip the cream. Beat the eggs with the sugar until light and lemon-colored. Combine egg yolk mixture with the jam. Carefully fold in the cream and 3/4 of the berries. Sprinkle the remaining berries in the bottom of a 1-liter (quart) ice cream mold. Pour over the cream mixture. Freeze. Serve with whipped cream and fresh berries.

ROSE HIP ICE CREAM

Serves 6

4 dl (1 2/3 cups) whipping cream
about 3 dl (1 1/4 cups) sweetened rose hip purée
lemon juice

Whip the cream. Fold the rose hip purée into the cream. Add lemon juice for balance. Pour into a 1-liter (quart) ice cream mold with a lid. Freeze.

LEMON ICE CREAM

Serves 5

10-12 lemons
5 dl (2 cups) water
3 dl (1 1/4 cups) sugar
1 liter (quart) sweet white wine

Wash the lemons well and grate the rind (no pith.) Squeeze the juice and strain. Combine juice, rind, water and sugar in a saucepan. Heat until the sugar dissolves. Cool. Add the white wine. Taste for sweetness. Freeze in an ice cream machine. The ice cream will be soft.

CREAM PUDDINGS

BARLEY CREAM

Serves 4

1 1/2 dl (2/3 cup) pearl barley
4 dl (1 2/3 cups) water
1 liter (quart) full fat milk
salt
1 dl (1/2 cup) sugar
2 dl (3/4 cup) whipping cream

Soak the barley in the water overnight. Simmer in the soaking liquid 30 minutes. Drain.
Add the milk and cook 30 minutes, until tender. Flavor with a few grains salt and sweeten with sugar. Chill.
Lightly whip the cream. Fold in the barley porridge.
Serve with sauce made from berry juice concentrate.

MADEIRA CREAM

Serves 4-5

2 1/2 dl (1 cup) whipping cream
2-3 egg yolks
3/4 dl (1/3 cup) sugar
1 dl (scant 1/2 cup) Madeira

Whip the cream.
Beat the egg yolks with the sugar until light and lemon-colored. Beat in the Madeira, a little at a time.
Fold the cream into the egg yolk mixture.
Serve immediately with cookies.

CLOUDBERRY CREAM

whipping cream
sweetened cloudberries

Lightly whip the cream.
Fold in the cloudberries, which should be a little too sweet.
Add additional sugar, if necessary.
Serve in individual bowls. Top with fresh or sugared cloudberries and serve with almond cookies.

RICE CREAM

Serves 4

Rice porridge:
4 dl (1 2/3 cups) water
1 3/4 dl (3/4 cup) round grain rice
1 liter (quart) full fat milk
1 teaspoon salt
sugar
2 1/2 dl (1 cup) whipping cream
1 teaspoon vanilla sugar (1/2 teaspoon extract)

Bring the water to a boil and add the rice. Return to a boil and simmer until all water is absorbed, 10-15 minutes. Add the milk and bring to a boil. Lower the heat, cover and simmer until the rice is tender, about 30-40 minutes. Season with salt. Transfer the porridge to a dish and sprinkle with sugar. Cool.
Lightly whip the cream.
Fold the porridge into the cream. Sweeten with sugar and vanilla sugar.
Serve with sauce made from berry juice concentrate.

TROLL CREAM

Serves 8

1 liter (quart) lingonberries
3 dl (1 1/4 cups) sugar
1 egg white

Combine all ingredients in a mixer bowl and beat until quadrupled in volume.

DYLLE

Serves 5

3 3/4 liters (quarts) full fat milk
1 1/2 dl (2/3 cup) rice

Simmer the milk slowly until it turns light brown and has a caramelized flavor, about 2 hours. Stir occasionally.
Rinse the rice. Add after the milk has cooked 90 minutes. Return to a boil and simmer until the mixture is a thick soup. Serve cold with cinnamon and sugar. This recipe yields about 1 1/4 liters (5 cups).

PUDDINGS

BREAD PUDDING

Serves 8-10

500 g (1 pound) white or light whole wheat bread
7 1/2 dl (3 cups) milk
3/4 dl (1/3 cup) sugar
1 1/4 dl (1/2 cup) flour
1/2 teaspoon cinnamon
1/2 baking powder
75 g (2 3/4 ounces, 1/3 cup) margarine, melted
2 eggs, lightly beaten
1/2 teaspoon lemon extract (optional)

Cut the crusts off the bread, cube and soak in milk 1 hour. Preheat the oven to 150°C (300°F). Combine the bread with the remaining ingredients. Pour into a greased 2-liter (quart) mold. Place a towel in the bottom of an oven pan. Place the mold on the towel. Fill with hot water to reach halfway up the sides of the mold. Bake 1 hour. Serve with sauce made from berry juice concentrate.

GRANDMA'S SHERRY PUDDING

Serves 5

5 sheets (5 teaspoons powdered) gelatin
5 dl (2 cups) whipping cream
1 1/4 dl (1/2 cup) sugar
1 1/2 dl (2/3 cup) sweet sherry

Soak the gelatin sheets in cold water (or sprinkle the powdered gelatin over 3 tablespoons of the cream) 5 minutes to soften. Squeeze excess water from the sheets (disregard for powdered gelatin). Melt the gelatin over low heat.
Bring cream and sugar to a boil. Cool slightly. Squeeze excess water from the gelatin sheets (disregard for powdered gelatin) and melt in the cream mixture. Stir until dissolved, then stir in the sherry. Strain into a 1-liter (quart) mold. Chill at least 3 hours.
Unmold and serve with sauce made from berry juice concentrate.

Madeira, cloudberry and troll (lingonberry) cream are three desserts which can be served with coffee.

Rice cram with chopped nuts and red berry sauce.

FLUMMERY

Serves 12

18 sheets (6 tablespoons powdered)
gelatin
1 1/2 liters (quarts) 35% fat sour cream
500-600 g (18-20 ounces, 1 - 1 1/4
liters, 4-5 cups) confectioner's sugar
juice of 2 lemons
1 1/4 dl (1/2 cup) sweet sherry

Soak the gelatin sheets in cold water (or sprinkle the powdered gelatin over 1/3 cup water) 5 minutes to soften. Squeeze excess water from the sheets (disregard for powdered gelatin. Melt the gelatin over low heat. Cool slightly. Whip sour cream and sugar. Add lemon juice and sherry. Stir the gelatin into the sherry cream. Pour into individual dessert dishes and chill.

CARAMEL PUDDING

Serves 8

1.
1 liter (quart) full fat milk
1 vanilla bean, split lengthwise
10 eggs
3 tablespoons sugar
Caramel to glaze the molds:
500 g (1 pound, 5 3/4 dl, 2 1/2 cups)
sugar
2 1/2 dl (1 cup) water

Preheat the oven to 150°C (300°F). Bring the milk and vanilla bean to a boil. Whisk the eggs and sugar carefully. Whisk the eggs into the boiling milk. Caramelize the sugar in a frying pan until golden. Add the water and cook until golden brown. Line 3 1-liter molds with the caramel. Strain the milk mixture, then divide among the molds. Place a cloth towel in the bottom of an oven tray. Place the molds on the towel (to keep them from moving). Add hot water to reach halfway up the molds. Bake 90 minutes. Refrigerate until completely cold, then unmold.

2.
4 dl (1 3/4 cups) sugar
1 liter (quart) whipping cream

3/4 dl (1/3 cup) sugar
1 vanilla bean, split lengthwise
15 egg yolks

Preheat the oven to 150°C (300°F). Caramelize the sugar in a frying pan until golden. Glaze the bottom and sides of a rectangular 2-liter loaf pan. Heat the cream, half the remaining sugar and the tiny seeds scraped from the inside of the vanilla bean, along with the bean itself to the boiling point. Beat the egg yolks with the remaining sugar. Carefully whisk in the hot cream. Strain into the prepared pan. Bake in a water bath (see the previous recipe) about 90 minutes. Refrigerate until completely cold, then unmold and decorate as desired.

MADEIRA PUDDING

Serves 10

12 sheets (4 tablespoons powdered)
gelatin
5 dl (2 cups) full fat milk
4 eggs
3 1/2 dl (1 1/2 cups) confectioner's
sugar
2 dl (3/4 cup) Madeira

Soak the gelatin sheets in cold water (or sprinkle the powdered gelatin over 3 tablespoons of the milk) 5 minutes to soften. Bring the milk to a boil. Squeeze excess water from the gelatin sheets (disregard for powdered gelatin.) Melt the gelatin in the milk. Cool slightly. Beat the eggs with the sugar until light and lemon-colored. Whisk into the milk mixture. Add the Madeira, then strain into a metal bowl. Chill until syrupy. Whip the cream and fold into the partially-set pudding. Pour into 10-12 rinsed individual dishes. Note: Other kinds of wine or orange juice can be used instead of Madeira.

MILK PUDDING

Serves 12

125 g (4 ounces, 1/2 cup) butter
1 liter (quart) 10% fat cream
1 1/4 dl (1/2 cup) flour

1 1/4 dl (1/2 cup) sugar
3 dl (1 1/4 cups) bread or cracker
crumbs
4 tablespoons (1/4 cup) ground
blanched almonds
grated rind of 1 lemon
1/2 teaspoon cardamom
3 tablespoons currants

Preheat the oven to 180°C (350°F). Bring butter, cream and flour to a boil, stirring constantly. Pour into a bowl and mix in remaining ingredients. Pour into a greased 1 1/2-liter (6 cup) mold and bake 1 hour. Serve with sauce made from berry juice concentrate.

POTATO PUDDING

Serves 4

125 g (4 ounces, 1/2 cup) butter
250 g (8 ounces, 2 medium) boiled
potatoes
2 teaspoons flour
1 1/2 dl (2/3 cup) full fat milk
1 1/4 dl (1/2 cup) confectioner's sugar
grated rind of 1 lemon
4 eggs

Preheat the oven to 200°C (400°F). Grease and flour a 1-liter (quart) mold. Melt the butter. Mash the potatoes and add with the flour. Beat in the milk. Cool. Stir in the sugar and the lemon rind. Separate the eggs and beat in the yolks, one at a time, beating well after each. Beat the egg whites until stiff but not dry and fold in. Pour into the prepared mold. Place a cloth towel in the bottom of an oven pan. Place the mold on the towel (to keep it from moving). Add hot water to reach halfway up the sides of the mold. Bake 40 minutes. Serve with sauce made from berry juice concentrate.

Homemade caramel pudding and a good cup of coffee is a perfect finale after a festive meal.

SHERRY PUDDING

Serves 8

9 sheets (3 tablespoons powdered)
gelatin
7 1/2 dl (3 cups) whipping cream
1 3/4 dl (3/4 cup) sugar
1 3/4 dl (3/4 cup) sweet sherry

Soak the gelatin sheets in cold water (or sprinkle the powdered gelatin over 3 tablespoons of the cream) 5 minutes to soften. Bring cream and sugar to a boil. Squeeze excess water from the gelatin sheets (disregard for powdered gelatin). Melt the gelatin in the hot cream. Cool slightly, then stir in the sherry. Chill until syrupy. Pour the partly-stiffened mixture into a rinsed 1-liter mold. Chill at least 3 hours. Unmold and serve with sauce made from berry juice concentrate.

TAPIOCA PUDDING

Serves 8-10

1 1/4 liters (5 cups) water
1 3/4 dl (3/4 cups) tapioca (not quick-cooking)
1/2 dl (3 1/2 tablespoons) sugar
2 1/2 dl (1 cup) ready-to-drink berry juice
sugar

Bring the water to a boil. Add tapioca, sugar and juice. Simmer about 20 minutes. Pour into a rinsed 1 1/2-liter (6 cup) mold. Sprinkle with sugar to keep a skin from forming. Refrigerate. Serve with light cream and sugar.

SEMOLINA PUDDING

Serves 10

3 dl (1 1/4 cups) semolina (cream of wheat)
1 liter (quart) full fat milk
75 g (2 2/3 ounces, 1/3 cup) butter
a few grains salt
2 1/2 dl (1 cup) confectioner's sugar
3 tablespoons butter
8 eggs, separated

Bring milk, 75 g (1/3 cup) butter, salt and sugar to a boil. Add the semolina and simmer 15 minutes. Preheat the oven to 160°C (325°F). Remove from the heat and add the remaining butter. Beat in the eggs, one at a time. Beat the egg whites until stiff but not dry and fold in. Pour into a greased 2-liter mold. Place a towel in the bottom of an oven pan. Place the mold on the towel and fill with hot water halfway up the sides of the mold. Bake 1 hour. Chill. Unmold and serve with sauce made from berry juice concentrate.

SNOW PUDDING

Serves 4

5 sheets (5 teaspoons powdered) gelatin
1 3/4 dl (3/4 cup) sugar
juice of 3 lemons
6 egg whites

Soak the gelatin sheets in cold water (or sprinkle the powdered gelatin over 2 tablespoons water) 5 minutes to soften. Squeeze excess water from the gelatin sheets (disregard for powdered

Lingonberries

gelatin) and melt over low heat. Beat sugar and lemon juice. Add the melted gelatin. Beat the egg whites until stiff but not dry and fold in. Pour into a rinsed glass bowl and chill at least 3 hours. Serve with vanilla or caramel sauce.

WINTER LINGONBERRY PORRIDGE

Serves 12

1.
3 dl (1 1/4 cups) pearl barley
1 liter (quart) water
1 1/2 liters (quarts) lingonberries
750 g (1 2/3 pounds, 8 3/4 dl, 3 3/4 cups) sugar

Soak the barley overnight. Simmer in the cooking water 1 hour. Add berries and sugar and cook to a thin porridge, 30-40 minutes. This porridge can be canned and stored. Note: Another, possibly Finnish, version of this dish substitutes rice or rye flour for the barley.

2.
1 liter (quart) water
660 g (1 1/2 pounds, 7 3/4 dl, 3 1/3 cups) sugar
2 1/3 liters (quarts) lingonberries
3 1/2 dl (1 1/2 cups) rye flour

Simmer water and sugar 5 minutes. Add the berries and simmer 10 minutes. Sprinkle the flour over the mixture, stir well and return to the boil. Simmer 5 minutes. Serve warm with light cream.

OTHER DESSERTS

BREAD PANCAKES

Serves 4

250 g (9 ounces) white bread
7 1/2 dl (3 cups) milk
1 tablespoon butter
3 tablespoons flour
2 eggs
1 teaspoon cinnamon
1/2 teaspoon cardamom
3 tablespoons sugar
butter

Cut the crusts from the bread and cube. Bring the milk to a boil and pour over the bread. Soak overnight. Mix to a batter. Add remaining ingredients. The batter should be rather thick. Fry small cakes on both sides in butter. Serve hot with jam.

BOILED RICE WITH LINGONBERRIES AND CREAM

boiled long grain rice
lingonberry compote
light cream

Serve rice in a bowl with lingonberry compote and cream.

RICE PORRIDGE PANCAKES

Serves 4

2 dl (3/4 cup) rice porridge
2 egg yolks
1 1/2 dl (2/3 cup) full fat milk
2 tablespoons sugar
1/2 teaspoon cinnamon
1-2 drops lemon extract
1 tablespoon chopped almonds
2 tablespoons raisins
2 egg whites
butter
bread or cracker crumbs

Mix the porridge with the egg yolks. Whisk in the milk. Add sugar, cinnamon, lemon extract, nuts and raisins. Beat the egg whites until stiff but not dry and fold in. Melt butter in a skillet. Sprinkle crumbs over the butter before spooning in the batter. Sprinkle top of pancake with crumbs before turning. Serve with jam or fruit compote.

SOUR CREAM DESSERT OMELET

Serves 5

2 1/2 dl (1 cup) whipping cream
2 1/2 dl (1 cup) sour heavy cream
2 tablespoons sugar
6 eggs, separated
1 3/4 dl (2/3 cup) flour

Boiled rice with lingonberries and cream is a simple and tasty dessert.

Sour cream dessertomelet.

Preheat the oven to 180°C (350°F). Whip the cream and sour cream with half the sugar. Beat the egg yolks with the remaining sugar until light and lemon-colored. Fold into the cream. Fold in the flour. Beat the egg whites until stiff but not dry and fold into the cream mixture. Pour into a greased ovenproof dish and bake until puffed, golden and set, about 15-20 minutes.

BAKED GOODS

FLATBREAD

Equipment needed for baking flatbread:
An oblong wooden bowl, a large plastic bowl or a large mixer bowl for mixing ingredients and kneading dough.

A baking board, a large wooden plate or marble slab is best.

A rolling pin, preferably patterned with rills or squares.

Wooden baking sticks, rather like long tongue depressors, or thin flat spatulas for lifting sheets of flatbread from the baking board and turning them on the griddle.

A smaller rolling pin with rills, squares or spikes to roll over the sheet of flatbread when it is on the griddle, to make tiny holes in the surface.

Flour brush.

Griddle.

A flat tray or wooden plate for the finished flatbread.

Tips for making flatbread:
Roll it out part of the dough to a 2 - 2 1/2 cm (1") thick sheet. Cut circles of dough with a 9 cm (3 1/2") round cookie cutter.

Roll out each dough circle with a patterned rolling pin to a thin sheet.

Dust the baking board with barley, whole wheat or oat flour.

Bake the dough sheets on a griddle over medium heat until lightly colored on both sides.

Fold the baked flatbread in half or cool as is. Store the baked flatbread in stacks under a light weight in a dry, cool room.

Flatbread is a must with hearty soups, dried meats and fermented fish.

FLATBREAD

1.

*500 g (18 ounces, 8 1/4 dl, 3 1/2 cups)
fine whole wheat flour
500 g (18 ounces, 8 1/4 dl, 3 1/2 cups)
oat flour
500 g (18 ounces, 8 1/4 dl, 3 1/2 cups)
flour
about 1 liter (quart) water
salt*

Combine the flours. Add water and knead to a stiff dough.

2.

*7 1/2 dl (3 cups) water
5 dl (2 cups) coarse whole wheat flour
1/2 teaspoon salt
7 1/2 dl (3 cups) fine rye flour
7 1/2 dl (3 cups) barley flour*

Bring the water to a boil and pour over the coarse flour. Cool. Add salt and most of the rye and barley flour. Knead to a pliable, not too stiff dough with the remaining flour.

3.

*about 3 liters (quarts) water
1 kg (2 1/4 pounds, about 3 liters (quarts)) oatmeal
2 teaspoons salt
1 kg (2 1/4 pounds, 16 1/2 dl, 7 cups) oat flour
dl coarse whole wheat flour*

Bring the water to a boil and pour over the oatmeal. Soak overnight.
Knead the oatmeal with the remaining ingredients to a stiff but pliable dough.

4.

*3 dl (1 1/4 cups) flour
1/4 teaspoon salt
1 tablespoon sugar
1 dl (1/3 cup) whole wheat flour
75 g (5 tablespoons, 1/3 cup) butter
1 1/4 dl (1/2 cup) milk*

Combine the dry ingredients. Crumble the butter into the flour mixture.
Stir in the milk, kneading until pliable.
Divide the dough into 8-10 pieces.

OAT BREAD

*2 kg (4 1/2 pounds, 33 dl, 14 cups) oat flour
about 12 dl (5 cups) water*

Make a firm dough of oat flour and water. Knead well. The dough will be firm and short.

LOAF AND LAYER CAKES

BERGEN RUMBALLS

Makes 12-14 balls

*Pastry:
3 1/2 tablespoons sugar
2 dl (3/4 cup) flour
75 g (2 2/3 ounces, 1/3 cup) margarine
Cream Puffs:
1 1/2 dl (2/3 cup) water
3 tablespoons margarine
1 1/4 dl (1/2 cup) flour
2 eggs*

Rumballs from Bergen.

Filling:
2 egg yolks or 1 egg
1 1/2 tablespoons sugar
1 3/4 tablespoons cornstarch
2 1/2 dl (1 cup) full fat milk
2-3 tablespoons rum
1 dl (scant 1/2 cup) whipping cream
12-14 cocktail cherries

Pastry:
Combine sugar and flour and cut in the margarine. Knead lightly. Form into a ball, wrap in plastic. Chill 1 hour.
Preheat the oven to 210°C (425°F).

Cream Puffs:
Bring water and margarine to a boil. Add the flour and stir until the mixture forms a ball. Remove from the heat. Cool slightly, then beat in the eggs, one at a time. The mixture should thick enough to just keep its shape. Make 12-14 balls with a spoon and place far apart on a greased baking sheet.
Roll out the pastry. Cut out round cookies with a 6-7 cm (2 1/2") cutter. Drape them over the balls and press carefully against the baking sheet. Bake until golden, 25-30 minutes.
Whisk together eggs, sugar, cornstarch and milk in a saucepan. Heat to boiling, stirring constantly. Do not allow to boil. Cool, stirring occasionally. Stir in rum. Whip the cream and fold into the rum cream.
Puncture the balls. Fill a pastry tube with rum cream and pipe the mixture into the balls. Top each with a cherry.

WHIPPED CREAM CAKE

4 eggs
2 dl (1 cup) sugar
1 dl (1/2 cup) flour
1 dl (1/3 cup) potato starch
1 teaspoon baking powder
fresh fruit juice
7 1/2 dl (3 cups) whipping cream
fruit or berries

Preheat the oven to 175°C (350°F).
Beat eggs and sugar until light and fluffy. Sift the dry ingredients and fold into the egg mixture. Pour into a greased 22 cm (9") springform and

Whipped cream cake is Norway's most popular cake. Fill and decorate according to taste.

bake on the lowest oven shelf about 30 minutes. Cool the cake completely before removing from the pan.
Divide the cake horizontally into 2 or 3 layers. Sprinkle fruit juice over the layers. Whip the cream. Use the top layer as the base with the baked side down. Spread with a layer of cream and fruit. Repeat, then top with the bottom layer of the cake, baked side up.
Spread whipped cream over the top and sides of the cake. Use a pastry tube to pipe stars around the edges.
Decorate with fruit or berries, or even chocolate figures.

AUTUMN CAKE

Cake layers:
6 eggs
2 1/4 dl (1 cup) sugar
3 dl (1 1/4 cups) flour
1 teaspoon baking powder
Filling:
5 dl (2 cups) lingonberries
7 1/2 dl (3 cups) cloudberries
confectioner's sugar to taste
7 1/2 dl (3 cups) whipping cream
Garnish:
750 g (1 2/3 pounds) marzipan
yellow food coloring

Wine jelly:
3 sheets (3 teaspoons powdered) gelatin
2 dl (3/4 cup) white wine
juice of 1/2 lemon
sugar to taste

Preheat the oven to 170°C (350°F).
Beat the eggs with the sugar until light and lemon-colored. Combine flour and baking powder and sift over the egg mixture. Fold the flour carefully into the eggs. Pour into a 24 cm (10") springform. Bake on the lowest oven rack about 45 minutes. Cool on a rack. When completely cold, divide horizontally into 3 layers.
Reserve a small amount of each berry for decoration. Mash the remaining berries separately. Sweeten to taste with confectioner's sugar.
Whip the cream. Reserve a small amount of whipped cream for decoration. Mix the lingonberry purée with half the remaining cream. Mix the cloudberry purée with the other half.
Place the bottom layer of cake, baked side down, on a plate. Spread with lingonberry cream. Top with the middle layer of cake and spread with cloudberry cream. End with the top layer, baked side up. Spread with a thin layer of whipped cream.

Couldberries are a prized delicacy. A good spot for picking cloudberries is usually kept secret.

Cut a circle of parchment paper slightly smaller than the cake and place on top of the cake. Roll out most of the marzipan to a round sheet and place over the cake. Color the remaining marzipan yellow. Roll it into a strip and place around the bottom of the cake. Cut the marzipan on top of the cake into a spoke pattern (see the illustration), but do not cut all the way out to the edge of the cake. Roll up each section away from the center point. Remove the parchment paper with a fork. Spoon a circle of lingonberries onto the center of the cake. Spoon the cloudberries around the lingonberries. For the wine jelly, soak the gelatin sheets (or sprinkle the powdered gelatin over 2 tablespoons cold water) in cold water 5 minutes to soften. Squeeze excess water from the sheets (disregard for powdered gelatin). Melt the gelatin over low heat. Combine wine and lemon juice and sweeten to taste. Stir in the gelatin. Strain. Refrigerate until just beginning to set. Spoon carefully over the berries. Smooth out with a knife dipped in boiling water. Refrigerate until ready to serve. This cake can be made 24 hours in advance. Just before serving, sprinkle with confectioner's sugar.

CANDY COOKIE CAKE

2 eggs
2 1/2 dl (1 cup) confectioner's sugar
3 tablespoons cocoa
2 tablespoons very strong coffee
250 g (8 ounces, 1 cup) coconut fat, melted
16 rectangular sweet biscuits
gumdrops
walnut halves

Beat the eggs with the sugar until light and lemon-colored. Add cocoa, coffee and the melted coconut fat. Beat well.
Line a 1-liter (quart) loaf pan with parchment paper. Pour a layer of chocolate mixture in the bottom, then a layer of biscuits. Repeat until all is used, ending with chocolate. Decorate with gumdrops and walnut halves. Chill overnight. Unmold and slice thinly with a sharp knife.

Opposite page: Autumn cake.

HONEY CAKE

4 eggs
2 1/2 dl (1 cup) sugar
1 dl (1/3 cup) melted honey, cooled
5 dl (2 cups) flour
1/4 teaspoon ground allspice
1/4 teaspoon ground black pepper
1/4 teaspoon ground ginger
1 teaspoon baking powder
3/4 dl (1/3 cup) chopped citron

Preheat the oven to 180°C (350°F).
Beat the eggs with the sugar until light and lemon-colored.
Stir in the honey.
Sift the dry ingredients together and mix into the batter. Add the citron.
Pour into a greased 1 1/2-liter (6 cup) loaf pan.
Bake 1 hour, cool 10 minutes on a rack, then remove from the pan.

APPLE CAKE

200 g (7 ounces, scant 1 cup) unsalted butter
2 1/4 dl (1 cup) sugar
4 eggs
1 teaspoon baking powder
3 dl (1 1/4 cups) flour
3 apples
2 teaspoons sugar
1 1/2 teaspoon cinnamon
pearl sugar

Preheat the oven to 180°C (350°F).
Beat butter and sugar until light and fluffy. Add eggs, one at a time, beating well after each.
Combine baking powder and flour and add, mixing well.
Pour half of the batter into a greased 24 cm (10") springform.
Peel and core the apples. Slice thinly and arrange 2/3 of the apple slices over the batter. Sprinkle with sugar and cinnamon. Cover with remaining batter.
Top with remaining apple slices and sprinkle with pearl sugar.
Bake on the lowest oven shelf about 50 minutes. Serve warm with whipped cream.

APPLE CAKE WITH SABAYONNE

Pastry:
250 g (8 ounces, 4 1/4 dl, 1 2/3 cups) flour
1 dl (1/3 cup) cold water
250 g (8 ounces, 1 cup) baking margarine or shortening
Sugar syrup:
1 dl (1/3 cup) sugar
2 dl (2/3 cup) water
apples
fresh black currants or jam
sugar
1 egg, beaten
Sabayonne:
8 egg yolks
2 dl (3/4 cup) white wine
1 1/4 dl (1/2 cup) sugar

Pastry:
Quickly combine all pastry ingredients in a food processor. Do not overwork.
Roll out the dough on a floured board to a 1 1/2 cm (2/3") thick sheet. Roll from the middle out to the edges.
Fold the rectangle into thirds, as with a letter. Wrap in plastic and chill at least 30 minutes.
Preheat the oven to 225°C (425°F).
Combine sugar and water and bring to a boil. Simmer 1 minute.
Roll out half the dough to a 2 mm (3/32") and place in the bottom of a 22 cm (9") springform and bake until golden, 7-8 minutes. Reduce the oven temperature to 175°C (350°F).
Peel and core apples and place close together on the dough. Fill the core holes with berries and sugar or jam. Brush the apples with sugar syrup.
Roll a slightly larger dough sheet to cover the apples. Make 3 cm (1 1/4") holes in the dough between the apples. Make dough rings to frame the holes. Attach with beaten egg. Brush the top of the pie with beaten egg. Bake until golden, about 30 minutes.
Whisk egg yolks and sugar in a double boiler until thick and lemon-colored. Beat in the wine. Pour the mixture into the holes on top of the apple cake, or serve alongside.

FINNØY CAKE

250 g (8 ounces, 1 cup) unsalted butter
250 g (8 ounces, 3 dl, 1 1/4 cups) sugar
4 eggs
2 teaspoons baking powder
250 g (8 ounces, 4 1/4 dl, 1 3/4 cups) flour
1/2 dl (3 1/2 tablespoons) raisins
1/2 dl (3 1/2 tablespoons) chopped dried apricots
1/2 dl (3 1/2 tablespoons) chopped almonds
30 g (1 ounce) chopped semi-sweet chocolate
2 dl (3/4 cup) confectioner's sugar
juice of 1 orange
juice of 1 lemon

Preheat the oven to 150°C (300°F). Beat butter and sugar until light and fluffy. Beat in the eggs, one at a time. Stir the baking powder into the flour and add along with the fruit, almonds and chocolate. Pour into a greased 2-liter (8 cup) loaf pan and bake 90 minutes. Melt the sugar in the orange and lemon juice. Pour over the finished cake. Make holes in the cake with a skewer so the mixture will soak in.

MRS. WALNUM'S BLACK CAKE

250 g (8 ounces, 1 cup) unsalted butter
400 g (14 ounces, 4 3/4 dl, 2 cups) sugar
2 eggs
500 g (18 ounces, 8 1/4 dl, 3 1/2 cups) flour
100 g (3 1/2 ounces, 1 3/4 dl, 3/4 cup) currants
100 g (3 1/2 ounces, 1 1/2 dl, 2/3 cup) chopped citron
2 teaspoons cinnamon
1 teaspoon cardamom
1/2 teaspoon ground cloves
1 teaspoon baking soda
1 teaspoon baking powder

Preheat the oven to 180°C (350°F). Grease and flour a 25-35 cm (10x14") rectangular pan. Beat butter and sugar until light and fluffy. Beat in the eggs, one at a time. Add flour and remaining ingredients. Pour into the prepared pan and bake around 60 minutes.

Apple cake is a typical dessert cake.

PRINCE'S CAKE

250 g (8 ounces, 1 cup) unsalted butter
1 1/2 dl (2/3 cup) sugar
1 egg
1 egg yolk
6 dl (2 2/3 cups) flour
Filling:
3 1/2 dl (1 1/3 cups) ground almonds
3 dl (1 1/4 cups) confectioner's sugar
2 egg whites
1/2 teaspoon rum extract
2 tablespoons water

Preheat the oven to 180° C (350° F).
In a food processor, combine butter, sugar, egg, egg yolk and flour until the dough forms a ball. Do not overwork.
Press 2/3 of the dough into the bottom and up the sides of a 22 cm (9") spring-form.
Combine ingredients for the filling and pour into the crust.
Roll out remaining dough to a thickness of 3 mm (1/8"). Cut into 12 mm (2 1/2") strips. Lay the strips in a lattice pattern over the filling. Place a strip of dough around the edge of the cake.
Bake about 50 minutes.

STRAWBERRY CAKE ROLL

2 eggs, separated
1 dl (1/3 cup) full fat milk
1 teaspoon sugar
1/2 dl (3 1/2 tablespoons) flour
melted butter
3 dl (1 1/4 cups) strawberries
sugar
confectioner's sugar

Beat egg yolks, milk, sugar and flour until smooth.
Beat the egg whites until stiff but not dry and fold in.
Brush a large, non-stick frying pan with melted butter. Pour in the batter, cover, and cook slowly over low heat about 10 minutes.
Slice the berries. Sprinkle with sugar. Spoon over the cake, then roll up.
Sprinkle the roll with powdered sugar and serve with berries, whipped cream or ice cream.

Prince's cake is a classic almond cake.

Strawberry cake roll is delicious with a cup of coffee or topped with ice cream.

KING HAAKON'S CAKE FROM HANKØ

4 eggs
4 dl (1 2/3 dl) sugar
2 tablespoons hot water
2 dl (1 cup) flour
2 dl (2/3 cup) potato starch
1 teaspoon baking powder
Buttercream:
250 g (8 ounces, 1 cup) unsalted butter
2 1/2 dl (1 cup) confectioner's sugar
1 egg yolk
1 tablespoon flour
2 1/2 dl (1 cup) full fat milk.

Preheat the oven to 180°C (350°F). Grease and flour a 22 cm (9") spring-form. Beat the eggs with the sugar until light and lemon-colored. Add the water. Sift in the dry ingredients. Pour into the prepared pan and bake about 30 minutes.

Buttercream:
Beat butter and sugar until light and fluffy. Beat in the egg yolk. Stir in the milk. Cook just until the mixture reaches the boiling point, but do not allow to boil. Cool.

Divide the cake into 2 layers. Fill and frost with buttercream. Garnish with crushed almond praline, if desired.

ALMOND RING CAKE

250 g (9 ounces, 6 dl, 2 1/2 cups) finely-ground blanched almonds
250 g (9 ounces, 6 dl, 2 1/2 cups) finely-ground unblanched almonds
500 g (18 ounces, 10 dl, 4 1/3 cups) sifted confectioner's sugar (sift first, then measure)
3 egg whites
Icing:
2 dl (scant 1 cup) sifted confectioner's sugar
1 egg white

Preheat the oven to 200°C (400°F). Combine almonds and confectioner's sugar in a large saucepan. Add the unbeaten egg white and mix to a firm dough. Place the pan over low heat and knead until the dough is so hot that it is almost impossible to handle. Grease the ring pans for a 16-18 ring cake. Spoon the dough into a cookie press or pastry tube with a wide round tip. Press

Almond ringcake

the dough into the rings, pressing the ends together to look as seamless as possible. Bake 12-15 minutes, until dry and firm outside, but still slightly soft inside. Cool slightly, then remove from the pans and cool completely. For the icing, sift the confectioner's sugar and combine with egg white to make a thick icing. Make a small cone of paper and cut off the tip. Pipe on garlands of icing and stack. Decorate with flags, bon-bons or candy.

KVÆFJORD CAKE

100 g (3 1/2 ounces, scant 1/2 cup) margarine
1 1/4 dl (1/2 cup) sugar
4 egg yolks
1 3/4 dl (2/3 cup) flour
1 teaspoon baking powder
3-4 tablespoons milk
4 egg whites
2 1/4 dl (1 cup) sugar
1/2 dl (3 1/2 tablespoons) chopped almonds
1 package (4 ounces) rum or vanilla pudding mix
3 dl (1 1/4 cups) full fat milk
3 dl (1 1/4 cups) whipping cream

Preheat the oven to 180°C (350°F). Beat margarine and sugar until light and fluffy. Beat in the egg yolks, one at a time. Sift the flour with the baking powder and add alternately with the milk. Pour into a greased 20x30 cm (8x12") pan. Beat the egg whites until stiff but not dry. Gradually add the sugar and beat until stiff and glossy. Spread over the cake batter. Sprinkle with almonds. Bake 20-25 minutes. Cool and halve. Prepare the pudding according to the package directions, but use only 3 dl (1 1/4 cups) milk. Cool. Whip the cream and fold into the pudding. Spread one cake layer with cream, then top with the other cake layer.

ALMOND OR NUT CAKE

4 eggs
1 3/4 dl (3/4 cup) sugar
1 teaspoon baking powder
4 3/4 dl (2 cups) ground almonds or other nuts

Preheat the oven to 170°C (350°F). Beat eggs and sugar until light and lemon-colored. Combine baking powder and nuts and fold carefully into the egg mixture. Pour into a greased 22 cm (9") springform. Bake 30 minutes. Cool in the pan. Serve with whipped cream or ice cream.

Kvæfjord cake is sometimes called the "world's best" with good reason.

Nut cakes can be filled with custard cream, buttercream, chocolate cream or, simply, flavored whipped cream.

RHUBARB CAKE

*150 g (5 ounces, scant 2/3 cup)
unsalted butter
2 dl (3/4 cup) sugar
3 eggs
4 dl (1 2/3 cups) flour
2 teaspoons baking powder
3/4 dl (1/3 cup) full fat milk
300 g (10 ounces, about 3 stalks)
rhubarb
sugar*

Preheat the oven to 200°C (400°F).
Beat butter and sugar until light and
fluffy. Beat in the eggs, one at a time.
Combine flour and baking powder and
add alternately with milk. Chop the rhubarb. Pour the batter into a greased
20x30 cm (8x12") pan. Top with rhubarb and sprinkle with sugar. Bake on
the lowest oven shelf 40 minutes. Cool.
Serve with a thick vanilla cream.

RICE CAKE WITH NUTS AND RAISINS

*1 liter (quart) full fat milk
1 dl (scant 1/2 cup) round grain rice
1/2 teaspoon salt
2 tablespoons sugar
3 tablespoons flour
1 3/4 dl (3/4 cup) raisins
2-3 teaspoons tumeric (for color)
2 dl (3/4 cup) chopped almonds
6 eggs*

Bring the milk to a boil. Add rice and
salt. Cook over low heat 30-40 minutes,
stirring occasionally. Cool. Preheat the
oven to 180°C (350°F). Stir sugar, flour,
raisins, tumeric and almonds into the
porridge. Beat in the eggs, one at a
time. Pour into a greased 1 1/2- liter (6
cup) loaf pan and bake 30-40 minutes.
Serve lukewarm with fresh berries and
whipped cream.

CHOCOLATE CAKE

*125 g (4 1/2 ounces) semi-sweet
chocolate
125 g (4 ounces, 1/2 cup) unsalted
butter
1 1/2 dl (2/3 cup) strong coffee
4 eggs
3 1/2 dl (1 1/2 cups) sugar
3 1/4 dl (1 1/3 cups) flour
2 teaspoons baking powder
Frosting:
125 g (4 1/2 ounces) semi-sweet
chocolate
1-2 tablespoons water
75 g (2 1/2 ounces, 1/3 cup) butter
3 dl (1 1/4 cups) sifted confectioner's
sugar
1 egg
liqueur or rum*

Preheat the oven to 180°C (350°F).
Grease and flour a 24 cm (10") springform.

Chocolate cakes always appear on the Norwegian cake table.

Lingonberry cake.

Break the chocolate into squares and melt with the butter over low heat. Add the coffee and cool slightly.

Beat the eggs with the sugar until light and lemon-colored. Sift the flour with the baking powder and fold into the batter. Stir in the chocolate.

Pour the batter into the prepared pan. Bake 45 minutes. Cool in the pan 10 minutes, then remove. Cool completely on a rack.

Frosting:

Break the chocolate into squares and melt over low heat. Cool slightly.

Beat butter and sugar until light and fluffy. Add the egg and beat well. Gradually add the melted chocolate. Beat until smooth.

Cut the cake horizontally into 2-3 layers and sprinkle each with liqueur or rum. Spread a thin layer of frosting between the layers. Cover top and sides with remaining frosting.

SILVER CAKE

80 g (2 3/4 ounces, 1/3 cup) margarine
1 1/4 dl (1/2 cup) sugar
4 tablespoons (1/4 cup) chopped blanched almonds
2 1/4 dl (1 cup) flour, sifted
1 1/2 teaspoons baking powder
4 egg whites

Preheat the oven to 180°C (350°F).

Beat margarine and sugar until light and fluffy. Add flour, baking powder and almonds.

Beat egg whites until stiff but not dry and fold into the mixture.

Pour into a greased 1 1/2-liter (6 cup) loaf pan. Bake 45 minutes, until golden. Cool on a rack 10 minutes before removing from the pan.

LINGONBERRY CAKE

4 1/2 dl (scant 2 cups) flour
1 1/2 dl (2/3 cup) sugar
1 tablespoon baking powder
150 g (5 ounces, scant 2/3 cup) unsalted butter
1 egg
2 dl (3/4 cup) lingonberry preserves
Streusel topping:
1 1/2 dl (2/3 cup) oatmeal
3 tablespoons butter
1 dl (1/2 cup) sugar
1 teaspoon vanilla sugar (1/2 teaspoon extract)

Preheat the oven to 200°C (400°F).

Combine flour, sugar and baking powder and cut in the butter with a pastry blender. Add the egg and mix well.

Spread into a greased 20x30 (8x12") pan. Spread the preserves over the batter. Combine all ingredients for the topping and sprinkle over the batter.

Bake 25-30 minutes, until golden. Cool in the pan.

YEAST BREADS

LONG BERGEN LOAVES

3 breads

1 1/2 liters (quarts) skim milk
50 g (1 3/4 ounces) fresh yeast
1 tablespoon salt
1 1/2 kg (3 pounds, about 3 liters,
12 1/2 cups) rye flour
1 kg (2 1/4 pounds, about 1 3/4 liters,
7 cups) flour
butter

Heat the milk to lukewarm and stir in the yeast.

Add salt and flour to make a firm dough. Knead until smooth. Form into a ball, sprinkle with flour and place in a bowl. Cover with plastic and a cloth and let rise in a warm place.

Knead dough thoroughly. Divide it into thirds. Knead and form each into a loaf. Place in a greased oven tray. Grease the sides of each loaf so that they will pull apart easily.

Let rise in a warm place 45 minutes. Preheat the oven to 200°C (400°F). Brush the loaves with water. Prick the tops with a fork. Bake on the lowest oven shelf 1 hour. 3 loaves.

Note: Save some of the flour for shaping. It might be necessary to add a little more milk if the dough is too stiff.

BERGEN ROLLS

12-16 rolls

5 dl (2 cups) water
50 g (1 3/4 ounces) fresh yeast
4 1/2 dl (2 cups) rye flour
2 dl (scant 1 cup) flour
2 teaspoons salt
2 dl (3/4 cup) flour for kneading

Heat the water to lukewarm and stir in the yeast.

Add flour and salt and knead well. The dough should be very loose. Sprinkle with flour and let rise 1 hour. Knead in most of the second amount of flour. Divide the dough into pieces and roll each into a ball. Press the center of the ball with the side of the hand, to almost divide in two. Place on a greased oven

sheet and let rise in a warm, dry place. Preheat the oven to 220°C (425°F). Bake 20 minutes.

Serve with butter and cheese, preferably a pungent variety.

BERGEN WATER PRETZELS

20 pretzels

3 1/2 dl (1 1/2 cups) water or milk
40 g (1 1/2 ounces) fresh yeast
60 g (2 ounces, 4 tablespoons, 1/4 cup)
butter or margarine
500 g (18 ounces, 8 1/2 dl, 3 1/2 cups)
flour
1/4 teaspoon salt

Heat the liquid to lukewarm and stir in the yeast. Melt the butter and add with flour and salt to make a firm dough. Divide into 20 pieces. Roll each into long sausages and form into pretzels. Preheat the oven to 220°C (425°F). Bring water to a boil in a wide pot. Add pretzels, a few at a time, and return to the boil. They sink to the bottom, then float to the top when fully risen. Remove with a slotted spoon and place on a baking sheet. Bake 10 minutes.

BERGEN SPICED BREAD

2 loaves

2 1/2 dl (1 cup) milk
1 dl (1/3 cup) dark corn or sugar syrup
1/3 liter (1 1/3 cups) dark beer
75 g (2 3/4 ounces) fresh yeast
1 dl (1/3 cup) sugar
2 teaspoons salt
1/2 teaspoon pepper
2 teaspoons ground star anise
500 g (18 ounces, 1 liter, 4 cups)
rye flour
500 g (18 ounces, 8 1/4 dl, 3 1/2 cups)
flour
1 dl (1/3 cup) raisins

Heat the milk, syrup and beer together to lukewarm and stir in the yeast. Combine sugar, salt, pepper and anise and add. Add most of the flour to the yeast mixture to make a stiff dough. Sprinkle with flour. Cover with plastic and a cloth and let rise in a warm place. Knead dough well. Knead in the raisins. Make

2 round or oblong loaves. Place on a greased baking sheet and let rise in a warm place. Preheat the oven to 200°C (400°F). Bake about 1 hour. Lower the temperature toward the end of the baking time, if the breads become dark. As soon as the breads are out of the oven, brush with water. Cool on a rack.

SWEET BUNS

24 buns

3 1/2 dl (1 1/2 cups) milk
70 g (2 1/2 ounces, 4 1/2 tablespoons)
butter
50 g (1 3/4 ounces) fresh yeast
1 egg
1 dl (1/3 cup) sugar
1/2 teaspoon cardamom
1 teaspoon salt
7 1/2 dl (about 3 cups) flour
raisins

Heat the milk and butter to lukewarm and stir in the yeast. Add remaining ingredients and mix lightly together. Let rise over steam. Divide the dough into pieces and roll into balls. Let rise. Preheat the oven to 225°C (425°F). Bake 10-15 minutes.

Opposite page: Many Norwegians prefer coarse, whole-grain breads, baked in many different shapes.

LENTEN BUNS

12-16 buns

1 3/4 dl (3/4 cup) milk
2 tablespoons margarine
25 g (1 ounce) fresh yeast
5 dl (2 cups) flour
3/4 dl (1/3 cup) sugar
1/4 teaspoon cardamom
Filling:
1 1/4 dl (1/2 cup) ground blanched almonds
1 1/4 dl (1/2 cup) sugar
1 egg white
beaten egg

Make a dough according to the directions in the previous recipe and let rise until doubled. For the filling, combine almonds and sugar. Lightly beat the egg white and add. Divide the dough into 12-16 pieces. Press each piece flat. Spoon a little almond filling in the middle of each and wrap with the dough. Roll into smooth balls. Preheat the oven to 225°C (425°F). Place the balls on a greased oven sheet. Let rise 20 minutes. Brush with beaten egg and bake 10-15 minutes.

SWEET BREAD
FROM BJØRKEDAL

4 dl (1 2/3 cups) milk
90 g (3 ounces) yeast
180 g (6 ounces, 3/4 cup) butter
4 tablespoons (1/4 cup) sugar
2 eggs
700 g (1 2/3 pounds, 12 dl, 4 3/4 cups) flour
Vanilla cream:
1 package (4 ounces) vanilla pudding mix
about 4 dl (1 2/3 cups) full fat milk
2 tablespoons sugar (optional)

Heat the milk to lukewarm and stir in the yeast. Melt the butter and add along with the sugar and eggs.

Stir in half the flour, then knead in the rest. Cover with plastic and let rise in a warm place. Prepare the pudding according to the directions on the package, but with the lesser amount of milk and extra sugar. Roll the dough into a rectangle. Spoon the vanilla pudding in the middle lengthwise.

Fold the sides over the pudding. Shape into a big pretzel, seam side down. Snip with a scissors and pull the dough points in alternating directions.

Let rise. Preheat the oven to 200°C (400°F). Bake 30 minutes.

Sweet bread pretzel.

Jelly doughnuts and lenten cream buns.

OAT BREAD

5 loaves

2 1/2 liters (quarts) skim milk
4 dl (1 1/4 cups) oatmeal
100 g (3 1/2 ounces, 1/3 cup) margarine
70 g (2 1/2 ounces) fresh yeast
1 1/2 kg (3 pounds, about 2 1/2 liters, 10 1/2 cups) whole wheat flour
1 tablespoon salt
2 tablespoons sugar
2 dl (3/4 cup) light corn or sugar syrup

Bring 5 dl (2 cups) of the milk to a boil. Cool slightly, then pour over the oatmeal. Soak overnight. Heat the remaining milk with the margarine to lukewarm and stir in the yeast. Add half the flour, salt, sugar and the softened oatmeal. Let rise. Knead the dough. Add syrup and remaining flour and knead to a medium-stiff dough. Let rise. Preheat the oven to 200°C (400°F). Form the dough into 5 loaves. Bake 1 hour.

CRESCENT ROLLS

16 rolls

4 tablespoons (1/4 cup) margarine
3 dl (1 1/4 cups) milk
50 g (1 3/4 ounces) fresh yeast
500 g (18 ounces, 8 1/4 dl, 3 1/2 cups) flour
2 tablespoons sugar
1/2 teaspoon salt

Melt the margarine and add the milk. Stir in the yeast. Add remaining ingredients to make a medium-stiff dough. Let rise twice. Divide dough in half. Roll each piece to form round sheets, about 30 cm (12") in diameter. Cut each into 8 triangles. Roll up from the wide end. Bend the ends slightly inward. Place the rolls on a baking sheet and let rest 10 minutes. Preheat the oven to 225°C (425°F). Bake 10 minutes.

CHRISTMAS BREAD

4 loaves

1 liter (quart) milk
100 g (3 1/2 ounces) fresh yeast
250 g (8 ounces, 1 cup) margarine
250 g (8 ounces, 3 dl, 1 1/4 cups) sugar
1 1/2 teaspoons cardamom
1 1/2 kg (3 pounds, about 2 1/2 liters, 10 1/2 cups) flour
100 g (4 ounces, 3/4 cup) raisins
100 g (3 ounces, 1/2 cup) chopped citron

Heat the milk to lukewarm and stir in the yeast. Melt margarine and sugar together and add with the remaining ingredients to form a medium-stiff dough. Let rise. Divide the dough into 4 parts. Knead and form into loaves. Let rise. Preheat the oven to 225°C (425°F). Bake about 1 hour.

CINNAMON ROLLS

20-24 rolls

3 1/2 dl (1 1/2 cups) full fat milk
50 g (1 3/4 ounces) fresh yeast
125 g (4 ounces, 1/2 cup) butter
500 g (18 ounces, 8 1/4 dl, 3 1/2 cups) flour
90 g (3 ounces, 1 dl, scant 1/2 cup) sugar
1/2 teaspoon cardamom
Filling and topping:
melted butter
1-2 tablespoons sugar
1-2 teaspoons cinnamon
1 egg, beaten
pearl sugar

Heat the milk to lukewarm and stir in the yeast. Melt the butter and add. Combine flour, sugar and cardamom. Add milk mixture and knead to form a firm dough. Let rise. Knead the dough and roll out into a rectangular sheet. Brush with melted butter. Sprinkle with sugar and cinnamon. Roll up. Cut with a sharp knife into 2 cm (1") slices. Place on a greased baking sheet. Brush with beaten egg, then sprinkle with pearl sugar. Let rise 10-15 minutes. Preheat the oven to 225°C (425°F). Bake 10 minutes. Cool on a rack.

TEA CAKE

5 dl (2 cups) full fat milk
50 g (1 3/4 ounces) fresh yeast
150 g (5 ounces, scant 2/3 cup) butter
500 g (18 ounces, 8 1/4 dl, 3 1/2 cups) flour
100 g (3 1/2 ounces, 1 1/4 dl (1/2 cup) sugar
4 drops lemon extract
3/4 dl (1/3 cup) currants
4 tablespoons (1/4 cup) chopped citron
melted butter
sugar
cinnamon
chopped almonds

Heat the milk to lukewarm and stir in the yeast. Melt the butter and add with the flour, sugar, lemon extract, currants and citron. Knead the dough. Roll out the dough on a greased baking sheet to form a round sheet. With a sharp knife, make 2 cm (1") deep cuts 1 cm (1/2") apart all around the edge of the dough. Fold these edges over the middle to make a raised edge. Let rise 45 minutes. Preheat the oven to 200°C (400°F). Brush with melted butter. Sprinkle with sugar, cinnamon and chopped almonds. Bake 30 minutes. Cut into wedges to serve.

WALNUT BREAD

2 loaves

100 g (3 1/2 ounces, 2 1/2 dl, 1 cup) chopped walnuts
100 g (3 1/2 ounces, 1 1/2 dl, 2/3 cup) cracked wheat
100 g (3 1/2 ounces, 2 dl, 3/4 cup) coarse whole rye flour
100 g (3 1/2 ounces, 2 dl, 1 cup) fine whole rye flour
2 dl (scant 1 cup) creme fraiche or whipping cream
5 dl (2 cups) water

Combine all the ingredients and refrigerate overnight. Heat the dough to about 30°C (86°F) and add:
50 g (1 3/4 ounces) fresh yeast
1 teaspoon salt
2 tablespoons walnut oil
800 g (1 3/4 pounds, about 13 1/4 dl, 5 1/2 cups) flour
Knead the dough. Form into 2 loaves. Let rise. Preheat the oven to 200°C (400°F).
Brush the loaves with:
beaten egg white
milk
Bake 1 hour.

Walnut bread

DEEP FRIED CAKES

JELLY DOUGHNUTS

12 doughnuts

5 dl (2 cups) flour
35 g (1 1/4 ounces) fresh yeast
1 tablespoon sugar
1 tablespoon cardamom
3 tablespoons margarine
2 eggs
1 dl (scant 1/2 cup) full fat milk
1 egg white
1 dl (1/2 cup) thick raspberry jam
shortening or oil

Combine flour, yeast, sugar and margarine.

Whisk the eggs into the milk and add. Knead lightly.

Roll the dough out to a 5 mm (1/5") thick sheet. Cut out with a 75 mm (3") round cookie cutter.

Lightly beat the egg white and brush around the edges of half the circles. Place a spoonful of jelly in the center of the circles brushed with egg white. Top with the other circles. Press the edges together.

Let rise 15-20 minutes.

Heat the shortening or oil to 180°C (350°F) and deep fry, a few at a time, about 5 minutes.

Drain on paper towels. Sprinkle with confectioner's sugar.

Illustration: Page 205.

POOR MAN'S COOKIES

50 cookies

5 egg yolks
4 tablespoons (1/4 cup) sugar
1 tablespoons cognac
1/2 teaspoon grated lemon rind
1/2 teaspoon cardamom
4 tablespoons (1/4 cup) whipping cream
3 3/4 dl (1 1/2 cups) flour
shortening or oil

Beat egg yolks, sugar, cognac, lemon rind and cardamom until light and lemon-colored. Whip the cream and add. Sift the flour over the egg yolk mixture and mix well. Form into a ball and cover with plastic wrap. Chill overnight. Work with small amounts of dough. Roll out as thinly as possible on a floured board. Cut into 3 cm (1 1/4") wide strips. Cut on the diagonal into 8 cm (3") long diamonds. Cut a slit in the center of each. Pull one corner through the hole for a twisted cookie. Heat the shortening or oil to 180°C (350°F). Cook several at a time until golden, 2-3 minutes. Drain on paper towels. Illustration: Page 219.

DEER ANTLERS

About 50 cakes

3 eggs
2 dl (3/4 cup) sugar
1 1/2 dl (2/3 cup) whipping cream
1 1/2 dl (2/3 cup) 35% fat sour cream
7 dl (3 cups) flour
2 teaspoons horn salt (or 2 tablespoons baking powder)
1 teaspoon cardamom
2 tablespoons melted butter
shortening or oil

Beat eggs and sugar until light and lemon-colored.
Whip cream and sour cream lightly together.
Sift the dry ingredients. Add alternately with melted butter and both creams to the egg mixture. Mix lightly together. Refrigerate overnight.
Roll the dough into 8 mm (1/3") sausages. Cut into 12 cm (5") lengths. Form into a wreath. Make 2 notches along the edges.
Heat the shortening or oil to 180°C (350°F). Deep fry, a few at a time, until golden, 3-4 minutes.
Illustration: Page 218.

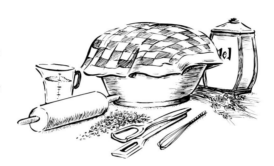

ROSETTES

About 30 rosettes

3 eggs
2 tablespoons sugar
2 1/2 dl (1 cup) full fat milk
3 1/4 dl (1 1/2 cups) flour
2 tablespoons melted butter.

Whisk eggs, sugar and milk lightly together.
Sift over the flour and mix. Add the melted butter, mixing well. Refrigerate 30 minutes.
Heat the shortening or oil to 180°C (350°F). Heat the rosette iron in the fat. Dip the iron into the batter. The batter should just reach the top of the iron, not over it. Deep fry in the fat until just stiff, about 1 minute.
Remove the rosette with a fork and drain on paper towels.
Sprinkle with powdered sugar or fill with cream or jam.

Rosettes

CAKE DOUGHNUTS

About 24 doughnuts

2 eggs
1 3/4 dl (3/4 cup) sugar
1 1/2 dl (2/3 cup) whipping cream
1 1/2 dl (2/3 cup) sour cream
1/2 teaspoon cardamom
1 teaspoon horn salt (or 1 tablespoon baking powder)
7 dl (3 cups) flour
shortening or oil

Beat eggs and sugar until light and lemon-colored.
Whip the cream, adding the sour cream when the cream holds soft peaks.
Stir the cream into the egg yolk mixture. Sift the dry ingredients over and mix. Knead lightly. Refrigerate at least 3 hours before baking.
Roll the dough out to a 1 cm (1/2") thick sheet. Cut out doughnuts with a doughnut cutter.
Heat the shortening or oil to 180°C (350°F). Deep fry, a few at a time, until golden, 3-4 minutes.
Drain on paper towels.

Cake doughnuts

5 1/2 cups) flour
1 teaspoon cardamom
600 g (1 1/3 pounds, 2 1/3 cups) butter

Whisk lightly together egg yolks, sugar and cream. Sift the flour and add.
Knead in the butter. Cover the dough with plastic wrap and refrigerate at least 2 hours. Roll out the dough in a cool room. Use small pieces. Roll out to thin sheets. Make cardboard templates the size of the goro iron. Cut out cookies using the templates as guides.
Bake on an ungreased "goro" iron.

CONES

About 18 cookies

2 eggs
1 1/2 dl (2/3 cup) sugar
1 1/2 dl (2/3 cup) flour
1 1/4 dl (1/2 cup) potato starch
125 g (4 1/2 ounces, 1/2 cup) butter
4 tablespoons (1/4 cup) water
1/4 teaspoon almond extract
butter

Beat eggs and sugar until light and lemon-colored.
Combine flour and starch and carefully stir into the egg mixture.
Melt the butter and add with the water and extract.
Refrigerate 30 minutes.
Heat a "krumkake" iron. Grease lightly for the first cookie only.
Bake until golden, then form into cones around a wooden cone shape or drape over cups to form cookie bowls.
Serve with ice cream or fruit or alone.

COOKIES
BAKED IN IRONS

WAFERS

About 50 cookies

2 dl (3/4 cup) whipping cream
4 dl (1 1/2 cups) full fat milk
4 dl (1 3/4 cups) flour

Combine cream and milk. Sift over the flour and combine. Refrigerate at least 30 minutes. Bake on a "krumkake" iron. To serve, spread with butter and sprinkle with sugar.

GORO

About 150 cookies

3 egg yolks
2 1/4 dl (1 cup) sugar
2 1/2 dl (1 cup) whipping cream
about 800 g (1 3/4 pounds, 13 1/4 dl,

Wafers and cones are thin crackerlike cookies baked in irons. Serve with sour cream or whipped cream for dessert or with coffee.

PATTERNED COOKIES

1 liter (quart) 35% fat sour cream
1 liter (quart) full fat milk
1 liter (quart) barley flour

A pastry scraper with a comb edge is needed for these cookies.

Combine sour cream and milk. Add barley flour. The batter should be thick enough for the combing effect to remain.

Place a spoonful of batter on a lefse (see those pages for recipes) and spread it to the edges. Make a pattern with the comb.

Fry on a griddle until golden.

WAFFLES

1. Ordinary
About 24 waffles

500 g (18 ounces, 8 1/4 dl, 3 1/2 cups) flour
100-150 g (3-5 ounces, 1 1/4 - 1 1/2 dl, 1/2-3/4 cup) sugar
1 teaspoon cardamom
3 eggs
1 liter (quart) full fat milk
250 g (8 ounces, 1 cup) margarine
2 1/2 (1 cup) whipping cream

Whisk flour, sugar, cardamom, eggs and milk until smooth. Melt margarine and add with the cream. Strain. Refrigerate 1 hour.

Bake in a waffle iron. Serve waffles with butter and jam.

2. Sour cream
About 12 waffles

4 dl (1 2/3 cups) whipping cream
1 dl (scant 1/2 cup) 35% fat sour cream
3 1/2 dl (1 1/2 cups) flour
4 tablespoons (1/4 cup) water
butter

Whip the two creams together. The mixture becomes very then just before it peaks. Sift the flour, add the water and some of the cream. Mix well. Carefully mix in remaining cream. Heat the waffle iron and grease with butter. Cook waffles until golden. Cool on a rack. Serve with butter and jam or cheese.

Waffles

CHOUX PASTRY

CREAM PUFFS

12 puffs

100 g (3 1/2 ounces, scant 1/2 cup)
margarine
2 1/2 dl (1 cup) water
2 1/2 dl (1 cup) flour
4 medium eggs

Preheat the oven to 220°C (425°F).
Bring margarine and water to a boil.
Remove from the heat and add the flour. Return to a boil, stirring until the dough forms a ball. Cool slightly.
Beat in the eggs, one at a time. The dough should be stiff enough to keep its shape without spreading.
Spoon into a pastry tube with a star tip. Pipe mounds onto a greased oven sheet.
Bake 20-30 minutes. Cool.
Cut off the tops of the puffs. Fill with whipped cream flavored with sugar and vanilla. Replace the top. Sprinkle with confectioner's sugar just before serving.

CREAM PUFF PRETZEL

cream puff dough
whipped cream
powdered sugar icing

Follow the recipe for cream puffs, but do not spoon the dough into a pastry tube. Spoon onto the greased oven sheet in the shape of a large pretzel.
Bake 30 minutes. Cool.
Divide in half horizontally and fill with whipped cream flavored with sugar and vanilla. Replace the top half
Glaze with a mixture of confectioner's sugar stirred into a little cream and flavored with rum extract.

LEFSE

Lefse for special occasions are made of fine rye flour, while those used every day are made from coarser flour. Potatoes are used in certain recipes. These should be boiled and then ground and mixed with milk and flour to make a stiff dough.
Lefse dough should be kept in a cold place and then divided into pieces which are rolled out into thin sheets. These are cooked on a griddle on both sides.
Lefse are stored in stacks under a light weight. Long ago, all dry lefse were softened with a damp towel before they were spread or filled.

ASKØY LEFSE

1 egg
1 1/2 dl (2/3 cup) sugar
1 1/2 dl (2/3 cup) melted butter
1 1/2 dl (2/3 cup) buttermilk
1 1/2 dl (2/3 cup) potato starch
about 3 1/2 dl (1 1/2 cups) flour
1/2-3/4 teaspoon baking powder
1/2-3/4 teaspoon horn salt (or 1 1/2-2
tablespoons baking powder)

Lightly beat the egg, add sugar, melted butter and milk. Sift the dry ingredients and add. The dough should be so loose that it is almost a thick batter.
Refrigerate 30 minutes to stiffen.
The size of the lefse depends upon whether it will be cooked in a pan or on a griddle. Roll out on a floured board.
Brush off extra flour before cooking.
Cook on both sides over low heat until golden with brown flecks.
Cool before placing in a towel.
Spread cold lefse with butter and sugar or butter and cheese. Fold into a rectangle.

WEDDING LEFSE

400 g (14 ounces, 8 dl, 3 1/3 cups)
fine whole rye flour
400 g (14 ounces, 6 3/4 dl, 2 3/4 cups)
flour
1 teaspoon baking soda
125 g (4 ounces, 1/2 cup) butter
5 dl (2 cups) full fat milk
4-5 dl (1 2/3 - 2 cups) buttermilk
Topping:
2 1/2 dl (1 cups) full fat milk
3/4 dl (1/3 cup) flour
1 tablespoon potato starch
1 small egg
1/4 teaspoon salt
Filling:
1 1/2 dl, 2/3 cup) sugar
2 1/2 dl (1 cup) full fat milk
3 tablespoons dark syrup
60 g (2 ounces) brown goat cheese or
3 tablespoons cajeta
1/2 dl (3 1/2 tablespoons) full fat milk
1 tablespoon flour
1 small egg

Sift flours and soda together and crumble in the butter.
Add both milks and knead to make a stiff dough.
Cover and refrigerate 1 hour.
Whisk together all ingredients for the topping.
Roll the dough into a sausage and cut into pieces of equal size.
Knead the dough until smooth, then roll out into not-too-thin sheets.
Cook on a griddle over low heat on one side only. Remove and let cool.
Brush topping on the uncooked side.
Return the lefse to the griddle, cooked side down. Cook over low heat until completely dry.
Stack the cooked sheets, using a pot lid as a weight.
Before using, sprinkle with water on the dry side.
Filling:
Brown half the sugar until light golden. Cool slightly. Heat the milk and add gradually. Add remaining sugar, syrup and cheese, stirring often. Whisk together milk, flour and egg. Stir into the mixture. Simmer 5 minutes to thicken. Cool.
Spread the lefse with butter and top with filling. Top with another lefse. Cut into triangles and roll up, starting with the large end, like crescents.

FJALER LEFSE

6 eggs
6 tablespoons sugar
1 1/4 teaspoon salt
2 1/2 dl (1 cup) milk
3 tablespoons butter, melted
6 dl (2 1/2 cups) flour

Whisk together eggs, sugar and salt. Add milk and melted butter. Knead in the flour.
Cover and refrigerate 30 minutes. Divide into pieces of equal size. Roll out to thin sheets.
Cook on a griddle on both sides.

OLD-FASHIONED LEFSE

5 dl (2 cups) full fat milk
3-4 teaspoons hornsalt (or 3-4 table-spoons baking powder)
3 dl (1 1/4 cups) 35% fat sour cream
2-3 dl (3/4 - 1 1/4 cups) buttermilk
about 1 kg (2 1/4 pounds, 17 dl, 7 cups) flour

Heat the milk. Add hornsalt, sour cream and buttermilk.
Add flour and mix to a stiff dough.
Cover and refrigerate 2 hours. Divide into 25 pieces of equal size. Roll out to thin sheets.
Cook on a griddle on both sides.
Stack the cooked sheets and place under a weight.
To serve, soften in a damp cloth. Spread with butter, sprinkle with sugar, cinnamon and brown goat cheese. Fold into a rectangle.
Note: These lefse were served on special occasions, such as Christmas, Easter and Whitsuntide.

GLAZED LEFSE

500 g (18 ounces, about 3 medium) potatoes
100 g (3 1/2 ounces, scant 1/2 cup) margarine
2 dl (3/4 cup) sugar
1 teaspoon salt
5 dl (2 cups) full fat milk
about 300 g, (10 1/2 ounces, 5 1/2 dl, 2 1/4 cups) barley flour

about 350 g (13 ounces, 6 dl, 2 1/3 cups) flour
Glaze:
5 dl (2 cups) full fat milk
2 dl (3/4 dl) sugar
2 eggs
1/2 teaspoon cardamom

Peel and slice the potatoes. Cook until tender. Mash.
Add margarine, sugar, salt and milk to the warm potatoes.
Knead in the flour. Divide the dough into pieces of equal size. Roll out to thin sheets. Cook on one side only on a griddle.
Combine all the ingredients for the glaze. Spread over the lefse, then cook until set.
To serve, spread with butter and sprinkle with sugar. Fold over and cut into serving pieces.

SALTEN GLAZED LEFSE

190 g (7 ounces, 3/4 cup + 2 table-spoons) butter
1 - 1 1/4 kg (2 1/4 - 2 1/2 pounds, 2 - 2 1/2 liters, 8 1/3 - 10 cups) fine whole rye flour
2 teaspoons hornsalt (or 2 tablespoons baking powder)
6 dl (2 1/2 cups) lukewarm water (35°C, 95°F).
2 dl (3/4 cup) light corn or sugar syrup
flour for rolling out
Topping:
10 eggs
4 dl (1 2/3 cups) sugar
1 1/2 liters (quarts) full fat milk
1/4-1/2 teaspoon hornsalt (or 3/4 - 1 1/2 teaspoons baking powder)
about 550 g (9 dl, 4 cups) flour

Crumble butter into the flour and horn-salt. Add water and syrup. Knead well on a floured board to make a stiff, short dough.
Divide into 45-50 g (1 3/4 ounce) pieces.
Make a 30 cm (14") cardboard circle to use as a template.
Roll out the dough into sheets using the template on a floured board. Use a rolling pin with rills. Cut along the edges.

Brush off excess flour.
Keep the sheets cold. When all are rolled out, turn the pile. The side with the rolling pin pattern is the "face."
Cook, face down, on a griddle. When all the sheets are cooked, preheat the oven to 250°C (450°F).
Whisk eggs and sugar until light and lemon-colored. Stir in the remaining ingredients to make a thick batter.
Spread topping on the sheets with a rubber spatula. Then use a spreading comb.
Bake 2-3 minutes.
Store in stacks in a dry place.
To serve, spread with butter, then sprinkle with sugar and cinnamon. Cut into diamonds or triangles and serve with gomme.

WHITE LEFSE FROM NORDLAND

1 kg (2 1/4 pounds, 2 - 2 1/2 liters, 8 1/3 - 10 cups) fine whole rye flour
1 tablespoon dark syrup
100 g (3 1/2 ounces, scant 1/2 cup) butter
1 teaspoon hornsalt (or 1 tablespoon baking powder)
about 1 dl (1/3 cup) water
Topping:
250 g (5 dl, 2 cups) rye flour
500 g (6 1/4 dl, 2 1/2 cups) potato starch
1 1/2 dl (2/3 cup) sugar
1 teaspoon vinegar
5 dl (2 cups) water

Combine all ingredients to make a stiff dough.
Divide into pieces of equal size and roll out to thin sheets.
Cook on one side only, then place under a weight.
Combine all ingredients for the topping. Spoon onto the uncooked side of the lefse. Spread over the entire sheet with a flat hand. It should be white and shiny.
Stack the lefse on a plate with white side up. Dry in an 80°C (175°F) oven.
To serve, soften on the dark side with lukewarm water. Spread with butter and sprinkle with sugar. Fold with the white side out.

"Lefser" come in many varieties, both thick and thin and in different shapes.

LEFSE

1 kg (1 3/4 liters, 7 cups) flour
4 teaspoons hornsalt (or 4 tablespoons,
1/4 cup) baking powder
1 dl (scant 1/2 cup) 35% fat sour cream
2 tablespoons sugar
7 1/2 dl (3 cups) buttermilk
Filling:
1 kg (2 1/4 pounds, 4 1/2 cups) butter
6 dl (2 1/2 cups) sour cream
650 g (7 1/2 dl, 3 1/4 cups) sugar
vanilla sugar
cinnamon

Combine all ingredients and knead
lightly to make a loose dough.
Shape the dough into a long sausage.
Cut into pieces of equal size. Roll out
into thin sheets.
Cook on one side on a griddle, but do
not allow to become hard.
Wrap the baked lefse in a cloth.
All the ingredients for the filling should
be at room temperature. Combine and
beat until smooth. Flavor with vanilla
sugar and cinnamon. Spread on the
cold lefse.

LEFSE FROM TROMS

8 dl (3 1/3 cups) full fat milk
2 dl (3/4 cup) sugar
2 dl (3/4 cup) semolina (cream of
wheat)
3 dl (1 1/4 cups) whipping cream
850 g (14 dl, 6 cups) flour
4 teaspoons horn salt (or 4 tablespoons,
1/4 cup baking powder)

Combine milk, sugar, semolina and
cream and cook a thick porridge, about
15 minutes. Refrigerate overnight.
Add remaining ingredients and knead
to make a firm dough.
Divide into 20 pieces of equal size. Roll
out to thin sheets. Cook on a griddle on
both sides.
Spread with sugar and sprinkle with
sugar or grated brown goat cheese (Ski
Queen).

LEFSEKLING

1 liter (quart) full fat milk
250 g (8 ounces, 1 cup) butter
1 kg (2 1/4 pounds, 16 3/4 dl, 7 cups)
flour
4 tablespoons (1/4 cup) 35% fat sour
cream
1 egg yolk

Bring the milk to a boil. Add the butter.
When the butter is melted, pour over
the flour.
Add sour cream and egg and mix well.
Cover and refrigerate overnight.
Divide the dough into pieces of equal
size. Roll out into thin sheets and cook
on a griddle on both sides.
When cold, spread with butter and
sprinkle with sugar. Cut into diamonds.

LEFSEKLING FROM TELEMARK

5 dl (2 cups) full fat milk
3 tablespoons margarine
500 g (8 1/4 dl, 3 1/2 cups) flour
flour

Bring milk and margarine to a boil.
Pour over the flour. Stir to make a thick
porridge.
Cover and refrigerate overnight.
Knead in flour to make a pliable dough.
Divide the dough into pieces of equal
size. Roll out into thin sheets and cook
on a griddle, rolled side down.
Immediately as the lefse are placed on
the griddle, sprinkle with lukewarm
water.
Cook until light brown on both sides
with small golden bubbles and crisp.
Store in a dark, cool place. These keep
well.
Before serving, soften in a damp cloth.
Spread with butter and sprinkle with
sugar if served with coffee. Use butter
only if served with fish.

LILEMS

200 g (7 ounces, scant 1 cup)
margarine
1 liter (quart) buttermilk
2 dl (3/4 cup) sugar
5 teaspoons baking powder

4 teaspoons horn salt (or 4 tablespoons,
1/4 cup baking powder)
1 kg (2 1/4 pounds, 16 3/4 dl, 7 cups)
flour
Filling:
500 g (18 ounces, 2 1/4 cups) butter
6 dl (2 1/2 cups) sugar

Melt the margarine and add the buttermilk.
Stir in the sugar. Sift the baking powder
and horn salt with part of the flour and
stir into the margarine mixture.
Add remaining flour to make a pliable,
easy-to-roll dough.
Divide the dough into pieces of equal
size and roll out into thin sheets.
Cook on a griddle until golden on both
sides.
For the filling, beat butter and sugar
until light and fluffy. Dip the sheet into
the mixture, then fold in half and cut
into diamonds.

MØSBRØMLEFSE WITH DIP

This lefse is served mostly during the
summer.

2 tablespoons butter
2 tablespoons light corn or sugar syrup
1 liter (quart) buttermilk
2 tablespoons sugar
1 tablespoon hornsalt (or 3 tablespoons
baking powder)
1 kg (2 1/4 pounds, 16 3/4 dl, 7 cups)
flour
250 g (9 ounces, 4 1/4 dl, 1 3/4 cups)
barley flour
250 g (9 ounces, 4 1/4 dl, 1 3/4 cups)
fine whole wheat flour
Dip:
500 g (18 ounces) grated brown goat
cheese (Ski Queen)
5 dl (2 cups) full fat milk
1-2 dl (2/3 cup) buttermilk
flour
light sugar or corn syrup
sour cream
melted butter

Melt the butter and add the syrup. Pour
over the milk.
Combine the dry ingredients and add
the liquid. Divide the dough into 40

pieces of equal size. Roll out to thin sheets immediately. Cook on 1 side only on a griddle over high heat.

Stack, cover with a cloth and press with a weight. Cool.

Combine cheese and both milk. Thicken with flour and sweeten with syrup. Place the lefse on the griddle. Spread with the dip. Top with sour cream and melted butter in the center.

Fold over all the sides to partially cover the center.

LEFSE FROM NORDLAND

1 liter (quart) buttermilk
100 g (3 1/2 ounces, scant 1/2 cup) margarine
1 3/4 dl (3/4 cup) light corn or sugar syrup
2 dl (3/4 cup) sugar
4 teaspoons hornsalt (or 4 tablespoons, 1/4 cup baking powder)
flour

Combine all ingredients, adding enough flour to make a pliable dough. Cover and refrigerate 30 minutes.

Preheat the oven to 250°C (450°F).

Divide the dough into pieces of equal size and roll out to thin sheets.

Bake 5-10 minutes in the oven.

To serve, spread with butter and sprinkle with sugar and cinnamon.

Store cold, preferably frozen.

LEFSE FROM NUMEDAL

2 liters (quarts) full fat milk
250 g (9 ounces, 1 1/4 cups) unsalted butter
250 g (9 ounces, 1 cup) lard
2 kg (33 1/2 dl, 14 cups) flour
2 tablespoons sour cream
2 egg yolks

Bring milk, butter and lard to a boil. Add remaining ingredients and knead while still warm.

Divide into pieces of equal size and roll out into thin sheets.

Stack with parchment paper in between until all are rolled out. Cook on a hot griddle, floured side down.

Store the cold lefse in a cloth to retain

Baking lefse

moisture. To serve, spread with butter on the floured side. Fold double, then fold again. Store cold.

POTATO LEFSE

1 kg (2 1/4 pounds, about 5 large) potatoes
6-700 g (1 2/3 pounds, 10 - 11 dl, 4-5 cups) flour

Boil the potatoes in their skins. Cool, then peel and grind.

Knead in the flour until the dough is stiff enough to roll out.

Divide the dough into pieces of equal size. Roll out to thin sheets. Cook on 1 side on a griddle.

Brush the uncooked side with water before the lefse is turned. Cook until dotted with brown on both sides.

To serve, sprinkle with water and wrap in a cloth until soft.

Spread with soft butter. Sprinkle with sugar or confectioner's sugar.

Stack and cut into pieces.

KLING FROM SIGDAL

600 g (1 1/3 pounds, 2 1/2 cups) butter
about 900 g (15 dl, 6 1/4 cups) flour
3 liters (quarts) full fat milk
6 dl (2 1/2 cups) 35% fat sour cream
6 egg yolks
4 egg whites
about 500 g (8 1/4 dl, 3 1/2 cups) flour
flour
Buttering:
500 g (18 ounces, 2 1/4 cups) butter, at room temperature
500 g (18 ounces, 2 1/4 cups) margarine, at room temperature
1 kg (2 1/4 pounds, 11 3/4 dl, 5 cups) sugar

Melt the butter in a big pot. Stir in the first amount of flour.

Heat the milk to 37°C (98°F). Gradually stir the warm milk into the butter-flour mixture to make a lumpfree batter. Simmer 3-4 minutes, stirring constantly, to make a thick porridge.

Transfer to a bowl. Cool.

Add sour cream, egg yolks and egg whites. Sprinkle with flour, cover with plastic wrap and a cloth. Refrigerate overnight. Knead in the second amount of flour. The dough should be pliable and easy to roll out.

Divide the dough into two equal parts. Refrigerate one piece of dough. Roll the other into a sausage.

Cut the dough sausage into 100 g (3 1/2 ounce) pieces. Press the pieces flat and round, then let rest on a floured board 60-90 minutes before rolling out. Cover the baking surface first with a flannel sheet, then with a cotton sheet. Sprinkle a generous amount of flour on the baking table. Roll the dough out to thin sheets about 50 cm (20") in diameter. Roll up on thin baking wands (rather like long chopsticks) and roll onto the griddle. Cool until golden on both sides over high heat, but do not allow to burn. When done, wrap first in a cotton sheet, then in a flannel sheet. Cover with plastic wrap to keep the kling soft. They should be completely covered. Beat butter and margarine until fluffy. Butter half of each kling. Sprinkle with sugar, then fold over the other half. Cut the edges. Divide each into 4 wedges. Kling freeze well. Pack airtight. Note: Kling are served with coffee on special occasions, such as Christmas, Easter, Whitsuntide, christenings, confirmations, weddings and funeral. Kling also is served with fermented fish or anchovies at Christmas breakfast.

SNEKA LEFSE

about 300 g (10 ounces, 3 medium) cold, boiled potatoes
about 600 g (10 dl, 4 1/4 cups) flour (1/3 of this can be rye flour)
beestings

Grind the potatoes and knead in the flour to make a soft dough. Divide the dough into pieces of equal size and roll out. Cook carefully. They should remain soft. Stack. Spoon some beestings on the soft lefse. Rub over the surface in a circular movement with a light hand. Return to the griddle and cook on the dry side. To serve, moisten the dry side with water. Spread with butter and sprinkle with sugar.

STRILE LEFSE

7 dl (3 cups) full fat milk
100 g (3 1/2 ounces, scant 1/2 cup) margarine
1 teaspoon salt
1 tablespoon sugar
1 kg (16 3/4 dl, 7 cups) flour
1 tablespoon ground anise

Bring the milk to a boil and add margarine, salt and sugar.

Combine flour and anise. Pour over the boiling milk mixture. Mix well. Cool about 1 hour. The dough should be stiff. Divide the dough into pieces of equal size and roll out into thin sheets. Place 1 sheet on the griddle. When it begins to steam, place another sheet on top. Turn and remove the first sheet. Packed the cooked lefse in a cloth. To serve, spread with butter and sprinkle with sugar or top with cheese. Note: These used to be serve with poached fish, but today, they are served with coffee.

THICK LEFSE

6 dl (2 1/2 cups) buttermilk
4 dl (1 2/3 cups) sugar
200 g (7 ounces, 2 dl, 3/4 cup) butter, melted
2 tablespoons hornsalt (or 6 tablespoons baking powder)
flour

Combine all ingredients with enough flour to make a stiff dough. Divide into pieces of equal size and roll out to 5 mm (1/5") thick sheets. Cut out, using a dish as a guide.

Cook on a grill or in a skillet on both sides. Sandwich 2 lefse with butter beaten with sugar. Cut into wedges.

VIKNA LEFSE

125 g (4 ounces, 1/2 cup) margarine
2 tablespoons light corn or sugar syrup
1 1/2 liters (quarts) buttermilk
4 tablespoons (1/4 cup) hornsalt (or 3/4 cup baking powder)
2 kg (33 dl, 14 cups) flour
100 g (3 1/2 ounces, 2 dl, 3/4 cup) fine whole rye flour

Melt margarine, add syrup and heat almost to a boil. Add 5 dl (2 cups) buttermilk. Stir in hornsalt and remaining milk. Combine the two flours. Stir into the milk mixture. Work the dough as little as possible.

Divide the dough into 40 pieces of equal size. Roll out and cook on a griddle on both sides, as described in previous recipes.

PANCAKES

BUTTERMILK PANCAKES

Serves 4

3 eggs
3 dl (1 1/4 cups) buttermilk
3/4 dl (1/3 cup) sugar
1 1/2 teaspoons baking soda
4 1/2 dl (2 cups) flour
butter

Whisk together eggs and milk. Add the dry ingredients and mix until smooth. Refrigerate 30 minutes.

Fry in a small amount of butter on a griddle or in a skillet. Spoon on batter. Spread out with a spoon and cook on both sides over medium heat. The pancakes should be thin.

Serve with butter, sugar and jam or sour cream.

PANCAKES

120 g (4 ounces, 1/2 cup) margarine
5 eggs
2 liters (quarts) full fat milk
2 teaspoons salt
650 g (about 1 1/2 pounds, 11 dl, 4 1/2 cups) flour
margarine

Melt the margarine and combine with the other ingredients. Refrigerate 30 minutes. Fry in a small amount of butter on a griddle or in a skillet. Make thin pancakes. Serve with jam, butter or syrup.

POTATO CAKES

1 kg (2 1/4 pounds, about 5 large) potatoes
250 g (9 ounces, about 2 medium) boiled potatoes
2 dl (3/4 cup) buttermilk
salt
butter

Peel and grate the raw potatoes, and mash the boiled potatoes. Add the milk and season with salt. Fry small flat cakes in butter on a griddle or in a non-stick skillet until golden on both sides. Spread the cakes with butter and sugar and roll up.

SOUR CREAM CAKES

800 g (1 3/4 pounds, 13 1/4 dl, 5 1/2 cups) flour
500 g (\8 ounces, 2 1/4 cups) butter
5 dl (2 cups) 35% fat sour cream
2 tablespoons sugar
sugar
cinnamon

Crumble flour and butter together. Add the remaining ingredients and mix to make a loose dough.
Roll the dough out into small thin sheets. Cook on a dry griddle. Sprinkle the uncooked side with sugar and cinnamon, then turn.
Serve with sugar and sour cream.

RAISED PANCAKES

175 g (6 ounces, 3/4 cup) butter
2 1/4 dl (1 cup) sugar
4 eggs
1 liter (quart) buttermilk
about 600 g (1 1/3 pounds, 10 dl, 4 1/4 cups) flour
1 teaspoon baking soda

2 teaspoons hornsalt (or 2 tablespoons baking powder)
1 teaspoon vanilla sugar (1/2 teaspoon extract)
butter

Melt the butter, add sugar and beat in the eggs and milk. Combine the dry ingredients and add, mixing well. Refrigerate 30 minutes. Fry in a small amount of butter on a griddle. Serve with butter and sugar.

COOKIES

BERLIN WREATHS

2 hard-cooked egg yolks
2 raw egg yolks
1 dl (scant 1/2 cup) sugar
250 g (8 ounces, 1 cup) butter
about 350 g (10 ounces, 5 3/4 dl, 2 1/2 cups) flour
1 egg white, lightly beaten
pearl sugar

Preheat the oven to 190°C (375°F).

Buttermilk pancakes, pancakes, potato cakes and raised pancakes are served with coffee throughout Norway. The latter are served on all ferry boats in western Norway.

Mash cooked and raw egg yolks together. Add sugar and beat until light and lemon-colored. Add butter and flour alternately. The dough should not be too stiff. Roll the dough into 8 mm (1/3") thick sausages. Cut into 12 cm (5") lengths and form into wreaths. Place on a greased baking sheet. Brush with beaten egg white and sprinkle with pearl sugar. Bake about 10 minutes. Makes about 70 cookies.

COOKIE STACKS

2 eggs
250 g (3 dl, 1 1/4 cups) sugar
2 tablespoons whipping cream
250 g (8 ounces, 1 cup) unsalted margarine
about 500 g (8 1/4 dl, 3 1/2 cups) flour
3 egg whites
4 tablespoons (1/4 cup) pearl sugar
125 g (3 dl, 1 1/4 cups) ground blanched almonds

Beat eggs and sugar until light and lemon-colored. Whip the cream. Melt the margarine and add alternately with the flour and cream. Mix lightly together. Cover and refrigerate overnight. Preheat the oven to 180°C (350°F). Lightly beat the egg whites. Stir in sugar and almonds. Roll out the dough into a thin, rectangular sheet. Cut out 3 1/2x23 cm (1 1/2x9") strips. Place on a greased baking sheet. Bake 10 minutes. Cool on a rack. Spoon a thin stripe of almond mixture along the middle of each cookie. Return to the oven, but leave the door open. Cook only until the almond mixture solidifies. It should still be white. Form a tower by stacking 2 cookies in 1 direction, then 2 in the other.

OAT CRACKERS

250 g (8 ounces, 1 cup) margarine
250 g (9 ounces, 7 dl, 3 cups) oatmeal
250 g (9 ounces, 4 1/4 dl, 1 3/4 cups) flour
150 g (5 ounces, 1 3/4 dl, 3/4 cup) sugar

1 1/2 dl (2/3 cup) full fat milk
2 teaspoons hornsalt (or 2 tablespoons baking powder)

Melt the margarine and add the remaining ingredients. Chill at least 1 hour. Preheat the oven to 190°C (375°F). Roll out into a thin sheet and cut out 3" round crackers. Bake until golden, about 10 minutes. Makes 60-70 crackers.

COCONUT MACAROONS

5 eggs
250 g (9 ounces, 3 dl, 1 1/4 cups) sugar
500 g (18 ounces, about 14 dl, 6 cups) flaked coconut
2 tablespoons flour
1 tablespoon melted butter

Preheat the oven to 190°C (375°F). Beat eggs and sugar until light and lemon-colored. Carefully add remaining ingredients. Form small mounds (slightly smaller than a walnut) with two teaspoons and place on a greased

Tiny almond pies and deer authers.

baking sheet. Bake 8-10 minutes. Makes about 60 cookies.

TINY ALMOND PIES

150 g (5 ounces, scant 2/3 cup)
unsalted margarine
2 1/2 dl (1 cup) flour, sifted
1 egg yolk
1/2 dl (3 1/2 tablespoons) cold water
1 tablespoon cognac
Filling:
3 dl (1 1/4 cups) ground almonds
2 1/2 dl (1 cup) sifted confectioner's
sugar
3 egg whites, lightly beaten

Divide the margarine into 3 pieces of equal size. Crumble one piece into the flour. Whisk the egg yolk into the water and add. Knead lightly and form into a square. Wrap in plastic and refrigerate 30 minutes.

Let the remaining margarine rest at room temperature.

Sprinkle the baking surface with flour. Roll the dough out into a thin rectangular. Spread half the remaining margarine over 2/3 of the dough. Fold over the plain section, then fold over the other section with margarine, like a business letter. This forms a rectangle with 3 layers of dough and 2 of margarine. Roll into a rectangle and fold into thirds again. Refrigerate 30 minutes.

Roll out the dough and spread with the remaining margarine. Fold into thirds, roll out again and fold into thirds. Refrigerate the dough 30 minutes.

Preheat the oven to 200°C (400°F). Grease "sandkake" (small fluted pie) tins. Roll the dough out into a 2 mm thin sheet. Cut into circles slightly larger than the diameter of the tins. Press into the tins. For the filling, combine almonds with powdered sugar and egg whites. Place about 1 1/2 teaspoons of filling in each form.

Cut out 8 mm (1/3") strips of dough and arrange in an "x" over the filling. Tuck the ends between the filling and the crust. Bake on a baking sheet on the lowest oven shelf about 20 minutes. Makes 12-14 cakes.

Serina cakes, peppernuts, poor man's cookies and coconut macaroons.

PEPPERNUTS

2 1/2 dl (1 cup) light corn or sugar
syrup
2 dl (scant 1 cup) sugar
65 g (2 ounces, 4 tablespoons) butter
1/2 dl (3 tablespoons) whipping cream
1 teaspoon ground star anise
1/2 teaspoon pepper
3/4 teaspoon baking soda
about 500 g (8 1/4 dl, 3 1/2 cups) flour

Bring syrup, sugar, butter and cream to a boil. Combine the dry ingredients and add, mixing well. Refrigerate overnight. Preheat the oven to 200°C (400°F). Make small, round nuts and place on a greased baking sheet. Bake 8 minutes. Makes about 120 cookies.

SAND CAKES

125 g (4 1/2 ounces, 1/2 cup)
margarine
125 g (4 1/2 ounces, 1/2 cup) butter
125 g (1 1/2 dl, 2/3 cup) sugar
1 egg
400 g (about 6 3/4 dl, 2 3/4 cups) flour
50 g (1 1/4 dl, 1/2 cup) ground
almonds

Beat margarine, butter and sugar until light and fluffy. Add egg, mixing well. Stir in flour and almonds. Cover and refrigerate 1 hour. Preheat the oven to 190°C (375°F). Grease "sandkake" (small fluted pie) tins. Divide the dough into pieces and press into the greased tins. Make as thin as possible. Bake on a baking sheet until golden, 10-12 minutes. Cool slightly, then remove from the tins. Cool on a rack. Makes about 60 cookies.

SERINA CAKES

150 g (5 ounces, scant 2/3 cup)
margarine
1 1/2 dl (2/3 cup) sugar
1 egg
1 teaspoon vanilla sugar (1/2 teaspoon
extract)
1/4 teaspoon hornsalt (or 3/4 teaspoon
baking powder)
3 1/4 dl (1 1/2 cups) flour
1 egg or egg white, lightly beaten
chopped blanched almonds

Beat the margarine with the sugar until light and fluffy. Beat in the egg. Sift over the dry ingredients and mix well. Cover and refrigerate the dough overnight.

Preheat the oven to 190° C (375° F).
Form the dough into a sausage. Cut
into equal parts. Form each into 3 cm (1
1/4") balls and place on a greased baking sheet. Press down with a fork.
Brush with beaten egg or egg white
and sprinkle with almonds.
Bake until golden, about 10 minutes.
Makes about 70 cookies.

GINGERSNAPS

2 dl (3/4 cup) sugar
2 dl (1 cup) dark corn or sugar syrup
200 g (2 dl, 3/4 cup) margarine,
melted
1 dl (scant 1/2 cup) cold water
about 500 g (8 1/4 dl, 3 1/2 cups) flour
1 teaspoon baking soda
1 1/2 teaspoons ground ginger
1 teaspoon cinnamon
1/2 teaspoon ground cloves
1/2 teaspoon grated nutmeg
about 2 dl (3/4 cup) blanched almonds

Mix sugar, syrup, margarine and water
until smooth. Combine dry ingredients
and add, mixing well. The dough should
be soft. Refrigerate overnight. Preheat
the oven to 190° C (375° F). Using small
amounts of dough, roll out to thin
sheets. Cut into diamonds with a pastry
wheel. Place an almond, split lengthwise, in the center of each cookie. Bake
about 8 minutes.

*Christmas coffee with cakes: goro, Berlin
wreaths, gingersnaps, cookie stacks, sand
cakes, cookie stacks and Christmas cake.*

INDEX

BIBLIOGRAPHY

Recipes have been collected by members of the Association of Norwegian Chefs throughout the country.

Alm, Jens M., DEN NORSKE DRAM, Chr. Schibsted Forlag, 1985.

Ambjørgrud, O., Børke, I., Jansen, J. and Moe, E., NORSK MAT, J.W. Cappelens Forlag, 1965.

Borgen, Annemarta, FISK FRA KJØKKENET PÅ KNATTEN, Gyldendal, 1982.

Bø, Olav, HØGTIDER OG MINNEDAGER

Dass, Petter, NORDLANDS TROMPET, Fabritius Forlag, 1962.

Erken, Henriette Schønberg, STOR KOKEBOK, Aschehoug, 1980 (facsimile from 1914).

Gjestvang, Kari and others, HÅRDASKOST OG HÆRDASMAT, Hedemark Bondekvinnelag, 1980.

Innli, Kjell E., FRA BESTEMORS KJØKKEN, KOM Forlag, 1991.

Innli, Kjell E. and Helmersen, Helge, YRKESLÆRE I KJØKKEN, Yrkeslitteratur, 1990.

Kaspersen, MATSKATTER FRA NORD-NORGE.J.W. Cappelens Forlag, 1986.

Nichtawitz, Walter, GOD MAT FRA SJØEN, Gyldendal, 1984.

NORGES HISTORIE, Cappelens Forlag, 1976.

NORSK MAT, TRADISJONER OG GAMLE MATRETTER, Landbruksforlaget, 1992.

Notaker, Henry, ALLE TIDERS KOKEBØKER, Aschehoug, 1989.

Visted and Stigum, VÅR GAMLE BONDEKULTUR I and II.

PHOTOGRAPHS:

In addition to the food photographs, the main photographers also have taken the following pictures:

Per Eide: cover, p. 3, 7, 10, 11, 13, 29, 42, 50, 53 below, 96, 103, 116, 170 below, 215.

Bengt Wilson: p. 6, 16 small, 30, 43, 172, 203, back cover.

OTHER PHOTOGRAPHERS:

Norsk Folkemuseum: p. 12 (Wilse), 14, 15 (Wilse), 21, 22 (Wilse), 23 (Wilse), 24, 25 above (Wilse), 33 above (Wilse), 36, 38, 39, 44, 53 above, 224.

Arnulf Husmo, Husmofoto: p. 16 large, 51, 88, 188.

Kristian Hilsen, Husmofoto: p. 25 below, 26 below, 92, 120.

Steve Halsetrønning, Samfoto: p. 9 and endpapers

Pål Hermansen, Samfoto: p. 18, 19, 78.

Asle Hjellbrekke, Samfoto: p. 20.

Mimsy Møller, Samfoto: p. 28.

Hans Hvide Bang, Samfoto: p. 34.

Espen Brattlie, Samfoto: p. 40 large.

Nils Aukan: p. 17.

Arve Stensrud: p. 4, 27, 32, 166, 173, 192.

Hedemarkmuseet: p. 45.

Øyvind Leren: p. 33 below, 62 small, 111, 148 small, 150, 157, 186.

Ragge Strand: p. 40 small, 82, 210, 220.

Terje Rakke, Image Bank: p. 54, 58.

Arne Knudsen, Knudsen fotosenter: p. 41.

Eiliv Leren, PR reklamebyrå, p. 64 small.

Tor Greiner Jarild, p. 77, 79.

Mikael M. Dubois: p. 122.

Mauritius, Mittet foto: p. 168.